Hidden
San Francisco

Hidden
San Francisco

A Guide to Lost Landscapes, Unsung Heroes, and Radical Histories

Chris Carlsson

PLUTO  PRESS

First published 2020 by Pluto Press
345 Archway Road, London N6 5AA

www.plutobooks.com

British Library Cataloguing in Publication Data
A catalogue record for this book is available from the British Library

ISBN 978 0 7453 4093 7 Hardback
ISBN 978 0 7453 4094 4 Paperback
ISBN 978 1 7868 0612 3 PDF eBook
ISBN 978 1 7868 0614 7 Kindle eBook
ISBN 978 1 7868 0613 0 EPUB eBook

This book is printed on paper suitable for recycling and made from fully
managed and sustained forest sources. Logging, pulping and manufacturing
processes are expected to conform to the environmental standards of the
country of origin.

Typeset by Westchester Publishing Services

This book is dedicated to my two-year-old granddaughter, Halloul Hassan, born in San Francisco, who I'm sure will someday take these threads of history and weave them into a vital, transformative intervention into our shared future.

CONTENTS

ACKNOWLEDGMENTS

This book started with Pluto Press's David Shulman, who encouraged me to do a radical guidebook to San Francisco. It may have been postponed for many more years without his instigation, so thank you, David. Huge thanks to Glenn Bachmann for his beautiful maps. We are old friends, so it's been a treat to have his collaboration on this project. Thanks to all the friends who took the time to read earlier versions of this and to write complimentary blurbs. Not only are you my pals, you are all inspirational resources for this project, many of you with books listed in my sprawling bibliography. So many people have helped me over the years, as authors and speakers, as collaborators and friends, numbering in the hundreds by now.

Shaping San Francisco began in the mid-1990s with Greg Williamson and Jim Swanson, and important contributions from Dimitri de la Marea, Marina Lazzara, Daniel Steven Crafts, and many others. I never would have arrived at this point a quarter century later without the important foundation they helped establish. Since 2006 or so, LisaRuth Elliott has been codirecting Shaping San Francisco the project. Her participation, her vision, her critical engagement, and her friendship have all been indispensable to making this book possible. Adriana Camarena entered my life in 2007, and we married a year later. She has been a great critic, a thoughtful reader, and a daily pleasure to share life with. It's hard to imagine writing a book without her everyday encouragement and support. My daughter Francesca has been unflagging in her enthusiasm for this book, which helped when headwinds threatened to sink it at one point. As always, thanks to my parents for their steady support and generosity all these many years.

Special thanks to the friends in parallel community history efforts across San Francisco, especially David Gallagher at the Western Neighborhoods Project and the incredible photo resource at OpenSFHistory.org. Slowly our half dozen neighborhood history groups have evolved into San

Francisco's Department of Memory, and it's only a matter of time before the City recognizes our irreplaceable role in preserving and presenting local history. Ongoing thanks to the librarians at the San Francisco Public Library, especially the staff in the History Center in the Main Library, colleagues at the California Historical Society, and the remarkable collection at the National Maritime Museum, an underappreciated treasure of local history. I am indebted to my colleagues at the Mission Creek Conservancy for bringing me in to learn so much about Mission Bay's long history. Rick Prelinger and the Internet Archive have generously hosted and freely shared a cinematic, documentarian dimension to San Francisco history for a long time, for which I am eternally grateful.

Thanks to our Shaping San Francisco donors who have provided crucial support for years. Without your steady help: no project, no book. Finally, gratitude and appreciation to the hundreds of people who have attended my bike and walking tours over the past 25 years, and through their attention and enthusiasm—or lack thereof—have helped me become a much better storyteller!

PREFACE

Hidden San Francisco, is based on Shaping San Francisco, the project, which began almost a quarter century ago. This book is an outgrowth of over 20 years of Shaping San Francisco's public programming, consisting of free public talks and walking and bicycle tours that have been attended by thousands of people. From the beginning we were committed to sharing history as a public resource, valuing it as a public space and as a fundamental element of political awareness. Our commitment has been carried out during years of walking, biking, and sharing stories.

Shaping San Francisco began in 1995 as an effort to create a digital game based on San Francisco history. By the time the first edition was released publicly at the beginning of 1998, the game had been abandoned in favor of a complicated, nonlinear history project, then on CD-ROMs and a half-dozen public kiosks around San Francisco. When we started pondering how to set up this project—using the technologies of the time—we spent many hours compiling histories and designing and shaping our presentations, learning as we went about digital technologies, storage media, and the emerging language of interfaces.

Several Shaping San Francisco developers were avid bicyclists and had been part of the group who started the bicycling phenomenon Critical Mass in San Francisco in 1992, so it was a logical extension to begin sharing the histories we were writing in the form of public bicycle history tours. The first labor history bike tour I organized in 1995 became the kernel of an expanding program of public bike tours. By the turn of the century, I had given a transit history bike tour during BikeSummer held in San Francisco in 1999, and an ecological history tour by bicycle soon after.

Facing a massive rent increase during the original dot-com boom forced us into a prolonged battle in 2000 to save our offices. And soon after, when Windows XP came out in 2001, our original Shaping San Francisco CD-ROM stopped working.

Years later we reemerged as part of CounterPULSE. In 2006, our Public Talks series began at the CounterPULSE theater, and bike tours became regularly scheduled in that same year. In 2009, our accumulated histories finally opened on the Internet at Foundsf.org. Over the past decade, we've added many new tours on bicycle and in recent years a whole spate of walking tours as well. Over 13 years of Public Talks are archived on our website at Shapingsf.org, furthering our mission of doing public history in public and making it available for free in perpetuity.

Our sprawling archive of the City's history at Foundsf.org has buttressed a deep and complicated knowledge of this place. Unfortunately, the serendipitous connections between disparate historical actors and events we've discovered and included in our archive aren't always obvious to visitors to the website. Foundsf.org is a nonlinear archive of more than 1,900 distinct pages at this writing, with more than 7,000 photos, hundreds of video and audio clips, and numerous hyperlinks that encourage accidental discoveries. But there is no guarantee that as one enters the site and begins to click links and follow any given path, that meaningful discoveries will be made. You may encounter surprises, or you might find yourself overwhelmed and baffled about how what you've seen holds together—especially if you enter without any idea of what you're looking for.

Giving tours to a dozen or more people 15–20 times a year for the past decade has helped me become a much better storyteller. It has also helped me understand the limits of a digital archive in providing a narration of history. It turns out that having a great digital archive is one thing, but creating meaning and understanding requires more than simple access—it takes storytelling, it requires presenting information in a coherent narrative arc. This is the basic truth discovered by every historian who has ever published a popular work of history.

Hidden San Francisco, is based on years of storytelling, which in turn is based on years of gathering and writing and presenting the complicated, overlapping histories we have collected on Foundsf.org. When we began gathering those stories, it wasn't always clear how a given piece should be characterized. Many topics have blurry boundaries. Is a strike on the streetcars in 1917 a labor story or a transit story? Is building a train southward that involves cutting a gorge through Irish Hill a transit story or an ecological one? In both cases the answer is of course both! We also tag our many screens with the decades they took place in, which neighborhoods they were in, and other thematic attributes. But even deciding what the boundaries were between neighborhoods turned out to be subject to dispute. All this is to say that the more we learned, the fuzzier the once-sharp edges around any given story became. Everything has a way of spilling into everything else, the longer and harder you look at it.

This book divides material into a series of chapters on ecology, labor, transit, and dissent. Dozens of "stops" (labeled with E, L, T, and D for the aforementioned topics, e.g., E3 or T8, etc.) allow me to present the stories I've been telling during our biking and walking tours that are collected here for the first time. But, as noted, a story in one chapter might have been put somewhere else depending on who wants to characterize the story. I've gone ahead and decided to put some things in the ecology chapter, the transit chapter, the labor chapter, or the dissent chapter, even if on another day one or another might have seemed more suited to a different location. I think you'll find most of my choices make sense, and if your sensibility suggests that something should have been somewhere else, I hope you'll indulge me and recognize that I might very well agree with you if we were sitting and arguing over a drink.

In Chapter 1, Openers, I give the basic themes that shape our historical thinking, as well as some of the history of making history that precede and undergird our approach. Chapter 2 offers an overview of local ecological history from the prehistory use of the land to the many social conflicts over our relationship to nature both inside and outside of the urban paradigm. Chapter 3 looks at San Francisco's epic class war over the decades since the City burst into life in 1849. The eight-hour day has come and gone many times, along with countless unions and federations of both labor and capital. Hopefully this labor history will give a fresh look at the contentious history of who did the work and how that work was shaped and channeled by the gyrations of markets and money. Chapter 4 collects stories of how San Franciscans arrived and moved around the land and sea, the vehicles, the rights of way, the ships, and the men (and occasionally the women) who worked on building and running the many forms of transit. The extension of the City across the dunes and hills depended on the evolving systems of streetcars and trains, and then eventually the complete urban takeover by the private automobile, punctuated by crescendos of bicycle activism at the end of both the nineteenth and twentieth centuries. Chapter 5 encompasses a wide variety of social movements, uprisings, riots, and contrarian dissenters. Though the longest chapter, no matter how much I included, a great deal has been left out. I wanted to grasp key moments and memorable movements, but I am sure there will be howls of indignation at episodes that are equally important to San Francisco's storied history of resistance and rebellion but were not included here. Each of the four main chapters (2–5) have an accompanying map showing the "stops" and providing a suggested bicycling route to visit most of them (they are too far apart to visit them all on foot, except over days). The appendix features five additional walking tours to provide you with another way of using the material gathered in this book while moving through San Francisco. You can use them at your leisure, and access the stories I tell at the sites on those tours by looking them up on the maps in each chapter. An extensive bibliography provides most of the sources, though we've chosen not to footnote the book extensively since it is not an academic project. Additional sources are also on our websites.

Though this book has a certain inevitable finality to it once printed, I don't propose it as the final word on what's divulged here. I worked hard to get the facts and nail down the stories, but I've learned that history can be a moving target. The truth about history is subject to debate and future modification as our knowledge increases and our critical thinking shifts. One of the great things about our archive at Foundsf.org is that it is a living archive, always growing and changing. We are occasionally given corrections on photo captions or factual errors that have crept into our material, and gladly make the changes once we verify them. We are always inviting people to write up their own experiences and insights to add to the collection. History is never finished, and as our motto "history is a creative act in the present" explains, the creative act is the making and contesting of meaning. Any collection—this one included—is subject to revision and correction going forward. Any collection, any historical account, can be improved with newly discovered information, new ways of thinking critically about sources and/or interpretations. This book is certainly subject to the same caveat.

That said, I hope that *Hidden San Francisco*, will not just be food for thought, but seeds for future discoveries. Let this collection be a contribution to the kind of critical historical thinking that is indispensable to our hopes to make a life worth living—in a world that we can be proud of having shaped together.

—Chris Carlsson, June 2019

I

OPENERS

The approach of this book embodies a commitment to history from below, to history as lived, to documenting our time, alongside critical, in-depth, sometimes controversial histories. The histories we present here will deepen your understanding of where you are and how the City got this way, and hopefully, help you see your own participation in the City's life—whether as a resident or a visitor—in a new light. In the following pages you will find a complicated and contrarian historical understanding, a dissenter's history of San Francisco framed by the belief that history is a creative act in the present.

We don't believe history is only made by politicians, business owners, and celebrities more than it is by the unsung and often ignored streetcar conductors, secretaries, ironworkers, organizers, dockworkers, musicians, cabbies, and all the people that really shaped San Francisco through the years. Most of us don't tend to think of history as something we are actively engaged in, but that doesn't make it any less so. We make history together every day, both by acting in the world and by interpreting and arguing over a contested past. As you walk or bicycle through the streets of San Francisco, you are contributing to the City's history. Stop and talk to someone, take a photo and share it online, spend some time in a park or plaza and watch the life of the City unfold before your eyes. Show up at a concert, a poetry reading, an art show, a political protest, and you too are indelibly etched into San Francisco's history. Who knows how your presence will alter your own life or someone else's, or maybe even the trajectory of the City itself?

This book peels back the layers of San Francisco history to discover memories, echoes, and ghosts of the City's storied past, often hiding in plain view. The pre-urban landscape, dramatically reconfigured by decades of digging, plowing, flattening, and filling, continues to undulate beneath the streets and buildings of twenty-first-century San Francisco. From farming to industry to towering offices, city neighborhoods have been reinvented and reinhabited again and again. Behind old walls and gleaming glass facades lurk former industries, secret music and poetry venues, forgotten terrorist bombings, and much more.

Philosophically, this book, and the project it has grown out of— *Shaping San Francisco*—are rooted in the so-called "new history" that prominently hit popular consciousness in the wake of the social upheavals of the 1960s and 1970s. This type of history telling starts with a resounding rejection of the older consensus histories that have prevailed since the founding of the United States: sagas that foreground wealth and power and the "important" people (overwhelmingly white men) who controlled it, and our approach casts doubt on the notion of there being a "grand narrative" that tells one Truth about history. Rather than one glorifying story featuring history's apparent "winners," we join with others to look at the lives of millions of people—women and men of all ages, races, and sexualities— who may not have made the social register, but whose activity is the real muscle and bone of the world we live in. *Hidden San Francisco* prefers to seek out multiple points of view to help us make sense of the many experiences and ways of knowing that are as historically relevant as the stories of generals, executives, and mayors. The roots of this sensibility extend back further, well into the 1930s when the French "Annales" school was founded by Marc Bloch and Lucien Febvre and then carried on after WWII by Fernand Braudel. They emphasized the long flow of history by closely analyzing the everyday lives of people embedded in social structures, seeking to understand the dynamics between common behaviors and attitudes and the maintenance of systems of power and reproduction. They were the first to integrate geography, history, and sociology into a comprehensive analytic synthesis, seeking to provide a more complicated and nuanced understanding of how history is made, and how it is remembered. Thus, this book is a guide to San Francisco from a different point of view. Cable cars, hippies, and the Golden Gate Bridge are here too—but through their lesser-known and more complicated undersides.

Perhaps more importantly, this book confronts an amnesiac culture, a society that prefers to forget—or even worse, to never know in the first place! In San Francisco, we stand on land once claimed by Mexico from the

Spanish, who claimed it from the original inhabitants. It's preferable to think that this land was transferred thereafter to the United States in an honorable and fair way, rather than the real story of venal manipulation and brutal forcible annexation. We have been told we have to believe that the settlers who arrived in the new State of California found a paradise that was largely depopulated and open—a completely false idea in an area that had one of the densest preconquest populations in North America before the arrival of European microbes. And the genocidal campaigns carried out in the first 25 years of California's U.S. history make a very dark and unforgivably barbaric foundation for the oft-told tales of Gold Rush fortunes and entrepreneurial geniuses who supposedly "built" the state.

History doesn't automatically grab everyone's interest. Especially here, we live in a culture obsessed with the new, with now, with the always beckoning possibilities of a glittering future. Some people use the expression "You're history!" as an epithet, to declare the irrelevance of a person or an idea. In this book we pierce Americans' propagandistic relationship with history (from which San Franciscans are far from exempt). San Francisco is very much an American city, which means we wrap ourselves in a self-righteous certainty that ours is the best of all possible countries, with the best of all possible political and economic systems. San Francisco also describes itself as a bastion of liberalism and tolerant open-mindedness, the "left coast" of a country that is distinctly to its right politically. This history has its bits of truth throughout, but what is glossed over, left out, and deliberately hidden tells a very different story and can be found in the pages of this book.

At the time this book is to be published, the City is undergoing a breathtaking demographic change (some describe it as a massive ethnic and class cleansing as soaring rents and a vicious wave of evictions drive lower-income residents out). Dense residential high-rises are popping up where gasworks and foundries once stood along the edge of the original bay shoreline. Those forgotten early industries comprised the City's original "tech boom," fueling the mining and agricultural fortunes that forever altered the state's storied mountains and valleys. Today, private "Google buses" (actually separate, dedicated luxury bus lines for each of more than a half dozen large tech firms like Facebook, Apple, Yahoo, Electronic Arts, Google, Genentech, and others) roll every couple of minutes during morning and evening rush hours through neighborhoods where working-class Irish, Germans, Italians, and Scandinavians built sturdy and elegant Victorians that housed multigenerational families. To rent or buy an apartment in these spruced-up, much-loved buildings now requires more than a six-figure salary, but many of them still house longtime San Franciscans who benefit from the rent control and eviction defense resources that have been established through decades-long, arduous political efforts.

We ourselves have struggled to stay in San Francisco during this tidal wave of displacement, forced out and nearly evicted from our homes. We barely hang on, but our work to produce the histories herein is an ongoing rebuke to the out-of-control forces that are destroying the City that was, imposing a sterile and homogenized urbanity drained of precisely the peoples and energies that gave it its vital soul. But it's a fragile new order and one that longtime San Franciscans know will subside eventually. This book and the histories we've worked so hard to collect are a vital seed bank to help germinate the complicated, contested, and passionate San Francisco that is still here despite everything, and will never be fully defeated.

LABOR AND ECOLOGY

Our view of local history starts with intersecting labor and ecology, categories that provide revealing windows into how the City came to be the way it is. People don't work in a vacuum; they work in a context of nature and the environment we've collectively created over generations. Historians rarely look at these fields together. Labor historians tend to focus on the history of unions, with occasional looks at broader public movements, labor parties, etc., but never connect the workers' movement with the natural environment. On the other hand, the burgeoning field of environmental writing focuses largely on earth sciences, climate change, and species/habitat loss. Even if willing to examine the political history of ecologically inspired activism, it is the rare environmental scribe who connects ecology to the work done in society at large. To properly understand the history of this place, we have to know what kinds of work have been done, how these tasks were organized and carried out, by whom, under whose direction, and to what end. Mostly these questions have been absent from twentieth-century workers' politics and definitely from the environmental movement (with a few exceptions among environmental justice activists in recent years).

San Francisco—the place—precedes all this industriousness. What was here when modern life suddenly burst over the hills, dunes, shorelines, and waterways of the bay? Who was living here and how did *their* activity shape the environment that greeted the Spanish? How did patterns of work and economic activity shape the landscape, and in turn shape the lived experience of the residents of this sudden city? As the decades accelerated and the City was rocked by earthquakes (1868, 1906, 1989, along with thousands of smaller ones) and burned by massive fires, how did the evolving relationship with hills, water, and transportation shape San Francisco, its possibilities, its ability to sustain a complex urban life?

From its frenzied 1849 origins in the Gold Rush, the city of San Francisco has been built up from scarcely a hamlet into a world city. The City's history coincides helpfully with the emergence of photography, providing a remarkable visual record of how human effort flattened and "improved" the dunes and swamps into a ground suitable for an industrializing city to grow. To feed the growing city, agribusiness emerged early to remake the delta and the inland valleys into major croplands, altering forever the ecological composition that preceded their arrival. Over a century and a half, the thriving and tempestuous rivers of California were dammed, channeled, and diverted into one of the world's most impressive—and inconceivably bizarre—plumbing systems. San Francisco residents provided the planning, coordination, and capital to orchestrate an elaborate regional economy with itself at the profitable center. Monopolists repeatedly sought to dominate transportation, fresh water, mining, forestry, and agriculture.

Neither the city government nor most San Franciscans benefited from this well-organized imperial control of the region. Workers repeatedly confronted concentrated economic power to extract a "fair share" though rarely to alter the trajectory of plunder and exploitation followed by the wealthy. White workers organized racially exclusive unions to challenge their conditions again and again, in nearly every industry and occupation. On at least two occasions in city history, self-styled "workers' parties" took power and temporarily broke the Democrat-and-Republican political duopoly, only to fall apart in a few years. Even the subterranean waters, long forgotten after being entombed in cement culverts, occasionally break out and flood the streets, proving that the decades of reshaping the peninsula haven't fully suppressed the original landscape underneath the pavement.

Genocide and Slavery

Genocide and slavery are two more closely aligned categories that we must understand together to grasp the social dynamics that gave rise to the City by the Bay. In the twenty-first century, both concepts seem very far removed from our lives, but in fact the traces of these double horrors are not so easily expunged. From the beginning of Spanish settlement on the San Francisco peninsula, the colonists depended on Indian labor to build the mission, farm the fields and harvest crops, tend the livestock, and fish and ensnare large birds. Ostensibly the Indians, called "neophytes" by the Spanish friars, were willingly contributing their labor in exchange for the great benefit of becoming Christians and subjects of the Spanish crown. In fact, if they chose to exit this grueling regime, they were chased down by armed soldiers and forcibly returned. It wasn't until 1829, years after Mexico had gained its independence from Spain, that Indian slavery was formally abolished. By the time the missions were fully secularized in the 1830s, it is estimated that the original population of California had already fallen by two-thirds due to a combination of disease, starvation, and colonial violence.

Slavery was a key element of early California history, long swept under the rug by historians determined to put a positive spin on a dark history. After Indians were officially emancipated, their role in sustaining the Californio/Mexican cattle economy was barely altered. The Mexicans were dependent on their labor and thus not committed to their wholesale slaughter as the Americans were from approximately 1846 to the early 1870s. But Americans, too, found that Indian slave labor was an indispensable need. Officially a "free state" after being admitted to the Union in 1850, the new state legislature passed laws authorizing the indenturing of Indian children without their parents' consent, as well as any Indians deemed "vagrant," legalizing Indian slavery in the state. Up to 25 percent of Northern Californian households held an Indian child in slavery in the 1850s (Madley: 2016). California was also obliged to enforce the Fugitive Slave Act, which made it complicit in the capture and return of many enslaved Africans who traveled to the state with their southern "owners" and may have escaped while here. It was Lincoln's signing of the Emancipation Proclamation that finally ended both the enforcement of the Fugitive Slave Act and formal Indian slavery in the state (but not the genocidal slaughter that carried on into the following decade). The booming agricultural and mining economy of California would have had difficulty sustaining itself without the coerced labor of indigenous workers, followed by indentured Chinese labor.

The enormous output of the state would have been stuck in isolated California were it not for the violently oppressed workers who sailed the high seas. Forgotten and glossed over was the status of sailors on the great fleet of ships that serviced San Francisco Harbor during the nineteenth century. Subjected to extremely sadistic and cruel violence by ship officers, sailors were deprived of basic rights. As late as 1897, the U.S. Supreme Court held that sailors were exempt from the Thirteenth Amendment's prohibition against involuntary servitude (Pickelhaupt: 1996). California, like so much of the capitalist world economy, made its famous leap into modernity in no small part thanks to enslaved and coerced labor of Indians, Chinese, and sailors!

WAR AND ANTIWAR

War boosted the Bay Area many times. From the American seizure of California in the unprovoked Mexican-American War of 1846–48, to the horrendous genocidal campaigns against the native peoples of California and the western United States, San Francisco has been the beneficiary and the home of war promoters.

When the Civil War broke out, most shipping to and from California was curtailed, which in turn led to a new boom in manufacturing locally. When the Comstock Lode's multimillion-dollar silver deposits were discovered in western Nevada, San Francisco benefited even more than it had from the original Gold Rush. But by the end of the 1870s, a general depression had the country in its grip, and the Comstock Lode had petered out. The Union Iron Works moved from its early location near 1st and Mission to Potrero Point, where a state-of-the-art industrial behemoth was built to make iron and all the tools and machinery required for the ongoing industrial revolution. But the owner, Irving Scott, saw that he needed a steadier demand for what his high-technology facility could produce. After a world tour when he visited shipyards in Europe and Asia, he returned to San Francisco with the determination to convince the U.S. government to become his main client.

Soon, the Union Iron Works gained enormous federal contracts to produce warships, ultimately building most of what became the "Great

White Fleet" (the same one President Teddy Roosevelt sent around the world in 1909 to "speak softly and carry a big stick"). Already the Presidio and Fort Mason at Black Point were longtime military bases, as was Alcatraz Island. Mare Island in Vallejo had been the main naval installation on the bay with privately owned "graving" docks at Hunters Point also serving the needs of both private and U.S. Navy ships. When the Union Iron Works went bankrupt in 1901, Bethlehem Steel took over the facilities and ran them through both world wars until the 1960s.

The war profiteers were met by dissent each time. This place is also an epicenter for resistance to war. Mark Twain and others formed the Anti-Imperialist League of the United States to combat the U.S. annexation of the Philippines after the Spanish-American War of 1898–1904. Anarchists and labor radicals, Irish and South Asians, all resisted imperialism and WWI in the Bay Area. Conscientious objectors resisted WWII and Korea, and of course the resistance to the Vietnam War in the Bay Area is well known. The Cold War found its dissenters in San Francisco in the 1950s and famously in 1960 at the HUAC hearings in City Hall. By the 1980s, the nuclear freeze movement had gone national, and war resisters were protesting nuclear weapons and nuclear power, many of the activists living in San Francisco. Efforts to return the USS *Missouri* and "homeport" it in San Francisco in the mid-1980s were stopped by a dynamic citizens' movement, including the "Peace Navy." Activists argued that the ship was being turned into a "first-strike" vessel, meant to carry nuclear-tipped cruise missiles that could not be detected under then-existing arms agreements and technologies, and thus would violate treaty agreements with the Soviet Union. Hundreds blockaded streets and offices in downtown San Francisco during the 1980s to thwart the Reagan administration's illegal wars in Central America and to protest the growing threat of nuclear war. In 1991, hundreds of thousands marched through city streets against George H. W. Bush's planned attack on Iraq over Kuwait. In 2003, 20,000 people shut down the City's key traffic intersections and over a dozen key offices in a day of action against the second Iraq War.

The role of federal military spending in sustaining the premier industrial facilities in the San Francisco Bay Area cannot be overstated. A half dozen key military bases, endless contracts to local industrialists, and a huge workforce employed directly in the military and indirectly working for the many suppliers in the area—taken together this represented a significant portion of the local economy for over a century. The much-touted high-tech sector can trace its existence to military funding, originally for advanced communications theories and technologies, and later to the Arpanet, which eventually became the Internet. Today the military bases are almost all gone, but the public money sustaining local high-tech defense firms, research institutions, NSA and other spies, among them Lawrence Livermore National Laboratory, is still quite enormous. The ostensibly private tech industry that was spawned by all this defense spending has also met its dissenters in San Francisco's streets.

MODERNISM VS. ROMANTICISM

Almost everyone harbors at least a bit of romantic nostalgia for the City that was—especially if they never lived in it themselves! As a young urban center, less than 200 years old, San Francisco tends to emphasize and glorify anything it can romantically claim as its history. In almost the same breath, San Francisco's long history of poets, writers, and iconoclastic journalists have repeatedly cast a sharp eye on the machinations of money and power here. Singers and musicians, many in San Francisco, wrote the soundtrack of the late twentieth century, a heady mix of heart, hedonism, and howling opposition to the dominant society. Monopolists and militarists, politicians and businessmen, have all been stripped bare by muckraking investigations and bawdy ridicule. This civic reflex comes into conflict with the untrammeled pursuit of the modern that San Francisco is also well known for. San Francisco is practically a laboratory of modern life from its origins in land seizure and enclosure to the massive exploitation of nature and cheap labor, to the efforts to stabilize and maintain a world based on gross inequality, a collapsing environment, and hair-trigger threats of war, based on a new foundation of "surveillance capitalism" (Zuboff: 2019).

San Francisco quixotically saved its iconic cable cars in 1947 and a decade later presciently fought off a bunch of freeways. But it also has the hideously designed—by Bechtel Corporation—modernist BART train system and grandiose plans to bring the future into the heart of the City with the long-planned California High Speed Rail system. Historically preserved and protected buildings are all over town amid the dull brutalism of new modernist palaces for the nouveau riche of the twenty-first century.

During the 1970s high-rise revolt, San Franciscans resisted "Manhattanization" of the City. Now skyscrapers crowd the monotonously expanding skyline, while resistance to height limits has shriveled in the face of a highly profitable and increasingly vertical "new urbanism." Downtown has more than doubled its acreage since the late 1960s when activists stopped U.S. Steel from building a 50-story monster in the bay just north of the Bay Bridge. From the top of Rincon Hill all the way to the Washington Street boundary on the north, from the bayshore to 5th Street, the whole South of Market has been annexed into a downtown/convention center office and residential high-rise zone. Just south in the former railyards of Mission Bay, a "city within the City" has popped up in the past 25 years, characterized by a sprawling expanse of glass-clad offices and condominiums around the 42-acre UCSF Medical campus. The full length of Market Street is undergoing an unprecedented transformation from old department stores, neighborhood shops, early twentieth-century offices, theaters, and apartments, into a shiny procession of new malls, high-rises, and luxury condominium developments. Victorian and Edwardian buildings are being rehabilitated into luxury dwellings all over town, preserving the old facades while modernizing the interiors. With its pseudo-historic streetcar line and Potemkin Victorians, San Francisco has been carefully coiffed and manicured to reinforce the local economy's dependence on tourism.

San Francisco is a global city repeatedly regaled as a trendsetter, a city at the edge of the continent where countless thousands have come to discard old identities and resurface with imagined pasts and uncharted futures. Innovators have been welcomed by a bohemian culture suspicious of fixed truths, ossified class boundaries, and imported traditions. Music, literature, poetry, technology, art, cooperation, and collective invention have all flourished in San Francisco. The same cultural dynamism has also provided a rich foundation from which huge corporations have grown to straddle the globe, while their owners have exercised an enduring control over the City's growth and development.

San Francisco holds a vital place at the heart of modern world history. The City's own saga is barely 200 years old, and yet those years straddle the U.S. imperial push across North America and into the Pacific, the industrial revolution and the emergence of class war, mass immigration and racism, technological breakthroughs from railroads to photography, agriculture to chemicals, machines to microchips, and more. It's also an epicenter for resistance to war, home to the beginnings of the antinuclear movement in the 1950s, the neighbor-driven campaign to Stop the Freeways in the 1960s, the unparalleled success of the Save the Bay movement in preserving and cleaning up the San Francisco Bay since 1963, and for changing how we live among ourselves by shattering norms of racial, sexual, and gender stereotypes. The City's immigrant ethnic groups continue to organize and resist the deep historical racism that has dominated elite policy-making here.

San Francisco manages to be both a beacon to malcontents and nonconformists and one of the most tightly run oligarchic municipalities in the country. The distribution of power and influence results from an endless tussle between competing interests, factions, organizations, and movements as they ebb and flow across time. Moments of contestation and conflict saturate our past whether we know it or not, as our predecessors made decisions that continue to reverberate down the years. A definitive portrait of how we got here is elusive, but by revisiting locations and histories across the ever-changing landscape, we can uncover continuities and contradictions, and present our version of how the City arrived at this moment. Like any history worth its name, it's not meant to be the last word but a contribution to our ongoing shared efforts to understand *how the hell it turned out like this!*

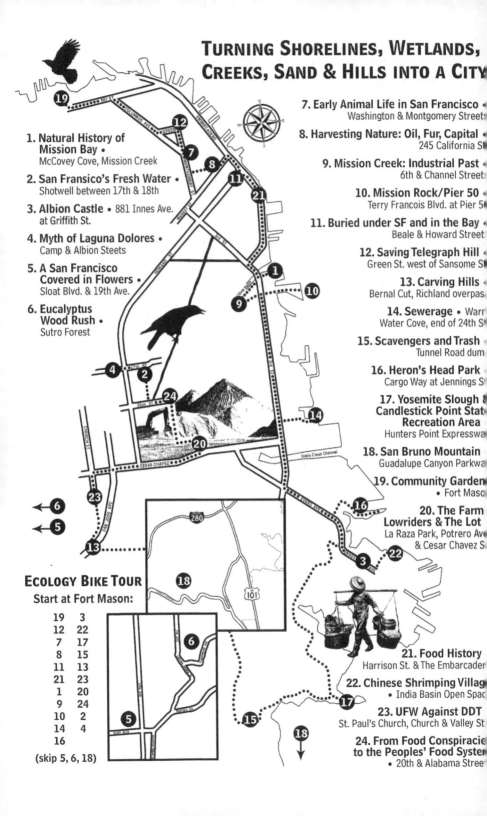

TURNING SHORELINES, WETLANDS, CREEKS, SAND & HILLS INTO A CITY

1. Natural History of Mission Bay • McCovey Cove, Mission Creek

2. San Fransico's Fresh Water • Shotwell between 17th & 18th

3. Albion Castle • 881 Innes Ave. at Griffith St.

4. Myth of Laguna Dolores • Camp & Albion Steets

5. A San Francisco Covered in Flowers • Sloat Blvd. & 19th Ave.

6. Eucalyptus Wood Rush • Sutro Forest

7. Early Animal Life in San Francisco • Washington & Montgomery Streets

8. Harvesting Nature: Oil, Fur, Capital • 245 California St

9. Mission Creek: Industrial Past • 6th & Channel Street

10. Mission Rock/Pier 50 • Terry Francois Blvd. at Pier 50

11. Buried under SF and in the Bay • Beale & Howard Street

12. Saving Telegraph Hill • Green St. west of Sansome St

13. Carving Hills • Bernal Cut, Richland overpass

14. Sewerage • Warm Water Cove, end of 24th St

15. Scavengers and Trash • Tunnel Road dump

16. Heron's Head Park • Cargo Way at Jennings St

17. Yosemite Slough & Candlestick Point State Recreation Area • Hunters Point Expressway

18. San Bruno Mountain • Guadalupe Canyon Parkway

19. Community Garden • Fort Mason

20. The Farm Lowriders & The Lot • La Raza Park, Potrero Ave & Cesar Chavez St

21. Food History • Harrison St. & The Embarcadero

22. Chinese Shrimping Village • India Basin Open Space

23. UFW Against DDT • St. Paul's Church, Church & Valley St

24. From Food Conspiracies to the Peoples' Food System • 20th & Alabama Street

ECOLOGY BIKE TOUR

Start at Fort Mason:

19	3
12	22
7	17
8	15
11	13
21	23
1	20
9	24
10	2
14	4
16	

(skip 5, 6, 18)

II

TURNING SHORELINES, WETLANDS, CREEKS, SAND, AND HILLS INTO A CITY

In San Francisco, material improvements were taking place. At Clark's Point, on the northern extremity of the city, huge precipitous rocks were quarried and removed, and the solid hill deeply excavated, whereby much new and valuable space was gained for building operations. New streets were graded, planked, and built upon, and new and finer houses everywhere erected. In the southern districts, the "steam-paddy" had been set to work and was rapidly cutting away the numerous sand hills that lay between the plaza and "Happy Valley." The rubbish was conveyed by temporary rails along the streets and emptied into the bay at those parts where already roads were laid out and houses built on piles. Sansome and Battery, with the intersecting streets to a considerable distance, were gradually filled up and firm foundations given for the substantial brick and stone houses that were beginning to be erected there. The town continued to move eastward, and new streets were formed upon piles farther out into the bay, across which the piers and wharves were shooting like the first slender lines of ice before the sheet of water hardens into a solid mass. Closer and thicker the lines ran, as house after house was reared on innumerable piles, while the steam-paddy and railway wagons, and horse-carts without number, were incessantly bearing hills of sand piecemeal to fill up the hollows, and drive the sea far away from the original beach.
—From the *Annals of San Francisco,* 1855

San Francisco in the twenty-first century is an iconic tourist destination. Few visit without being struck by its physical beauty: the quality of its

Southerly view from approximately Sacramento and Taylor Streets, St. Anne's Valley in foreground (today's Tenderloin) with South of Market, Mission Bay and Potrero Hill in distance. (Courtesy OpenSFHistory.org wnp37.00897-L [Marilyn Blaisdell Collection / Courtesy of a private collector])

light, the sparkling bay and the ocean beaches, the majestic bridges connecting the city to the rest of the Bay Area, the fresh air blowing in from the Pacific Ocean, and the amazing views from its hilltops. Photos of San Francisco are taken by the millions every year, promulgating an ever more familiar view of the City.

Nowadays, many locals are invested in the setting and involved in various ecological efforts, from native plant restoration to community gardens, bicycling and urban planning, expanding use of solar energy, an ever-expanding urban forest, and protected endangered species and habitats. San Francisco is probably greener in the early twenty-first century than it has ever been.

Nineteenth-century visitors, however, often complained that San Francisco was particularly ugly—its dunes and muddy roads made for a miserable stay, and the surrounding bay was a putrid dump full of sewage and refuse. The San Francisco peninsula was a sandy, boggy, hilly place often covered in fog and whipped by cold ocean winds. It wasn't nearly as nice a place to live as the areas south, east, and north of it. But the protected cove between Telegraph and Rincon Hills was a place where ships could shelter from the sea, wind, and fog, and it was there that the earliest traders established themselves on a sandy slope not far from the beach.

In spite of its inhospitable initial conditions, San Francisco grew and changed enough over the years to now be considered one of the world's most beautiful cities, a place where more and more people want to live, and where travelers come to visit from all over the world. How did it turn out like this? The answer to that question is a particularly curious story—intermittently infuriating and inspiring—of modern urban development.

San Francisco today is not only a gorgeous city draped over dramatic hills on a small peninsula straddling bay and ocean; it is also the historic heart of a sprawling metropolitan region that surrounds the bay and extends upriver into the heart of California. Within a few years of the start of the Gold Rush, the City already had its economic and political hands around a great deal of the Pacific Rim and most of the western edge of North America. The wildlife of land and sea were being mercilessly slaughtered to fill the coffers of early business empires headquartered in San Francisco, solidifying the link between urbanism and nature in a bloody, one-sided marriage. The plunder of metals, minerals, and waters furthered the city's essential dependence on the countryside, while the City's burghers grew fat on the profits (Brechin: 1999).

Four or so decades into this rapacious process, in 1892 the Sierra Club was founded in San Francisco as one of the nation's first environmental organizations. Farsighted locals like William Kent who saved Muir Woods at the beginning of the twentieth century worked alongside citizens who pushed to turn Mt. Tamalpais in Marin County and Big Basin in the Santa Cruz Mountains into parkland. Later, in the 1930s, during the depths of the Depression, East Bay leaders had the foresight to acquire large areas of the local hills to develop into a unique chain of urban regional parks, including Tilden and Redwood Parks. All of these set a precedent for the push to set aside, preserve, and protect urban and suburban open space.

In the 1960s, a dynamic local *ecology* of activist organizations and committed individuals emerged, determined to check the power of the monied and propertied to exploit nature without restraint. Rejecting the authority of scientists who uncritically supported the agenda of the chemical, nuclear, transportation, mining, and agribusiness industries, a flurry of magazines, political campaigns, and organizations arose to inform and advocate. Their campaigns ultimately blocked the construction of freeways, nuclear power plants, the use of agricultural chemicals, and helped to save the bay from disappearing under endless mountains of trash. Development plans of all kinds came under repeated scrutiny and opposition from mobilized citizenry, resulting in the San Francisco Bay Area we know today. While far from perfect—scarred in many places by unsightly corporate campuses, toxic waste sites, and architectural insults—it is one of the most beautiful metropolitan regions in the United States.

San Francisco's ecological history is a tale of human occupation and radical redesign, the liquidation of most of its original species and habitats, and the creation of a new mix of flora and fauna with the built environment of an urban society. The natural history of San Francisco is inextricably intertwined with the story of humans here, whose industrious transformation of land, shorelines, and waters has remade nature as steadily as the weather and the lumbering seismic shifts that perpetually shake this continental edge. It's also true that the human impact has been greatest for a relatively short time, since the City only really got started as urban space after 1849. Prior to that, the landscape had been shaped by wind and fog, storms and earthquakes, babbling brooks, floods, and rising and falling seas, for thousands of years. Humans, too, shaped that pre-urban world with annual fires and careful landscape management in ways that were invisible to civilization until very recently.

Perhaps the most dramatic stories involve two basic features: the shorelines and the hills, both of which have been more radically changed by human effort than by any of the region's frequent earthquakes. With the population influx of 1849 began a century-long effort to fill the bay, to make land by "reclaiming" mudflats, and so on, which drastically altered the size and shape of San Francisco. To cross the City today is to traverse creeks, wetlands, and bays, and crisscross old shorelines. Numerous sand ridges and dunes, often as tall as 100–200 feet, were leveled in the nineteenth century to fill in the coves, beaches, and bogs. Subterranean timbers from buried ships, brick foundations from burned-down buildings, and dense layers of industrial waste are all layered beneath the streets and structures of today's City.

In 1776, thousands of miles west of the nascent United States, this land we know as San Francisco was part of New Spain, but inhabited by tens of thousands of first peoples who lived in hundreds of villages and settlements both permanent and temporary throughout Northern California. Up to 100,000 people may have lived in the larger Bay Area and Sacramento-San Joaquin Delta (though less than 1,000 in the windy, foggy tip of the peninsula that became the site of San Francisco), one of the most dense pre-conquest populations in North America, divided into dozens of language groups (Milliken: 1995; Mann: 2005).

When Europeans first arrived in the late eighteenth century, they found a bay one-third larger than the size of today's bay. It was swarming with waterfowl, aquatic mammals, fish, and crustaceans, fed by dozens of creeks and rivers running from dense forests of oak and redwood in the surrounding hills. The water was so crowded with large fish that early European sailors claimed one could walk across the water!

The many local cultures that shared this space lived in relative peace and coexisted with grizzly bears, elk, whales, walruses, wolves, foxes, beavers, and hundreds of birds, small mammals, fish, etc. The skies were filled for days at a time by the overflight of billions of birds who depended on the bay, the biggest estuary on the Pacific Coast. The bay itself teemed with life, from seals, porpoises, and whales to massive sturgeon and literally millions of salmon that pulsed through the Golden Gate on three annual migrations back and forth from the high Sierras via the intricate and dynamic river systems that fed the bay.

After the Spanish arrived, layers of recorded history began to accumulate. The Spanish settlers centered their lives around Mission Dolores or at the Presidio. In the 1830s, a small number of people eventually settled on the sandy hill sloping westward from the bay at what was then called Yerba Buena Cove. The local economy depended on cattle and agriculture, twin scourges to the traditional food sources and land use patterns of the indigenous population. Cows were perhaps the most devastating import in early California, bringing with them European grass seed in their hooves and excrement, grasses that soon began to race across the landscape, overrunning the native plants that were familiar to the local population. The change in flora that the cattle wrought with their grazing and pooping quickly began to alter all sorts of long-settled patterns of life. Large predators like grizzly bears and wolves were systematically hunted by the Spanish to protect their livestock. Herds of elk were radically reduced by the hunters, and their traditional pastures were taken over by herds of cattle and sheep (Dreyfus: 2008).

Oak groves and willows offered limited wood supplies, and when the population exploded after 1848, local redwood forests down the peninsula and in the East Bay hills—along with the enormous oak forest that gave Oakland its name—provided the fuel and first building materials for the expanding City. Quarries on local hills provided bricks for buildings, gravel for roads, and ballast for ships. Devastating fires wiped out the new city a half dozen times in its first few years, encouraging a turn to iron and stone building materials. Then a major earthquake in 1868 that flattened many of the City's largest buildings pushed builders back to wooden structures that could better withstand the regular shaking that rocked local settlements.

The baroque, ornately built San Francisco that took shape in the gaslit nineteenth century came to an abrupt end in the massive earthquake and three-day fires of April 1906. An elaborate plan to reorganize the city's thoroughfares, parks, and neighborhoods had been submitted to the City a year before the earthquake, but even with its land cleared by disaster and a rare opportunity to remake the urban fabric, the men who controlled the rebuilding of San Francisco chose not to engage in grand efforts to reinvent it. Instead, they used their power to cement control over the city's political and economic trajectory.

The dirty, smoky, soot-filled industrial city that collapsed and burned in 1906 soon came roaring back to life. Faced with an outbreak of bubonic plague, San Francisco went on a massive campaign to kill rats and remove horses and agricultural animals from the City, closing over 400 stables and shutting down the domestic chicken trade. Dr. Rupert Blue was in charge of the campaign and declared that "the disease must be built out of existence . . . in time the City will be one block of concrete throughout." Rat-proofing involved removing all wooden floors from yards and filling all basements with wall-to-wall concrete. Almost six and a half million square feet of concrete was poured over San Francisco's sidewalks, basements, and remaining stables during the two years following the 1906 earthquake and fire (Dyl: 2017).

Streetcars were quickly rebuilt, and with the steady expansion of automobility (thanks in part to the removal of so many horses) in the postquake years, the city's ruins quickly gave birth to a new urbanism and, within a decade, a rapid extension of the City into its "outside lands" west of Twin Peaks. It would take until to the mid-twentieth century for the sand dunes to be completely transformed into the Sunset District, covered in single-family homes, San Francisco's own version of Levittown's 1950s suburban ideal.

Meanwhile, the shifting sands of the world economy combined with the rapid post-WWII regionalization of the Bay Area led to a mid-century reconfiguration of San Francisco's urban space. When the International Longshore and Warehouse Union agreed to the "Mechanization & Modernization" agreement in 1960, that led to a rapid shrinking of the Port of San Francisco. What had been a dominant shipping hub for over a century, in just a decade shrank to practically nothing as containerization methods took hold, shifting traffic to the spacious and rail-friendly Port of Oakland. But the demise of San Francisco's Port was only the most visible harbinger of a new economy moving into San Francisco, displacing manufacturing, printing, shipping, and food processing in order to expand the city's Financial District, giving rise to a downtown filled with the offices and headquarters of multinational corporations.

Railyards south of downtown were built from the 1870s on the former Mission Bay, gradually filled in and finally finished with the rubble of the 1906 earthquake and fire. By the 1960s, those railyards were obsolete too, and once removed, an expanse of empty land sat waiting for its next incarnation until the end of the century. The part of town now called Mission Bay has been a booming construction site from 1996 to the present, and is now home to the UCSF Medical campus, offices, stadiums, and apartment buildings.

Contemporaneous with the postwar economic (and ecological) transformation of the city, epic political struggles were placing San Francisco and the Bay Area at the epicenter of a newly emergent ecological sensibility. In the mid-1950s, Northern California's utility monopoly Pacific Gas & Electric (PG&E) began building a nuclear power plant on the Pacific Coast at Bodega Bay, north of San Francisco. But a citizens' movement made up of farmers and housewives in rural and small-town Northern California showed up in force to object at Sonoma County Board of Supervisors meetings. How could PG&E be allowed to build a nuclear power plant directly on the San Andreas fault? It took many years, many public hearings, demonstrations, and meetings, but finally by 1964 the plan was abandoned. The antinuclear movement had begun; atmospheric nuclear testing was halted by international treaty, and by the 1970s, a growing movement to block nuclear power plants began to win. Antinuke activists, organizations, lawyers, writers, and workers were clustered in San Francisco where the statewide Abalone Alliance had its offices, as the movement finally began to bear fruit.

Also in the mid-1950s, San Franciscans became aware of the California Department of Highways' plans for building elevated freeways through many of the city's neighborhoods. Neighborhood groups were founded as people came together to combat freeway plans in the Haight-Ashbury, the Sunset District, Glen Park, the Mission District, Telegraph Hill, and nearly everywhere that was a target for the construction plans. Middle-class women were the backbone of this movement, doggedly opposing plans to put freeways through Glen Canyon, Golden Gate Park, the Panhandle, and around the entire bayshore of the city (Germain: 2016). By 1959, the City's Board of Supervisors had blocked most legs of the comprehensive freeway plan, but it wasn't until 1965 that the two key pieces—the Panhandle/Golden Gate Park freeway and the shoreline Golden Gate Expressway—were finally blocked by tumultuous and controversial votes at the Board.

In 1963, the Save the Bay movement began. Locals were shocked in 1959 when the Army Corps of Engineers published a map showing the San Francisco Bay in the year 2000 shrunk to barely a wide river, with thousands of acres of shallow bay waters filled in by future developers. Three women—Sylvia McGlaughlin, Esther Gulick, and Kay Kerr—came together to launch the movement to save the bay after being encouraged by other local environmental groups to start their own group. By 1965, so many people across the region had enthusiastically embraced the effort, including thousands of school children who were brought out for cleanup days at the shoreline, that the State Legislature passed the McAteer-Petris Act establishing a regional management agency. The Bay Conservation and Development Commission (BCDC) has gone on to prevent further filling of the bay, open shorelines around the entire bayshore, preserve and restore natural areas, and more.

On the southern edge of San Francisco, surrounded by Brisbane, Daly City, South San Francisco, and San Bruno, sits San Bruno Mountain. By the late 1960s, a few thousand people had come together to save San Bruno Mountain, the last great open space between the nearly fully urbanized city and the suburbs to its south. Plans had been concocted to blow off the top one-third of the mountain and send it on miles-long conveyor belts into the shallow bay waters between the mountain and the San Francisco airport. A new state freeway would run down the next eastern shoreline, a mile and a half farther east than today's Highway 101, and all the bay between the two highways would be filled and turned into new suburbs, warehouses, and factories. Citizens organized to preserve the mountain as parkland, and eventually thousands of acres of rare habitat holding a half dozen endangered species (though, crucially, not all of the mountain) became San Bruno Mountain County Park. By the late 1970s, the citizens' movement had fractured, and out of it came the unscientific compromise known as Habitat Conservation Plans, a key loophole added to undermine the Endangered Species Act during the early Reagan administration.

Chemicals lost their postwar allure by the late 1960s in the wake of Rachel Carson's seminal *Silent Spring*, the carpet-bombing of Vietnam with Dow Chemical's carcinogenic defoliant Agent Orange, and the rise of the United Farmworkers in California's Central Valley campaigning against DDT alongside new national environmental groups. Pelicans and other birds were suffering reproduction problems as DDT impacted their food chains, and farmworker allies in supermarket parking lots convinced working- and middle-class Americans that chemically soaked food was bad for the workers and consumers. Combined with the radical efforts to short-circuit the commercial food business by food conspiracies and a left-wing People's Food System, healthy and organic foods became a booming business within a couple of decades.

The 1971 oil spill that resulted from two oil tankers colliding under the Golden Gate Bridge galvanized a generation of activists, many of whom were already in motion. Thousands of people turned out to rescue and clean birds and marine mammals from the devastating oil washing up on local shores. Meanwhile, Gulf & Western, a big oil company, saw their development plan for the Marin Headlands fall apart due to conflict with their development partner that delayed construction long enough for a new Board of Supervisors opposed to their plans to take office in 1970. Today what was supposed to be Marincello, a city of 30,000, is instead the bucolic Gerbode Valley, part of the Golden Gate National Recreation Area (GGNRA).

The GGNRA is one of the nation's only urban national parks, and one of the most biologically diverse parks in the country. Created through legislative jujitsu in 1972 by local representative Philip Burton, it was a product of a mobilized citizenry with a strong commitment to open space and parklands. Alongside its steady absorption of surplus federal lands that came available in the ensuing decades (notably the Presidio), it has also benefited by the acquisition of various coastal ranches that have been purchased and added to it, saving in perpetuity great swaths of agricultural and open lands abutting the Pacific Ocean.

Meanwhile, San Franciscans voted in 1974 to use a property tax to create an Open Space Fund that has allowed the City to acquire most of its open hilltops, and to steadily add land to its Recreation and Park Department. In 2016, the City finally approved a decades-long process to create a Natural Areas Program to preserve and extend as much as possible of the original habitats and species that once filled the San Francisco peninsula.

When examining urban history through an ecological lens, we confront the results of our collective labors. In the recent past, these collective labors have begun to include urgent efforts to undo and roll back some of the worst depredations wrought by earlier periods of untrammeled development. A strong majority now supports both defending and creating natural spaces in our urban lives. A radical redesign of how we live, what we do and why, with an integrated eco-logic running through it, is not only possible, but many key components of such a transformation are already being field-tested and carried out in San Francisco and the Bay Area. The current efforts in habitat restoration and community gardening, among others, are a window on our creative, cooperative possibilities. Even the Public Utilities Commission is reconsidering how to use the groundwater that fills the aquifers beneath the City, while it mandates a new system of gray water collection and reuse for all new developments going forward. Mission Bay, the new city-within-the-City south of downtown, was built with the first separated stormwater and sewer systems in San Francisco, an important development in local infrastructure. Mission Creek, at its northern edge, is home to one of San Francisco's most surprisingly successful ecological restoration stories. Efforts to daylight creeks and to open more space for urban agriculture are proceeding alongside persistent attempts to reclaim urban space from motordom and the private car.

E1: Natural History of Mission Bay

3rd Street Bridge/McCovey Cove/Mission Creek

All that's left today of the original Mission Bay is the Mission Creek channel, extending from San Francisco Bay past the Giants ballpark to an area under the freeways. Mission Bay was once a vast estuary, combining freshwater and saltwater marshes, tidal mudflats, and shallow bay waters. Nearest its original shoreline—in what we now think of as the relatively flat South of Market area—were acres of swampy bogland lying between

1852 U.S. Coastal Survey Map. Note swamp that extends northwesterly and crosses the line of Mission Plank Road ('T2) at approximately today's 7th Street. The deep channel that enters Mission Bay is approximately Townsend and 8th Streets today. (Courtesy David Rumsey Map Collection)

large sand ridges that had blown in from the ocean over thousands of years. While there were some willows along the banks of the main channel of Mission Creek, it was a relatively treeless landscape.

In what is today the north Mission part of town, freshwater streams poured down from the eastern flanks of Twin Peaks to mix with tidal surges through the Mission Creek wetlands that filled the area from approximately today's 19th Street on the south, Guerrero and Valencia Streets on the west, and Division Street (where the elevated freeway is now) on the north. While there were some willows along the banks of the main channel of Mission Creek, there were few trees in this area either. San Francisco's original landscape was largely scrub-covered dunes in the valleys on either side of the large northwestern diagonal of Franciscan bedrock that underlies our tallest hills (running from Hunters Point in the southeast through Bernal Heights, Mt. Davidson, Twin Peaks, and Mt. Sutro, and out to Lands End and the Golden Gate in the northwest corner of the City).

Fresh water also bubbled from artesian springs on the northern slopes of Potrero Hill to tumble into the Mission Bay estuary. A great quantity of fresh water poured in from Mission Creek itself, originating from two tributaries, one that started on the slopes of Twin Peaks, and the other that began not far west of today's Market and Church Streets. An underground river of fresh water that still moves southeasterly through the city's subterranean soils surfaced in countless ponds and swampy bogs and added millions more gallons of fresh water every week to the saltwater Mission Bay. The area teemed with a wide variety of life.

We tend to think of such a "natural history" as something that evolved separate from human intervention, but anthropological and archaeological studies of the pre-Columbian Americas indicate a remarkably anthropogenic landscape. That is to say, the people who lived here for thousands of years before the arrival of Europeans were not simply consuming the natural riches of the area, but were undoubtedly fully engaged in shaping their environment to suit their needs and preferences, using everything from seasonal burnings to careful cultivation of plants. A food-rich, accessible estuary like the one that occupied the eastern shore of the San Francisco peninsula was managed too, but in ways that are all but impossible to reconstruct.

In fact, the wet, shifting geography of the tidal zones makes a full archaeological investigation quite difficult, and the extensive landfilling along historic shorelines destroyed the earth mounds and shellmounds that once existed in this zone. We know that precontact dwellers here lived in small seasonal villages. Shellmounds—sites holding generations of discarded shells and other household debris, which were usually also burial sites—can be found around San Francisco Bay along nearly every creek and river. Unfortunately, any evidence of shellmounds around Mission Bay was destroyed during San Francisco's early, pell-mell urbanization process. Within a couple of years of the Gold Rush, the shoreline of Mission Bay was already being radically altered by shipbuilding and other early industries, and the dumping of landfill to "make land" using the sand, rock, and debris from the hills being leveled in the nearby South of Market area. A natural landscape was scraped away, covered over, and ripped apart to make space for the new city of San Francisco.

E2: San Francisco's Fresh Water

Shotwell between 17th and 18th Streets

San Francisco is surrounded on three sides by water, but the City's own creeks, ponds, and springs are mostly forgotten and buried. There are two surface creeks still visible to the intrepid hiker, one in Glen Canyon (Islais Creek) and the other at the edge of the Presidio (Lobos Creek). In recent years, restoration efforts have brought forth El Polin Spring in the Presidio and the headwaters of Yosemite Creek in McLaren Park to greater accessibility as well. But today most of the city's creeks are buried in culverts and merged with sewers. The deep tidal inlet that allowed watercraft to navigate into the heart of the Mission District as late as the 1860s is buried under city streets around Shotwell, Folsom, 17th, and 18th.

Similarly, the once rushing torrent of Islais Creek, with tributaries from Glen Canyon and further west at the end of Cayuga Street, is now a trickle, most of the water blocked and/or shunted into culverts near its sources. Long buried beneath the streets are large cement tunnels carrying the water to the bay, now hidden under Interstate 280. But once upon a time, the Burnham Plan for San Francisco proposed to turn Islais Creek and its riparian corridor into a parkway, which might have saved the wetlands east of Bernal Heights and south of Potrero Hill (fed also by Precita Creek) for fishing and recreation instead of burying them in culverts under endless drab warehouses.

Frank R. Quinn (1985) wrote down his memories of growing up in the Mission District and describes his childhood adventures in the Islais Creek watershed:

> Islais Creek fascinated us. Located east of what is today Highway 280, this huge area of marshland, full of numerous stagnant ponds and junk of all kinds, fed by streams of water from the hills, attracted us as a magnet does a nail. It was in this marshland that we boys would go rafting, sailing the malodorous

waters as though we were jolly tars on the Spanish Main. Islais Creek was fed, in part, by a stream that flowed down from the hills by way of what is today Alemany Boulevard. It was in this creek that we boys would catch pollywogs and bring them home, much to the consternation of our mothers. Today that stream is a busy highway carrying a heavy stream of automotive traffic.

In San Francisco's earliest days, fresh water was available from Mountain Lake on the edge of today's Presidio, and horse-drawn carts would bring barrels of fresh water to the City, far to the east. Similarly, William Richardson, San Francisco's first entrepreneur, acquired the southern Marin County lands now known as Richardson Bay and used ships to bring fresh water in by the barrel. A variety of water companies were founded to serve the city's exploding population during the Gold Rush years, but by the 1870s they had been consolidated into the Spring Valley Water Company, which brought fresh water to the City via redwood flumes, first from Mountain Lake and later from the Crystal Springs reservoirs in San Mateo. Spring Valley's owners prudently bought up all the watersheds and water sources in the vicinity of San Francisco, and with monopoly control, enjoyed a profitable period during the last quarter of the nineteenth century. Chronic battles between Spring Valley and the city government over water rates led James Phelan to apply for the water rights to the Tuolomne River in the Sierra Nevada Mountains, rights he then turned over to San Francisco when Congress passed the Raker Act in 1913. San Francisco was granted permission to build and maintain a dam and power plant in Hetch Hetchy canyon inside Yosemite National Park. In exchange for this public resource, San Francisco agreed to provide low-cost public water and public electricity to its residents in perpetuity, a deal only partially fulfilled. San Franciscans now get their water from the city-owned SF Water Department, which in turn is managed by the Public Utilities Commission. In spite of public ownership, water and sewage rates have been soaring in the City as a multiyear, multibillion-dollar effort is carried out to upgrade the Hetch Hetchy system and to ensure state-of-the-art sewage treatment.

Public water arrived in 1934, but public power has never arrived except to service MUNI and a few public facilities, while citizens have been paying top dollar for expensive electricity to PG&E in direct violation of federal law—and in contempt of a 1941, 8-1 U.S. Supreme Court decision—for nearly a century.

E3: ALBION CASTLE

881 Innes at Griffith

The Albion Castle, so called because of its unique architecture on the northern slopes of Hunters Point facing India Basin, sits atop a flourishing freshwater supply, a natural spring that produces close to 20,000 gallons of fresh water a day. The water was used to slake the thirst of San Francisco in the early 1850s, and to make beer and other alcoholic beverages in the 1870s after the construction of the underground cisterns; after Prohibition, the sweetly delicious fresh water was marketed by the Mountain Spring Water Company.

The Albion Ale and Porter Brewery was founded in 1870 by John Hamlin Burnell. Born in East Hoathly, Sussex, England in 1849, Burnell came to San Francisco via British Columbia. Having failed to make his fortune in the fur trade business, Burnell became interested in producing ales and porters comparable to those in England. A supply of fresh water was a critical ingredient for developing a brewery in the English tradition. This Burnell found in abundant supply in the underground springs that run beneath the property. Tunnels used for storing the ale were cut approximately 200–300 feet into the hillside.

The structures comprising the brewery covered fully half the lot, although little remains today but the reconstructed main brewery building, where fermenting kettles and malt mills were once located. This stone building with its three-story tower was probably modeled after the Norman castles of England constructed by skilled masons.

The brewery ceased operation altogether in 1919, after Mrs. Burnell's death and the advent of Prohibition. After 1920, the property was held by trust deeds and continued to deteriorate until 1938 when Adrien Voisin, a sculptor, bought it. Using old photographs and drawings, Voisin restored the main building's stonework to its original quality and used the premises as a residence and studio. Later, the Mountain Spring Water Company purchased the water rights from Voisin; and in 1964, the company purchased the brewery itself, allowing Mr. Voisin to retain life tenancy. In the twenty-first century, the water is not being used and is allowed to drain to the bay. The castle has been bought and sold as a private residence several times.

E4: Myth of Laguna Dolores

Camp and Albion Streets

Imagine the views from the original Mission Dolores in early 1800. To the south, the land dropped precipitously to the rushing Mission Creek, today running in a culvert beneath 18th Street. A deep ravine full of willows flourished on either side of the creek to the southeast (and became a working-class resort in 1850s San Francisco called "The Willows"). To the east spread the tidal slough and saltwater wetlands where birds, fish, and mammals lived in dense abundance. Small oak groves dotted local gulleys sheltered from wind by the hills, but most of the nearby hills were treeless and covered in dune scrub landscapes. To the north, another small creek burbled out of the hills and cascaded down to the swampy area that

The lake, invented in 1912 by a mapmaker, on a plaque on Albion Street. (Chris Carlsson)

is today's north Mission and covered by the Armory and the Central Freeway. Mission Dolores itself was built on dry, arable soil with easy access to nearby water, key qualities required for the Spanish Mission model. Rudimentary agriculture easily took hold in the surrounding acres in the decades before a town started to grow far east in Yerba Buena Cove.

In 1876, during centennial celebrations, two California historians debated the presence of a freshwater lake near the Mission. In 1912, Zoeth Eldredge published a map with the claim that a lake covered the area between 15th and 20th Streets, Valencia and Howard Streets, and was called originally *laguna de manantiel*. While working at the Oakland Museum of California, aquatic biologist Christopher Richard debunked the claim that a freshwater lake existed west of the known tidal inlet. A plaque that stands at Camp and Albion Streets shows a map of the supposed lake, and claims it stands on the bank of said lake. But core samples taken by Richard from beneath the recently built condominiums directly east of the plaque show that there was never a body of water standing in that area. Deciphering the early Spanish journals, *laguna de manantiel* refers to a spring-fed lake; and according to Richard's careful reading of new translations, it designated instead a body of water that later became known as Washerwoman's Lagoon at Gough and Vallejo Streets near the Marina District.

Nevertheless, the myth of Laguna Dolores persists, from some claiming it was destroyed by the tens of thousands of cattle and sheep owned by Mission Dolores in 1810, to others who simply post maps showing its existence in local business windows.

E5: A San Francisco Covered in Flowers

Sloat Boulevard and 19th Avenue

It's difficult enough to imagine the San Francisco shoreline consisting of an open expanse of bay water, ebbing and flowing over rich mudflats with the daily tides. Our imagination is challenged even further when we include the flora and fauna that flourished in this area prior to the arrival of European settlers. We don't know exactly what was here, but luckily we have the observations of Hans Herman Behr, a young German physician and naturalist who settled in San Francisco in 1850, and wrote down his observations some 40 years later (Behr: 1891). He describes freshwater ponds that pocketed the zone around today's 7th and 8th Streets near Harrison:

> Near the formerly well-known Russ Gardens there were extensive marshes abounding especially about their borders in interesting plants. Here grew the large-flowered dogwood, buckbean, stream orchids, the delightfully fragrant white-flowered bog orchid, and cotton grass. In the same vicinity I found in a single locality five specimens of leather grape-fern and the lady fern grew luxuriantly, often forming rootstocks two feet high, simulating tree ferns.

Behr goes on to describe a swampy bog with sand ridges running in parallel at a diagonal above the water. Where fresh water met the salty bay waters, a salicornia flat developed, providing a rich habitat for wetland critters. Long before city builders overran the area south of Mission Street, Behr observed a number of plants that would soon become rare or extinct in San Francisco, including spotted water hemlock, evening primrose, water pennywort, pondlily, and the once ubiquitous cattails. A dense stand of wax myrtle, blueblossom ceanothus, coast silktassel, and several kinds of fern clustered near today's 5th and Howard Streets, far inland from today's shores. At various locales in the area South of Market, subterranean fresh water broke to the surface providing sustenance for a wide variety of flowering plants, including fleabane, asters, rosilla, twinberry, and occasionally elderberry and wild currants. Even bog orchids flourished in the pre-urban saltwater marsh, where cordgrass was abundant, along with pickleweed and saltgrass, which is enjoying a comeback thanks to restoration efforts around the bay's shores in the past couple of decades.

Early San Franciscans marveled at the rich, colorful diversity of the flowers that would carpet the slopes of the undeveloped parts of the peninsula. Writing in the early twentieth century, Lillian Purdy describes going to Lake Merced to take in the show:

> Time was when you could gather wild flowers almost from your doorstep in San Francisco. Vacant lots and the nearest hills were alive with poppies and buttercups and lupines. But the city's growth has crowded these flowers from their haunts and

you must now travel several miles of railroad and tramp over hills and fields before you can be repaid with a harvest of blossoms. And, when you know the way into this garden of glories, no walk will be too long, no fatigue too great to compensate for the feast of eye and soul that awaits you. The road into this natural garden of San Francisco, where nearly every species of our flora grows in reckless profusion, is found by taking the San Mateo [street] cars, which carry you out through Sunnyside and on the border of the valley of vegetable gardens. Finally, at Ocean View, you leave the cars behind you and, walking southward along the railroad track for about half a mile, you cut across the field toward the ocean. From this point a most picturesque view spreads out before you. In the foreground is a variegated field—patches of gold, blue, rich, deep red and cream blended almost into rainbow effect—and beyond the green-carpeted hills, Lake Merced and a bit of ocean. (Purdy: 1902)

Restoration efforts on local hilltops and at the Presidio in the Golden Gate National Recreation Area are beginning to bring some of this floral profusion back to the City.

E6: Eucalyptus Wood Rush

Sutro Forest

Eucalyptus trees are ubiquitous in San Francisco and the Bay Area. They are not native to California originally, but many identify them as quintessentially Californian after more than a century of spreading across the landscape here. First brought by horticulturists who saw the fast-growing trees as ideal for windbreaks and as ornamental additions to their rural estates, it was at the beginning of the twentieth century that a promoter hit upon his strategy to get rich quick. Articles appeared in the press lamenting the U.S. "hardwood famine," and suggesting the eucalyptus, a timber tree in Australia, with its rapid growth and easy adaptation to California, was the perfect solution. The State Forester glowingly predicted: "It would appear that this State will become within the next twenty years the base of hardwood supply and the home of hardwood manufacturing. The new industry will produce a greater wealth than oranges."

Environmental writer Harold Gilliam (1966) described what happened next:

> Promoters jumped in by the score. They bought up big tracts of land at prices around $15 an acre, set out eucalyptus seedlings that cost them only $5 a thousand and sold the land for $25 an acre, promising that within a decade the timber would be worth ten times that price. Modest proposals appeared in newspaper and magazine ads: "Put your surplus into eucalyptus and after ten years you can live on the income the rest of your life, and when you are gone your children and your children's children will perpetually reap the same."

Thousands of people wanted to get rich quick and plunked down money to buy an acre of surefire trees. Eucalyptus seedlings were planted all over California. In the East Bay, one hopeful entrepreneur established a nursery with 30,000 seedlings along a rural Telegraph Avenue. After an eight-year frenzy, somebody made the embarrassing discovery that there was more than one kind of eucalyptus. There were, in fact, in Australia a staggering 600 species. And the principal kind imported here, the blue gum, was no good for timber, even in Australia. The Forestry Service of the U.S. Department of the Interior issued a report that popped the bubble. The blue gum eucalyptus was commercially useless (Farmer: 2013).

But by then, tens of thousands of the fast-growing trees were spreading across the hills and valleys of the state. Many people love how they look and smell, but the tree is not friendly to native plants or most animals, given that at its base the soil tends to turn very alkaline, and they monopolize any groundwater in the vicinity.

In Sutro Forest, the Presidio, and the East Bay hills, the forests turned out to be good at catching summer fog drip and adding to the water table. But the planted forests are reaching their old age now, leading many to clamor for their removal. Within the existing eucalyptus forests there tend to be dense ivy patches choking the trees and all else, in a macabre dance of invasive species. Worse is that the trees tend to freeze and die when winter temperatures fall below freezing, and that can lead to extreme fire hazards in the following summer months. Twice the East Bay hills have been engulfed in firestorms, once in 1923 and more recently in 1991, both times leading to hundreds of homes being burned to the ground, homes that were built on wooded hillsides and subdivisions that were carved out from the former eucalyptus plantations.

E7: Early Animal Life in San Francisco

Transamerica Pyramid/Montgomery and Washington Streets

One of the best anecdotal accounts describing wildlife along the bayshore takes place in the as yet unfilled Yerba Buena Cove. William Richardson was the first person to build a home near the shore in today's San Francisco in 1837. It also served as the center of his thriving business as a middleman between the cattle economy of the missions (mostly produced with enslaved Indian labor) and the visiting sailing ships from Britain, Russia, France, Spain, and eventually Mexico and the United States. His son Stephen wrote in his own memoir, *Days of the Dons*:

> One thing about the cove of Yerba Buena, or San Francisco, as it very soon came to be called, was the great number of good-sized fish that swam close in shore and were stranded by the outgoing tide. These were the natural food of all sorts of predacious animals, which existed in enormous numbers and, being little interfered with by man, for that reason were indifferent to his presence. I often used to sit on the veranda of my father's house and watch bears, wolves and coyotes quarreling over their prey along what is now Montgomery Street. (Miller: 1995)

Animal bones found in the shellmounds excavated in the early twentieth century give us a view of what lived here, and what was eaten here too—deer, elk, sea otter, beaver, squirrel, rabbit, gopher, raccoon, badger, skunk, lynx, bear, seal, sea lion, porpoise, turtle, wolf, goose, cormorant, canvasback ducks. The most commonly discovered molluscan remains in the shellmounds were the soft-shelled clam and the soft-shelled mussel (Nelson: 1909).

Three-spined stickleback and steelhead trout spawned in Mission Creek. Massive runs of sturgeon and salmon filled bay waters, occasionally becoming beached on the mudflats as the tides went out. When the tide was in, the mudflats beneath the water came to life. The snails, slugs, and other mud-dwelling critters were the ideal food for many of the birds that filled the skies and the waters.

Bird life on the bay was inconceivably thick. The waters of Mission Bay, and further south in India Basin and the waters around Hunters Point, were a happy hunting ground for ducks, geese, herons, egrets, clapper rails, marsh wrens, American bitterns, northern harriers, and many migratory birds. In the mudflats, birds with differently shaped bills of different lengths fed at different niches in the supermarket of mudflat creatures. The long-billed curlew in particular loved to feast on the ghost shrimp that once were abundant in Mission Bay. Sandpipers, plovers, and avocets were abundant, along with the wading black-necked stilts. The American coot looks like a black duck but is a distinct bird that still makes its nest among the cordgrass at water's edge. Brown pelicans, cormorants, loons, California gulls, and western grebes were also common to bay waters.

The abundance of game—on land, flying in from the skies, and in the sea—provided an ample diet for the humans living on the shores of the bay. But that abundance was already being diminished under the Spanish-imposed mission economy, with its landscape dominated by humans, cattle, and the invasive European grasses they brought with them. Aquatic life in the bay continued to thrive until industrial methods were applied to fishing and agriculture. Native Americans had hunted seals, sea lions, and sea otters as part of their culinary options, but European fur and hide traders had other plans. By the 1830s, the sea otter population had plunged, and at the beginning of the twentieth century there were only 14 sea otters left at Point Sur. As a result of preservation, protection, and cleanup efforts, river otters have been spotted on both sides of the Golden Gate in recent years, and sea otters have established a thriving presence in Monterey Bay to the south. Seals, sea lions, dolphins, and whales have all returned to the San Francisco Bay and are seen regularly thanks to decades-long efforts to clean and protect the bay.

E8: Harvesting Nature: Oil, Fur, Capital

Union Bank Building, 245 California Street (formerly Alaska Commercial Company)

San Francisco's early history is inseparable from a voracious exploitation of nature, not just within its own city limits or on the peninsula at the top of which it sits, but extending from Alaska to Hawaii, and most of western North America. Companies founded in San Francisco were at the heart of the systemic harvesting of animals and their conversion into products and eventually into capital itself. Much of that capital ended up taking the form of real estate in San Francisco or other land holdings around the West.

The earliest boom predated the city of San Francisco. Fur hunting brought British and Russians to the Pacific Coast in search of sea otters, which were slaughtered by the thousands. Once a common sight in the bay, by the 1830s their numbers were falling precipitously, thanks to the enormous demand for otter hides by Chinese and European clothiers, who prized its water resistance and heat retention qualities. By the late nineteenth century, sea otters had been hunted to what was feared to be their extinction—it wasn't until the 1940s that an isolated group of sea otters was discovered off the central California coast near Big Sur. Since that time, the otter has rebounded, though never to the abundant numbers it once enjoyed.

Similarly, the whaling business that began in earnest in the early 1700s in the Atlantic, centered around New England, had spread by the nineteenth century into the Pacific. Whalers crowded the city of Honolulu in Hawaii for supplies and repairs; and as the fleets ventured farther and farther north in pursuit of their prey, the harbor at Yerba Buena saw a slow increase in visitors too. By the 1880s, San Francisco was the capital of whaling on the West Coast, and was home to several large whale processing facilities, the most noteworthy being the Arctic Oil Works at the end of 16th Street on the bayshore established in 1883 to produce refined oils from seals, whales, and elephant seals. They maintained a large T-wharf, oil storage tanks, and open yards for drying baileen or whalebone, used for buggy whips and women's corsets.

In our epoch of fossil fuel use, it's easy to forget that before petroleum was discovered in the 1880s, the source of oil was primarily living beings of the sea—whales, walruses, sea lions, and seals. Forgotten too is the early growth in demand for whale oil. In the early 1700s, crime in the streets in London and Paris was out of control. Darkened nighttime streets made muggings all too easy, so a clamor went up to light the streets. Before long it was discovered that oil from right whales burned the brightest and longest of all known fuels; and as oil lamps were built through city streets, demand for whale oil soared (Dolin: 2007). By the late 1700s, countless new devices were appearing, and the industrial revolution was on the verge of a takeoff. Whale oil was a key ingredient in lubrication of all this new steam-powered machinery, and the extended workdays provided by illumination also gave impetus to the emerging capitalist economy.

In 1868, the Alaska Commercial Company was founded to take advantage of the vast seal herds of the Pribilof Islands, acquired as part of the 1867 purchase of Alaska from Russia. The company—founded by William Ralston, Louis Sloss, and crucially, General John F. Miller, collector of the Port of San Francisco (and great friend of President Ulysses Grant)— became the world's greatest fur supplier in the late nineteenth century. Miller acquired exclusive rights to harvest the Pribilof seal herds from Grant's administration, and went to Washington in 1881 to serve as California's senator and to defend the company's ongoing interests. The Pribilofs were then home to 80 percent of the world's fur seals, and they were harvested according to government regulations written by Miller himself. By 1889, when its lease ran out, the company had harvested a reported 1,850,000 seal skins, for which it had paid the U.S. government nearly $9.5 million. Its stockholders had harvested a reported $18 million in profits over the same period.

As historian and geographer Gray Brechin has described it:

> Treating the Arctic as a classic mining region, the Alaska Commercial Company extended its transportation and supply routes until it had 91 stations in Alaska, the Yukon and Siberia. Through these posts, trappers kept the company well supplied, not only with seal furs, but with red, white, blue and silver fox, otters, marten, mink, wolf, wolverine, bears (including polar), muskrat, ermine, lynx, beaver, sable, ivory, swanskin and whalebone. Furs and feathers were shipped to London for auction, then reshipped to the United States for processing and resale. (Brechin, 1999)

After the Pribilof lease expired, the Alaska Commercial Company reinvested capital in a variety of enterprises, including salmon canneries, a tannery, mines, transportation, utilities, and especially land reclamation and speculation in California. Central Valley railroad projects employed mining engineers who were once involved in hydraulic mining operations on the Yuba River; after these operations were outlawed in 1884, the engineers turned their expertise to long-range electrical transmission, which would in turn serve to drain marshes, milk cows, build cities, and power enormous gold dredges on the Sacramento River's tributaries. Engineers and entrepreneurs were virtually all tied with the syndicate that assembled Pacific Gas and Electric (PG&E) or its rival, Great Western Power, whose corporate goal it was to develop the resources of California and attract ever more immigrants to fill up the state's empty spaces.

Business leaders complained at the beginning of the twentieth century about California's vast size and resources and relatively low population, not larger at the time than that of the city of Chicago. Brechin again:

> It was to fill this vacuum that PG&E, Great Northern, the Northern Electric Railroad, and the various land reclamation companies such as Natomas were formed at the turn of the century, partly with profits derived from the skins and tusks of northern mammals. Capital made from the consumption of Arctic resources turned then to the consumption [development] of California land in the commodity form of real estate. (Brechin: 1999)

Leaping ahead to October 1989, the Loma Prieta 7.1 earthquake hit the Bay Area. Within days of this major seismic upheaval, several sea lions settled on the docks of Pier 39, a recent tourist-industry development on the waterfront at Fisherman's Wharf. Thanks to the 1972 Marine Mammal Protection Act, the owners of Pier 39 were not allowed to disturb these wild animals. More and more sea lions showed up on the docks, and after months of squatting at the valuable yacht harbor, the Pier 39 owners had to concede the space to them. Making the best of it, they established an observation deck and brought in docents to help people understand the remarkable sight of dozens of wild sea lions resting and occasionally fighting each other in a busy tourist destination on the north shore of San Francisco. For at least two decades, the sea lions of Pier 39 were themselves a major tourist attraction, though remaining a fully wild population. In 2015 or so, the numbers of sea lions began to drop, some days completely disappearing, but the population had rebounded by 2018.

Given the sordid history of human slaughter of marine mammals, for at least a few years, this surprising assertion of control by wild animals seemed to reverse fortunes and claim a bit of justice from a dark history.

E9: MISSION CREEK: INDUSTRIAL PAST

Huffaker Park, 6th and Channel Streets

Mission Creek is the remnant waterway of what was once a much larger inlet known as Mission Bay. Between 1860 and 1910, the area was filled in and put to use. Mission Bay was deeded to the railroads in exchange for building rail into San Francisco in the 1870s. After decades, the area was filled, and for half a century the "made land" of Mission Bay was home to huge railyards, including a large roundhouse. Banana companies like United Fruit Company and Del Monte unloaded tons of fruit along the banks of Mission Creek for decades.

Nearby was the old hay wharf, where at its peak over 300 tons a day of hay was unloaded from scow schooners (the flatbed trucks of their time). Tens of thousands of horses were waiting for this vital fuel as they worked the hills of San Francisco, pulling streetcars, wagons, and coaches full of people and cargo (T5). In a happy ecological cycle of the nineteenth century, the tons of manure that filled the streets of San Francisco were put to use on the sand dunes of western Golden Gate Park, creating better soil able to grow a variety of trees and plants on what had previously been a sand dune ecology.

Lumberyards, paint factories, warehouses, and other industrial concerns also established themselves along the banks of Mission Creek. In the 1970s, the industries were gone and the north side of Mission Creek was covered by an eight-lane-wide ramp for a freeway that dead-ended at 3rd Street (it was a stub meant to connect to the Bay Bridge, but the last section was never built). The Southern Pacific Railroad (now Caltrain) occupied the railyards north of the freeway. To the south of Mission Creek on the old landfill was a derelict warehouse district that had once included vast railyards, along with a cement plant, a firehouse, and later, a golf driving range.

In 1972, the Port of San Francisco asked houseboat dwellers on Islais Creek if they would move north to Mission Creek in exchange for a

Unloading lumber into carts in 1897 at a yard west of the 4th Street Bridge on Mission Creek. (Courtesy San Francisco Maritime National Historical Park [A12.29.727n1])

long-term lease, which they accepted. Thus began the houseboat community on Mission Creek, which has had a long and effective life—both in protecting their own housing and in improving the surroundings. The Mission Creek Conservancy was founded by members of the community to protect and improve the local ecology, habitat, and species diversity.

Their efforts have succeeded at bringing Mission Creek back to life. Its shores have dense native foliage, and more than 80 species of birds, dozens of fish, crustaceans, sea mammals, and other wildlife have come home to Mission Creek (Olmsted: 1986 and 2002).

The houseboat dwellers also built Huffaker Park along the southern shore, one of San Francisco's well-hidden treasures of public space for many years. But for more than 20 years, one of the biggest development projects in the history of San Francisco has been filling up the entire Mission Bay area, which has now become a new neighborhood, home to dozens of high-rise apartment buildings and offices, a 42-acre bio-medical campus of the University of California, with still more under construction.

By the time you read this, the park will have been subsumed into a normal municipal design, but for decades its eclectic character has graced the south side of Mission Creek, a product of the activism and commitment of the houseboat residents. Their efforts to affect the massive Mission Bay development also led to major restoration efforts along the creek. New approaches to stormwater and sewage were agreed to as part of the project and infrastructure for a gray water system was built in from the start.

E10: MISSION ROCK/PIER 50

Terry Francois Boulevard at Pier 50

Mission Rock was once a tiny island sitting east of today's shoreline at the edge of Mission Bay, although today it lies under the extended Pier 50. After it was purchased early in San Francisco history it was flattened and expanded, becoming a place where grain shipments from the Central Valley and delta were brought in and unloaded by scow schooners. Temporarily stored in a warehouse on Mission Rock, the grain was then reloaded onto speedy clipper sailing ships, and later on to steam-powered schooners, that would bring the California wheat to markets as far away at Australia and Europe.

The island served this purpose and other agricultural storage activities until its demise in January 1946. During those early post-WWII months, the U.S. Navy, in cooperation with the Port of San Francisco, burned the island's facilities to clear the way for its annexation to the port. Pier 50 with the large sign *Port of San Francisco* encompasses the former Mission Rock near the far eastern end where the U.S. military maintains a ready-reserve ship most of the time.

E11: Buried under San Francisco and in the Bay

Beale and Howard Streets

Beneath the gleaming new apartment tower at Folsom and Main Streets sits what was once a shipwrecking yard at the edge of Rincon Hill. When excavation began in the early 2000s, the wooden hull of the *Candace* was discovered about a half-floor beneath street level, where it had been left sunken in bay mud for 150 years. This was just the latest in what has been a steady rediscovery of sunken ships beneath downtown San Francisco. Over 70 ships have been discovered over the years, many of which have been left in situ as transit tunnels and building foundations have been erected around and on top of them.

Not far away, at Beale and Howard Streets, a gray office building was built in the late 1990s; and when its foundation was being excavated, builders came upon a layer 2.5 feet thick of tar, giving proof to the old nickname for this part of the City as "Tar Flat." In the early industrial city, the San Francisco Gas Works had its plant near this area, and the tar by-product of gas production was thought to be useless and allowed to flow into the nearby mudflats at the shoreline. (Today, of course, tar is used for roofing material among other things.)

Buried in the sand and soil beneath all the new construction are countless artifacts of nineteenth-century San Francisco, from clay pipes to glass bottles, to coins and buttons, and much more. When the first sailors jumped ship to head to the gold fields in the Sierras, they began a process that inexorably filled Yerba Buena Cove with a thickening foundation of debris that eventually became the land on which sits today's Financial District and downtown. The abandoned ships were the first warehouses and boardinghouses and restaurants of the sudden City. After several terrible fires destroyed most of the earliest structures, the hulls of ships burned to the waterline simply sank from view, and more pilings and structures were built over them.

While this accretion of layers was taking place in San Francisco, an opposite but perhaps more lasting process was under way in the mountains.

Soon after the placer mining was exhausted, major capital flowed into the river gulleys of California where gold was lodged in ancient streambeds high in the granite walls of the canyons. Technological breakthroughs in metallurgy and metalwork led to the creation of monitors—nozzles that directed gravity-fed streams from redwood flumes into canvas hoses and through the new hi-tech nozzles to blast away the mountains. Hydraulic mining of this sort steadily washed away the hills for 25 years, leading to the equivalent of three and a half Panama Canals worth of debris being washed down into the rivers of California, pulsing slowly but steadily into the San Francisco Bay itself (Isenberg: 2005). Within those vast quantities of soil and rock was a great deal of mercury, mined originally from the Almaden mines above the Guadalupe River south of San Jose, and used to amalgamate with gold in the hydraulic mining process. So much mercury was washed down the rivers that today's bay mud remains heavily contaminated by methyl mercury, one of the worst consequences of the Gold Rush to remain with us today. (The original mine also continues to contaminate the Guadalupe River, which flows into the south bay, thus worsening an already bad toxic mess.)

In 1884, the hydraulic mining process was finally halted on the Yuba River by the Sawyer decision in the North Bloomfield Mine case (and subsequently applied to other rivers by later court decisions). After years of state courts upholding the original rights of miners versus the claims of farmers and landowners downstream, a federal court upheld an absentee owner's right near Yuba City to NOT have his land swamped by 65 feet of mining debris. The farmer's property rights were deemed of equal value to the mining company's property rights to its mine, and thus the miners could no longer freely dispose of their wastes by sending them downstream to inundate other people's property. The Sawyer decision has been hailed in recent years as an early environmental decision as it did halt hydraulic mining in this case, but its foundation in property rights belies that notion. Moreover, it took further lawsuits on each river system to block other mining companies from continuing the practice; and once it was generally banned in California, the techniques of hydraulic mining were quickly exported to other parts of the world, where a number of countries are still using them today.

E12: SAVING TELEGRAPH HILL

Green Street west of Sansome Street

Telegraph Hill once extended beyond Battery Street to the east, and the early piers of Fisherman's Wharf extended into the bay from its eastern slopes. George and Harry Gray employed men who dug at the east face of Telegraph Hill for about 20 years, persevering through bankruptcies and occasional barrages of rocks from irate Irish and Italian hill dwellers whose small homes would sometimes come tumbling down the cliffside after a quarry explosion. The Gray brothers ignored and bribed their way through court orders and wide social opposition, which even included shootings of quarry personnel.

The movement to save Telegraph Hill was spearheaded by a group of women, mostly from other parts of San Francisco. In 1890, Alice Griffith, Elizabeth Ashe, and eight other women formed the Willing Circle, which eventually became the Telegraph Hill Neighborhood Association. Their efforts focused on stopping the quarrying of the hill, but also they aimed to improve the neighborhood by providing classes in homemaking, a Boys' Club, and a settlement house at the crest of Vallejo Street that provided two nurses for locals' needs. Alice Griffith was the persistent force, badgering city officials, local societies, and merchant associations. She found lawyers to take on the Gray brothers and enlisted the aid of John McLaren to plant flowering shrubs atop the then-barren Pioneer Park at the hill's summit. It took years, but their efforts finally caught the public's attention; and in 1903, the City's Board of Supervisors passed an ordinance banning the quarrying of Telegraph Hill. However, that ordinance was quietly ignored by the Gray brothers, who, under the cover of the 4th of July fireworks in 1909, set off a large dynamite charge that brought down part of Calhoun Terrace. It wasn't until 1914 that the City banned the removal of rock and debris from Telegraph Hill, which finally brought the quarrying of the hill to an end (Myrick: 1972 and 2001).

Today the hill is covered in million-dollar homes and is one San Francisco's most luxurious addresses. But at the foot of Green and Sansome Streets you can still see the scars of the quarrying that the Willing Circle stopped in the early twentieth century. In the disturbed hillside, exotic plant species are dominant, with eucalyptus, fennel, German ivy, and pampas grass spread across the cliffs. Curiously, the eucalyptus trees growing here invoke a whole other story, that of the early-twentieth-century Eucalyptus Rush (E6).

The Filbert Steps, running from Sansome Street to the top of Telegraph Hill, is home to one of San Francisco's most loved and venerated community gardens. Grace Marchant petitioned the Board of Supervisors in 1946 for permission to burn the garbage dump along the Filbert Steps. It burned for days, and after that Marchant began developing the garden. The flourishing gardens along the century-old wooden stairway on the eastern slope of Telegraph Hill created by the neighbors are open to the public, an outstanding example of citizen-generated urban design. Gary Kray and others have followed Grace Marchant, and her own daughter led the way on a parallel process for the Greenwich Steps just north of the Filbert Steps. The gardens have also become home to a flock of wild parrots—cherry-headed conures to be precise—made famous by the work of Mark Bittner, author of the book *The Wild Parrots of Telegraph Hill*, and Judy Irving, director of the film by the same name.

In sharp contrast to the profusion of flowers and cozy spots to sit in the Marchant Gardens, at the foot of the steps and across Sansome Street is Levi's Plaza, the design award-winning corporate campus. The architecture blends in with the surrounding nineteenth-century brick buildings it partially absorbed (including the Italian Swiss Colony Wine Company building and warehouse), with public plazas and parkland filling out the property. In an ironic juxtaposition, the artificial brook and gardens are built on the site of a Depression-era soup kitchen known as the White Angel Jungle. The tidy, controlled atmosphere of the bucolic park-like corporate campus is well liked for its relationship to the old brick warehouses of the area, but is the antithesis of the welcoming, neighbor-designed gardens along the old wooden steps just to its west.

E13: Carving Hills

Bernal Cut, Richland Overpass

San Francisco would not be a gridded, urbanized space without the remarkable efforts made to cut down, cut through, and flatten the dunes and hills that were here when urbanization began. One of the earliest dramatic examples of this process took place on Rincon Hill when it was the richest neighborhood in the City. Covered in elegant mansions, many of which

Northerly on 2nd Street from Bryant in 1869 after cut through Rincon Hill. (Courtesy San Francisco Maritime National Historical Park [A12.28.752n])

belonged to Confederate sympathizers such as Senator William Gwin, it was an unlikely place to be ripped open. But John Middleton, a landowner on the southern flanks of the hill along 2nd Street, had his own ideas. Winning election to the state legislature in 1868, he was intent on fulfilling his main goal: to cut 2nd Street's grade down and make it more passable and thus make his own land more commercially viable between the location of the City's commercial center and the shipyards and gas works near Steamboat Point.

He successfully passed a state law authorizing the Second Street Cut; and before long, crews of men and horses were digging into the hill and creating a deep east-west chasm while Rincon Hill still rose up 100 feet on either side. At first a bridge was built across the divide at Harrison Street, but eventually, over decades, most of the hill was brought down in size. While the Second Street Cut was underway, William Ralston and Asbury Harpending convinced the state legislature to authorize the leveling of the entirety of Rincon Hill, but the intransigent opposition of Governor Henry

Haight stopped that plan from coming to pass, with the legislature eventually reversing itself. (When the Bay Bridge anchorage was established on the remaining summit in 1936, the remainder of the hill was finally fully integrated into the urban grid.)

During the 1860s, Broadway was cut through the dense rock and steep slopes of Telegraph Hill. The eastern slopes of the hill were already being systematically quarried by several companies, who were bringing down tons of rock and selling them to road builders and for ship ballast among other uses. Broadway was opened to make access to Clark's Point and the Vallejo Wharf from solid land. Just to its south was the Barbary Coast, then still largely built on old ships and piers jutting over the waters of Yerba Buena Cove, so the Broadway cut provided a road to move goods in horse-drawn wagons into the City directly.

Two decades later, after the Long Bridge was built across the mouth of Mission Bay (today's 3rd Street), the railroad that used the bridge needed to create a way through the easternmost part of Potrero Hill (which is actually comprised of three different hills) known as Irish Hill. The steam paddys went to work and carved a route through the hill to connect the railroad to another long trestle crossing the wetlands of Islais Creek before reaching land at Hunters Point. Today's Dogpatch neighborhood sits astride the flattened land that was once a slope running up steeply from the shoreline and connecting to today's Potrero Hill. As recently as the 1930s, a big piece of Irish Hill still stood at the corner of 22nd and Illinois Streets, where it took 92 steps to reach the top on an old rickety stairway. The thousands of cubic yards of soil and rock from the original cutting of a passage through Irish Hill, and later its general demolition, all went to filling Mission Bay, the shipyards, and the Islais Creek basin to the south. Today a tiny remnant serpentine cliff of Irish Hill is still standing near 22nd and Illinois Streets amid the massive rebuilding and renovation of the Pier 70 shipyards.

Driving in or out of San Francisco's Mission District on San Jose Avenue, one passes through the Bernal Cut. Originally Bernal Heights was continuous with the hills to its west, today's Fairmount Heights, and farther Gold Mine Hill and Diamond Heights. The Southern Pacific Railroad built its line through the low point in this small hill range in the 1860s for its San Jose-San Francisco line. When they first opened it up, and for many years after, it was only the width of one railroad track, but in the 1920s the

City decided to radically widen the passage and add automobile traffic. That's when the overpasses at Highland and Richland Avenues were built. At one point this was projected to the southern end of the proposed Mission Freeway, but actual plans to plow through Valencia and Guerrero Streets with an elevated freeway were defeated by 1959, and San Jose Avenue has served as a high-speed car corridor ever since, until the addition of bike lanes and the J-Church streetcar in the twenty-first century.

E14: SEWERAGE

Warm Water Cove, eastern end of 24th Street at bayshore

During most of the late nineteenth and early twentieth centuries, the shoreline was a dumping ground for the organic and industrial waste of the new city: the offal from early slaughterhouses along Mission Creek, the raw sewage that poured in from houses and buildings that sat near its original shoreline, and the debris and waste from shipbuilding, power plants, and factories. San Francisco's original waterways—mostly consisting of small creeks running down hillsides into nearby tidal outflows—served as the original sewage-carrying system for the early residents. Nearly every creek eventually got the name Shit Creek because of its unquestioning use as an open sewer. Precita Creek under today's Cesar Chavez Street, Mission Creek under 18th Street, Islais Creek under Glen Park and Highway 280, all earned that delicious sobriquet.

It was along Precita Creek between the Mission District and Bernal Heights that San Francisco built its first formal box sewer, 13 feet across and 10 feet tall. Due to the seasonal variation of heavy rains in the winter and dry weather summers, the box sewer didn't function as planned. In 1995, Steven Bodzin described the result:

> A couple years after its construction, an internal inspection found the box to be a stinking mess. Solid wastes had built up where laterals, or residential hookups, connected to the big box. Strange foliage grew in the darkness, fertilized by the human waste and compost that congealed on the floor. Indeed, the ecosystem inside the box was so efficient at removing nutrients, the water flowing out at the east end of the sewer near today's General Hospital was clean enough to drink.

Lacking an easy way to use gravity for its sewer system, San Francisco had to figure out a new way to keep the shit flowing. One suggestion at the time proposed leaving the creeks at the surface to feed a system of reservoirs that could then be used to drain into the sewers to keep wastes moving, ending in sludge to use as fertilizer on nearby farms. But no such rational plan was enacted, due to the haphazard system of building that characterized early San Francisco, and the many different sewers already built, already experiencing serious problems. Mission Creek, for example, had 13 sewers dumping into it, and the resulting smell was eye-watering. Worse, the outflow was into tidal waters, and whenever high tides came up, they blocked the outflow, leading to back-gassing into people's homes, and worse.

Earlier, in 1893, the City commissioned a master plan for a new sewer system, but promptly shelved it as they did with a subsequent 1899 plan. After the 1906 quake destroyed 25 percent of the City, the surviving sewers were only known through a set of notebooks from public works engineers who tried to survey the pipes after the quake, along with the summary reports of the various master planners.

From 1908 to 1935, a zone system sent sewage to the bay or ocean in one of the 35 outfalls. New Deal federal money led to the second wastewater master plan, released in 1935, which was the first time "primary treatment" was called for. (Primary treatment consists of a screen across outflow pipes to catch large items like dead bodies, etc.) In 1938, the first treatment plant, at the end of Golden Gate Park, went into operation. In 1951, two more plants were built. One plant, at North Point, filtered effluent and pumped it into the bay near Pier 39, while sending the leftover sludge south for further treatment. A bigger plant at Phelps Street and Jerrold Avenue processed the waste from the southeast corner, including most of the City's industrial waste. It dried sludge into soil, including that from North Point, notably insulated from wealthy white noses.

In dry weather, all of these plants dumped primary-treated effluent directly into the bay or ocean. However, in wet weather, they—along with all the old outfalls at Mission Creek, Mile Rock, Marina Green, Fort Funston, Griffith Street, and elsewhere—spewed raw sewage into the bay, reinforcing a general aversion to being near the water. Big pools of discolored, toxic water were often visible, swimming was unthinkable, and fishing was a toxic roulette.

The Clean Water Act that passed as one of the major federal environmental initiatives at the beginning of the 1970s forced San Francisco to modernize its sewers again. In 1971, the City came up with its third master plan for the sewers. It called for a series of massive boxes to be built around the City's waterfront, intercepting old outfalls like a moat. The boxes would be big enough to hold the water of normal rains, delivering it slowly enough to the treatment plants that they could treat it properly before releasing it. The captured water would be sent to modernized treatment facilities at Jerrold Avenue and at a new southwest plant by the zoo. Overflows in the east would not be dumped into the bay, but rather sent by a tremendous tunnel to the southwest plant. That plant would spit its waste—which would always receive at least a primary treatment—out into the ocean 4.5 miles from land. This grand vision called for big money—initial cost estimates were $1.1 billion to $1.4 billion, the biggest public works project in city history.

Construction of the new sewers began in the mid-1970s, and after 20 years was largely finished. Huge box sewers run the length of Great Highway, and around the waterfront from Marina Green almost uninterrupted to Candlestick Park. Mission Creek's old outfalls now pour into a box sewer, which is pumped south to Jerrold Avenue. The outfalls at China Beach and Mile Rock are no longer active, as they deliver waste to the southwest plant by the Richmond Transport, a big tunnel under Sutro Heights.

The scale of the new system is worthy of ogling. The twelve miles of transport/storage tunnels, which reach sizes of 50 feet wide by 48 feet deep, dwarf the old downtown wooden tubes the way a freeway dwarfs a dirt road; the last known wooden sewer was replaced in 1985. The combination of all the boxes will be able to hold 200 million gallons, ostensibly enough to keep even a five-year storm from overflowing the treatment plants. In other words, the system should only overflow every five years, if rainfall continues its 70-year trend. The Southwest Ocean Outfall is a cement pipe on the ocean floor, which carries waste from the southwest plant. It is as much as 80 feet under the ocean surface, constructed to withstand a 15-foot movement along the San Andreas Fault (which it crosses). It may someday carry all effluent from San Francisco's nearly 900 miles of sewer mains.

In the 2000s, San Francisco faced yet another multibillion-dollar round of repair, reinforcement, and modernization of its sewage treatment facilities. By this time, citizens in the Mission District had embarked on ambitious efforts to create sidewalk gardens that serve as green sewers. That is, they capture rain and allow it to percolate into the aquifer rather than force it into the overburdened stormwater/sewage system. Through efforts by Jane Martin and her organization PlantSF, a new city permit was created to allow homeowners to open the sidewalks in front of their homes and plan drought-tolerant gardens. When she started this project, Martin was living on Shotwell Street between 17th and 18th Streets, at the low point of the original tidal inlet in the heart of the Mission District, an area prone to severe flooding in every major rainstorm. Permeable sidewalks, new water pumps beneath the street, and cement berms at either end to prevent inflow of rainwaters have alleviated the problem on that block. But the surrounding areas have been inundated several times in the 2010s, and efforts to prevent flooding so far have not succeeded. Nevertheless, the Department of Public Works (DPW) has planted medians in most major thoroughfares in the area, new street trees have been extensively planted, and the DPW has also established a series of swales to capture rainwater and direct it into the ground and away from the sewage system, all as a way to reduce the need to expand the system of box storage that sits beneath the City's shorelines.

As mentioned elsewhere, the build-out of the new Mission Bay neighborhood has proceeded with stormwater and sewage separated by design, and a new gray water system to capture and reuse lightly used waters has been built in from the beginning too. Still ahead is the need for a new water treatment facility to be built somewhere on the eastern side of the City to handle the flow of gray water and recycle it into proper uses.

E15: Scavengers and Trash

Tunnel Road Dump (Recology)

San Francisco's garbage collection began with families who claimed various territories for this activity for themselves. They would pass through these areas with horse-drawn wagons gathering refuse from the households along the way. Long ago, nearly everything had a potential use or was made of organic materials and could be decomposed. The various clans—a large number of them Italian immigrants—slowly amalgamated into two great syndicates, Sunset Scavenger and the Scavenger's Protective Association. In 1921, each was given an exclusive refuse collection license covering a specific part of the City, and each was organized as a cooperative of its members. Interestingly, the co-op structure was so thorough that everyone was given the same wages and benefits, from the workers on the route to the secretaries and executives in the office.

The two companies founded a third entity in 1935, the Sanitary Fill Company, which ran the dump on Tunnel Road, slowly filling in Brisbane Lagoon over the course of a half century. It was the stench of the garbage here that blew south across the flanks of San Bruno Mountain and by an ironic twist of fate, probably saved the mountain from rampant development in the mid-twentieth century. By 1965, the use of the bay as a garbage dump was over. The Scavenger's Protective Association changed its name to Golden Gate Disposal, while Sunset Scavenger kept its name. The companies began shipping solid waste to large dumps in surrounding hills.

In the early 1970s, the co-op structure that the companies had maintained since their founding a half century earlier was dismantled and replaced with an Employee Stock Ownership Plan. Wages that had been identical for decades now began to vary depending on more typical considerations. Many of the original shareholders sold their shares, and the company became a regular managerial corporation with investors owning the majority of shares. Seeking to expand into the lucrative trash business throughout Northern California, Golden Gate Disposal changed its name to Norcal Solid Waste Systems in 1983. In 1986, Norcal was sold back to the original Employee Stock Ownership Plan, and a year later it absorbed the former Sunset Scavenger, becoming one company.

Soon after, Norcal Waste, certain that their clients would never recycle, and institutionally opposed to the "hippie" approach to solid waste, sought to build a massive incinerator just south of city limits in Brisbane. Supervisors of both San Francisco and San Mateo approved the plan, as did the city council of Brisbane, but Brisbane citizens revolted. A popular initiative was put on the ballot, and the NIMBYs of Brisbane defeated the planned incinerator (which would have spewed toxic exhaust over their town), foiling the plans of Norcal and PG&E (who would have generated electricity with the burned trash). Combined with the California statewide mandate to reduce waste due to overflowing landfills, the re-named Recology had to establish curbside recycling in San Francisco, now taken for granted by City residents (Carlsson: 2011; Gravanis interview).

E16: HERON'S HEAD PARK

Cargo Way at Jennings Street

Today's Heron's Head Park at the end of Cargo Way just south of Islais Creek is one of San Francisco's little-known treasures, a nine-acre spit of land and shoreline restoration project that juts well into the bay on the northern edge of India Basin, across from the Hunters Point Naval Shipyard. The Port of San Francisco first proposed a 48-acre bay fill project here in the late 1960s, and received a permit in 1970 from the Bay Conservation and Development Commission (BCDC) to begin filling the subtidal bay lands by pointing to the economic benefits that would accrue to a new modernized shipping pier, Pier 98, and a second bay crossing, that is, another Bay Bridge.

By 1977, when the Port aborted the project and halted construction of the pier, container ships had mostly deserted San Francisco for Oakland, and the idea for a Southern Crossing was dead. In the early 1970s, the Port had made a fatal error when it bet on a new shipping technology known as LASH (Lighter Aboard Ship) instead of the now ubiquitous container cranes. By the time it got around to building its few modern container facilities, it was too late, and the vast majority of shipping had moved to the rapidly expanding and modernizing Port of Oakland (L16). As for the Southern Crossing, also by the early 1970s, highway planners promoting an additional Bay Bridge ran head on into a well-organized opposition that had already won the epic battles to stop the Panhandle/Golden Gate Park Freeway and the Golden Gate Expressway, and further freeway construction in San Francisco had been completely halted (T12).

BCDC ordered the Port of San Francisco to remove the debris they had put into the bay, and when the order was rejected, a lawsuit ensued between the two agencies. In the 15 years it took for the BCDC and the Port to resolve their differences about the legality of the bay fill, San Franciscans discovered a recreational and ecological treasure along their bayshore, and Pier 98 became a valuable recreational resource for the citizens of Hunters Point and the Bayview District. As storm waves and tidal action eroded the fill along the southern edge, it became habitat for migratory birds. A complex of tidal wetlands and intertidal ponds reemerged; after decades of absence, marsh plants could once again be found in San Francisco. Over 118 bird species have been observed in the last 20 years. American avocets and killdeers both nest at the site, and many other large charismatic shorebirds frequent the bucolic peninsula.

In the midst of these working-class neighborhoods where over a hundred years of heavy industry has created brownfield sites and hazardous waste sites, and where fuel storage tanks leak underground, exposing residents to a wide range of pollutants, a local activist group, Literacy for Environmental Justice (LEJ), guided by the principles of environmental justice and sustainability for urban youth, built the EcoCenter, a visitor's center for the remarkable restoration project. Heron's Head Park is one of a series of shoreline open spaces that ring India Basin, and extend south to the Candlestick Point State Recreation Area and its wetlands around Yosemite Slough (slowly being restored too), and north to the amazing rebirth of both Mission Creek and Islais Creek. The Bay Trail integrates many of these shoreline open spaces into its ambitious plan to ring the entire bay with a 400-mile open trail along its shores.

E17: YOSEMITE SLOUGH AND CANDLESTICK POINT STATE RECREATION AREA

Hunters Point Expressway

Along the southeastern shoreline of the bay within San Francisco city limits sits a forgotten creek and wetland now called Yosemite Slough. In the 1920s and 1930s, this area had some of San Francisco's most pristine bayshore beaches; in particular, a beach beneath the bluffs at the end of Egbert Street was once a much-loved childhood play area. But WWII led to an intense and toxic industrialization of this neighborhood. Yosemite Creek, with its headwaters in McLaren Park (recently restored), was culverted in the 1910s when most San Francisco waterways were buried beneath city streets and combined with sewage outflows. Adjacent to the Naval Shipyard's most toxic parcels, the eastern end of the Bayview neighborhood also housed a number of small metal shops and other industrial sites, all of which left behind a toxic stew in the ground. Several national Superfund sites dot the area today, and memories of beaches and access to a healthy bay are long forgotten.

View west from Candlestick Point State Recreation Area toward Bayview Hill.
(Chris Carlsson)

Along the southern shore of Yosemite Slough and due east of the former stadium site sits Candlestick Point State Recreation Area, the only urban state park in California. It is built on 100 percent landfill. Few remember now that the Candlestick Point park was created by a neighborhood campaign, some of whom remembered the old shoreline before development, while others saw the junkyard and debris that had accumulated offshore as an opportunity to create something special. Urban scavengers and artists built weird sculptures, and even for a time a curious Stonehenge built of concrete pieces and rebar took shape out there. Eventually the predominantly African American neighborhood pushed in public hearings for a natural park that would bring the bayshore and the bay into neighborhood reach. A park that had space for nature, for birds and seals and mudflats, public art, and unplanned uses was prioritized over basketball courts and ballfields. And new beaches were created that are today in heavy use on any given weekend or holiday, along with numerous barbecue pits that dot the park.

Ironically, perhaps bitterly, the gentrification pressure on Bayview is leading to a demographic shift even in the last black San Francisco neighborhood. As people cash out and move away, the population—once the largest percentage of homeowners in the City—is changing. The new shoreline parks in Yosemite Slough and north in India Basin are slowly taking shape after decades of deindustrialization, and also as part of the Bay Rim Trail. There is a general rethinking of the bayshore going on; in spite of inevitable sea-level rise, parks, wetlands, and publicly accessible space have been created all along the bayshore. The painful irony is that most of the people who once lived near here thanks to inexpensive housing are being pushed out and will not get to enjoy the improved, more accessible shoreline.

E18: San Bruno Mountain

Guadalupe Canyon Parkway, San Bruno County Park, walk up Radio Ridge from parking area

San Bruno Mountain sits astride the peninsula, the natural dividing line between San Francisco and the lands to its south. The political boundary was drawn further north, though, and most of San Bruno Mountain lies south of San Francisco's border. The mountain is visible to all who drive anywhere near it or fly above it coming in or going out of San Francisco's airport. From the south, big white letters saying SOUTH SAN FRANCISCO: THE INDUSTRIAL CITY sit on Sign Hill, a small extension south of the main flank. But most of San Bruno Mountain appears barren to the millions of eyes that pass in cars every day along Highway 101 or Interstate 280 on either side of it. In fact, San Bruno Mountain is teeming with life and represents the last land of its size that still is home to something like the original eco-niche that covered the San Francisco peninsula before the arrival of Europeans. Ironically, the reason the mountain was saved from the usual pattern of carving, flattening, and building that other parts of the City fell to was that it smelled bad (E15)! Brisbane was established in the northeasternmost valley of the mountain, probably the warmest spot, and just over the hill from evidence of a thousand-year-old indigenous pre-colonization village. At the foot of the dusty town was the bay, with the railroad line running along the shore (Caltrain still follows the same route today). For over 50 years, San Francisco's scavenger companies systematically dumped the City's refuse into the northern part of Brisbane Lagoon, the part of the bay south of Candlestick Point (Highway 101 is built on a causeway that crossed in a straight line across the mouth of Brisbane Lagoon—today most of it is fully landfilled). The prevailing northerly winds blew the smell of rotting garbage across the water directly to Brisbane.

San Bruno Mountain looking southeast from the air, SFO airport at upper right.
(Adriana Camarena)

Being subject to the stench of San Francisco's garbage made San Bruno Mountain undesirable for development.

In 1884, Charles Crocker, one of the Big Four builders of the Central Pacific Railroad, acquired San Bruno Mountain. After his 1888 death and the distribution of his estate, the mountain passed to the Crocker Estate

Company, later the Crocker Land Company. They held the mountain continuously to the recent past. From 1965 to the present, several proposals for the development of San Bruno Mountain were made. The Rockefellers were teaming up with the Crocker family, who owned a good deal of the mountain, with plans to lop off the top third and run it on conveyor belts into the bay to build another freeway 1.5 miles east of Highway 101, filling all the space between to landlock the airport and radically fill the southwest bay. This plan was the impetus for organized opposition, leading to the Committee to Save San Bruno Mountain and later San Bruno Mountain Watch. In 1970, mountain real estate was transferred to Foremost-McKesson Inc., which in turn passed it along to Visitacion Associates, a consortium of Foremost-McKesson and Amfac Inc. Visitacion Associates then co-owned 3,600 acres of San Bruno Mountain with the Crocker Land Company. Visitacion Associates proposed a massive development in 1975, slated for 8,500 residential units and 2 million square feet of office and commercial space. Years of contentious litigation and lobbying ensued. In 1978, Crocker Land Company settled litigation with San Mateo County by donating 546 acres and selling the county 1,100 acres of land along the main ridge, which later became San Bruno Mountain County Park. The State of California later bought and donated 256 more acres, making the park 1,900 acres.

In the late 1970s, the U.S. Fish and Wildlife Service listed the mission blue butterfly as an endangered species, and that made any further development on San Bruno Mountain illegal, since what remained of the mountain was habitat for the mission blue (and later the elfin and silverspot butterflies, as well as the San Francisco garter snake). Commercial development pressure led to the collapse of the Save San Bruno Mountain organization in the mid-1970s. After incorporation as a nonprofit, the self-appointed officers of Save San Bruno Mountain threw most of the membership out of the organization because they opposed a plan to compromise with local developers that the officers supported. The expelled members created yet another new organization, San Bruno Mountain Watch, and that group has carried on the fight to save endangered habitat and species, to run volunteer weed removal projects, and to campaign on behalf of saving the mountain from wanton development. The lawyers in control of the original organization helped invent a legal loophole that was incorporated as part of the Endangered Species Act in 1982 under Reagan's Interior Secretary James Watt. The idea was to create a Habitat Conservation Plan (HCP), showing how a "better" habitat elsewhere will be paid for by allowing commercial development on an existing habitat. This designation of HCP was invented for the northeast ridge south of Guadalupe Canyon Parkway, a prime habitat for the endangered mission blue butterfly. The sunny, sheltered area is now filled with suburban townhouses, and hundreds of thousands of dollars have been provided to make a suitable habitat on the saddle, an area full of gorse (a European invasive and not a host plant for the butterfly) and usually in cold windy fog.

The whole HCP concept sits on shaky scientific grounds, since the science of ecology and species stability/evolution is seriously understudied. In the case of San Bruno Mountain, the plan to create new habitat for the mission blue, San Bruno elfin, and callipe silverspot butterflies has failed utterly. "There are now more invasive plants occupying greater areas and displacing more native plants than at the HCP's inception," said Ray Butler and Jake Sigg, officials of the California Native Plant Society writing in the Summer 1993 issue of *Endangered Species*. Two large areas of the mountain, Paradise Valley and the Northeast Ridge, have meanwhile been bulldozed and graded. In June 1994, they stood barren and dusty, denuded of their once rich life, and are now filled with housing. Fortunately, more than 1,000 acres still teem with life in a dozen microclimates. Several dozen species of native plants, although threatened, persist along with endangered butterflies and snakes.

San Bruno Mountain is also home to several of the last intact indigenous shellmounds, making it a rare archaeological and anthropological treasure too. Today the pressure to develop is still wielded by a number of property owners who control parcels on the lower flanks of the mountain, especially in Daly City. Defenders of San Bruno Mountain are vigilant too, and enjoy widespread social and legal support. Much of the mountain is already incorporated into the County and State Park, and people continue to organize so that more and more of the mountain can be brought under permanent public control.

E19: COMMUNITY GARDENS

Fort Mason Community Garden

Starting in 1980, the San Francisco League of Urban Gardeners (SLUG) led the effort, largely volunteer driven, to establish over 100 community gardens in San Francisco. This effort did not appear out the blue, but was deeply rooted in a history that had been germinating in San Francisco for a half century or more. In 2003, due to a budget scandal and mismanagement, SLUG was succeeded by the San Francisco Gardener Resource Organization (SFGRO), which continues to this day. Its home is Garden for the Environment at 7th Avenue and Lawton Street in the Inner Sunset.

Important direct precursors to the contemporary urban gardening movement were the Victory Gardens of World War II. In Laura Lawson's masterful history of community gardening, she cites a 1944 U.S. Department of Agriculture report: "By 1944, M. L. Wilson, director of extension programs for the U.S. Department of Agriculture, could report that between eighteen and twenty million families had Victory Gardens that collectively provided 40 percent of the total American vegetable supply" (Lawson: 2005). In San Francisco alone there were some 70,000 Victory Gardens by the end of the war, a fraction of the several million across the United States and Canada. The know-how developed by local gardeners during the wartime effort was not entirely lost as the parks and public grounds were returned to their previous non-garden uses after the war. In San Francisco in particular, a city with dozens of microclimates and soil conditions, WWII gardeners were instrumental in the reemergence of community gardens in the 1970s.

Annette Young Smith, a 66-year old Alabama native who has lived in San Francisco's Bayview District for 34 years, applied her rural roots to the rock-hard median where she lives on the 1700 block of Quesada Avenue. Since she and her friend Karl Paige started removing debris and planting a garden in 2002, the entire block has been transformed. Neighbors all know each other now, and the garden that anchors the community has won awards and attracts visitors and helpers from all around. The block is a quintessentially San Franciscan street, "[Y]oung and old. Gay and straight. Black, white, Asian, and Latino. Newcomers and oldtimers. Immigrants and native born" (Yollin: 2004). Gardening provides a common language and context in an urban environment that usually promotes private property and individualism.

The renewed impetus for community gardening can be traced to the upheavals of the 1960s. In *The Omnivore's Dilemma*, Michael Pollan situates the problem of choosing what to eat in a new historic context created by the industrialization of food and the rebellious malcontents confronting it. Pollan traces today's gourmet ghettoes, vegetarianism, passion for organic foods (and antipathy to processed food) to April 20, 1969, when the Robin

Hood Commission tore down the fence surrounding a vacant lot owned by the University of California in Berkeley, California. They laid down sod and planted trees and put in a vegetable garden, and declared the establishment of "People's Park." One declared intention of the "agrarian reformers" with the new park was to grow their own uncontaminated food and give it away to the poor, echoing the seventeenth-century English Diggers who had also reclaimed common lands to feed the destitute of their era (often themselves!).

The successful opening of People's Park fired imaginations across the counterculture. San Francisco's Diggers had already helped shape the underground with its free stores, free food, and wild public events in 1966 and 1967. Acid tests, rock-n-roll, marijuana, long hair, and a rejection of "straight" culture fused with draft resistance, antiwar protests, and rising black and brown power movements to challenge the American Dream at its roots.

Pam Peirce is a crucial character in the specific San Francisco history of gardening and food politics. Pam got her first garden in 1975 in a friend's backyard, while she was editing the People's Food System newsletter *Turnover*. She had been an early member of the Ongoing Picnic Food Conspiracy where she helped buy food for a whole group at the Saturday Farmer's Market in San Francisco, and describes it as "an experiment in grassroots democracy, which is what community gardens are too." Peirce lived through the era and in the trenches of political wars that tore apart the movements addressing food politics. At the end of the 1970s, when federal support for urban gardening was radically reduced, a dozen community gardens were suddenly without the federally paid workers they had come to count on during previous years. Peirce refused to see the painstakingly built and maintained community gardens disappear for lack of infrastructural support. She made a list of local garden coordinators and began holding potlucks, building momentum for a new nonprofit organization to knit together the diverse and disparate community gardens in San Francisco.

During the 1970s, the U.S. Department of Agriculture funded an Urban Garden Program, which provided funds for Comprehensive Employment and Training Act (CETA) workers in most major cities. This allowed thousands of families to have plots in community gardens in the 1970s. By 1980, the federal Urban Garden Program had served nearly 200,000 urban residents, including approximately 65,000 youth. In 1982 alone, an estimated $17 million worth of food was produced (Hynes: 1996). The Reagan administration shrank government support for gardening, capping national funds at $3.6 million per year. By 1992, funding vanished entirely when a longtime congressional supporter retired. The end of government support meant gardens—and a whole panoply of nonprofit organizations—were forced to turn to private philanthropy and foundations for support. This in turn drove many toward models of greater economic self-sufficiency, which also meant more businesslike behavior. San Francisco's SLUG became more dependent on city funds, and redoubled its efforts to provide inner-city youth with training and jobs, but to some critics this also diminished their garden-support purpose.

In the 1990s, local residents from the Alemany Housing Projects, Bernal Heights, and other parts of southeastern San Francisco teamed up with SLUG to turn an illegal dump site into a productive 3.5-acre urban farm. For eight years they ran youth programs, training young people in organic agriculture and landscaping skills. They distributed fresh, healthy produce to low-income residents who normally would have little access to such important staples. The farm became a cornerstone of the local community and an example of a new paradigm of urban sustainability. Unfortunately, in 2003 SLUG lost its city funding and had to abandon the farm. Without money to pay workers and run educational programs, the farm collapsed. But within a few years new volunteers had resuscitated Alemany Farm. It is today a showcase of urban agriculture, growing and distributing 60–70 tons annually of fresh, organic produce.

Over 100 community gardens thrive in every corner of San Francisco, with city-provided water and widely varying self-governance models. Today's gardens remain important arenas for multigenerational circuits of communication, memory, and experience. Urban gardening initiatives resituate basic food security in local communities, or at least start the important process of relocalization and the skill development that local food security depends on. Secondly, by bringing together activists and neighbors and excluded communities, new relationships emerge based on the practical work of producing food and tending land.

E20: The Farm/Lowriders and the Lot

La Raza Park, Potrero Avenue and Cesar Chavez Street

At the eastern end of today's La Raza Park, a bucolic green space nestled near Highway 101 featuring a much-loved skatepark in its midst, sits a cluster of corrugated metal buildings next to a community garden called Potrero del Sol. Potrero Avenue passes to the west, Cesar Chavez Street dips down beneath the Highway 101 overpasses adjacent to its southern edge. From 1974 to 1987 this was known as Crossroads Community (the Farm), or the Farm by the Freeway. For a couple of years in the mid-1980s it was a storied punk rock venue, famously hosting some of the most out-of-control, raucous shows during the peak of the hardcore punk scene.

The former dairy on this site closed down for good in the late 1960s and sat derelict before its demolition. In 1974, Bonnie Ora Sherk and Jack Wickert met while she was waitressing at Andy's Donuts on Castro Street and he was a taxi driver. Together they decided that the empty property was calling out to be reclaimed as an urban farm and community center, and they leased the 1.5-acre concrete lot. They soon began depaving the site and launched the "farm in the city" as a Living Art Project. Everyone who entered the Farm—plant, human, or animal—was treated as an integral part of the ecosystem, participants in a project of artistic and environmental transformation. Chickens, goats, pigs, and hundreds of school kids passed through in following years. A large garden was created that survives today as the Potrero del Sol Community Garden.

Moreover, conceptualizing the impetus for the Farm as a "life frame" echoed the Diggers' "Free Frame of Reference" of the previous decade, and sought to make the Farm a more sustained effort beyond the temporary art installations Sherk had been known for. The whole farm became a classroom where artists, musicians, dancers, and ecologists acted as instructors. Children performed acts of their own creation on the theater stage. Noted performance artist Rhodessa Jones characterized the Farm as "one of the earliest industrial multipurpose, multidisciplinary, multicultural spaces in San Francisco" (Blankenship: 2011).

The Farm provided important meeting and rehearsal space for a wide range of initiatives, including the Frisco Bay Mussel Group, an early effort at creating a dynamic eco-activist group in 1978 that also gave rise to the Reinhabitory Theater. Also using the space were the San Francisco Mime Troupe, the Pickle Family Circus, Make-a-Circus, and the Jones Family, along with numerous artists, poets, dancers, and activists.

To its immediate north the remaining empty lot was used by Lowriders in the 1970s as a hangout. Between 1974 and 1975, Bonnie Sherk and other organizers gathered several thousand signatures from neighbors to demand the City purchase the adjacent 5.5 acres, and in 1976 the City did, promising to establish a new park. Thanks to activism and organizing from the Lowriders themselves, along with support from the Galería de la Raza, and other local organizations, the efforts to establish La Raza Park bore fruit in 1980. In the same year, the Lowriders were being heavily repressed by the police along Mission Street. At its peak in 1978–80, Latino youth took over Mission Street every Friday and Saturday night in endless parades of lowriders stretching at their peak from 14th Street all the way to Geneva Avenue in the outer Mission District. The BART plazas were key meet-up points in the days before cell phones, with different cliques claiming payphones and arranging romantic rendezvous as the slow procession of cars rolled by. Police set out to control this unauthorized use of public space by making left turns off Mission Street illegal after 9 p.m., as well as making countless arrests for loitering and other trumped-up charges, in order to ostensibly criminalize the community. A lawsuit filed by lowrider organizers later blocked the arbitrary police harassment of the era (Hernandez: 2015).

The Farm continued under its nonprofit umbrella until finally being evicted in 1987, in part because the property owner thought he could build on the punk rock venue the Farm had provided and make it into a successful nightclub. Extensive efforts by many neighbors and local organizations to save the Farm ultimately failed. The site has since been home to a private elementary school dedicated to African American–centric education and a changing cast of artists, entrepreneurs, and start-ups.

E21: FOOD HISTORY

Harrison Street and the Embarcadero

In the last three decades the food business and food politics have both exploded on the scene. The Slow Food movement started in Italy when an American fast-food restaurant was opened at the foot of the Spanish Steps in Rome, a movement that has become a global guardian of disappearing heirloom species and artisanal production methods. Urban farms have given rise to an ideology of locavorism, while debates over vegetarianism, veganism, and Michael Pollan's *Omnivore's Dilemma* have fueled a greater awareness of food—its place in the economy, in our daily lives, and our cultural sensibilities—than perhaps ever before.

In Sonoma, Marin, San Mateo, Santa Clara, and Alameda counties, local farms produced a landscape of diverse agricultural commodities.

Hay remained one of the top ten crops of local farms from the nineteenth century right into the 1990s, along with cattle, grapes, dairy, eggs, and cotton. Other crops rose and fell over the decades: plums/prunes, oranges, tomatoes, lettuce, pears, walnuts, almonds, barley, and rice. By 1997, California produced more than any other state with 76 crops, from alfalfa and almonds to a variety of lettuces and melons, peaches and persimmons, to strawberries, spinach, Asian vegetables, and walnuts. Moreover, California has been the #1 state in terms of agricultural revenue for the last 50 years (and that doesn't even count the billions from marijuana cultivation!).

A cornucopia of food production shaped the early landscape of the Bay Area and California more broadly, as it has come to shape our tastes and imaginations too. The literal state of abundance in San Francisco is staggering, and the more you open yourself to it, the more abundant it seems. The long, sordid history of racism, exclusion, and genocide that have dominated most of California's history, with its focus on racial and cultural purity, have not affected our cuisine. Since the 1970s, the famous California cuisine has emerged, based on fresh and abundant local vegetables, and over time, an ever more vigorous embrace of diverse food heritages all wrapped in a commitment to organic and healthy production.

Mission Dolores was the first agricultural settlement in San Francisco. Between the Mission and the bayshore, the historic marshes and farms once helped feed the City. North and west of the Ferry Building was once the heart and soul of the food business in San Francisco. From the once-thriving fishermen of the eponymous wharf to the finger piers along the northern waterfront, food poured into San Francisco and mostly landed somewhere here in the old Produce Market district. Today we see the four big corporate towers of the Embarcadero Center, and to its north the first Redevelopment Area in the City, occupied by the Golden Gateway Apartment towers. But until 1960, this was the thriving heart of the Italian North Beach, an ethnic community centered around the food business.

Further south the old giants of the U.S. coffee business—Hills Brothers, MJB, and Folgers—are now almost forgotten, their buildings turned into modern offices. One of the first world-spanning conglomerates of processed foods, the Del Monte corporation, has its roots in San Francisco where its global headquarters used to be in the old Southern Pacific Railroad building at the foot of Market Street. Their China Basin banana operations were centered on Mission Creek (aka Channel Street), where a great deal of hay was also offloaded to fuel the horse-based transportation system that kept San Francisco moving (and eating) for its first decades (T5).

With the publication of *Silent Spring* in 1962, many people started on a path away from agribusiness-dominated food supplies. In the 1960s and 1970s, major grocery chains were consolidating their hold on the national food market. Local grocers and small chains were being gobbled up by Safeway, A&P, Krogers, and Lucky. The march of homogenization was flattening diversity, making food tasteless, and saturating consumers with chemical-laden food. The search for the natural was on. Warren Belasco provides an excellent overview:

> Venturing into a health food store in late 1968, *San Francisco Express Times* food advisor Barbara Garson assumed the manager would be another one of those "proverbial little old ladies in tennis shoes." Yet in explaining why Garson should not eat sugar, the manager recounted the sordid role of US refineries in Cuba since the turn of the century. Previously wary of health food "cults," Garson was pleased—and surprised—that honey, whole wheat, soy noodles, organic raw milk, unusual herbs, and other health food staples could have a progressive context. Other freak explorers of the health food underground reported similar discoveries: dusty copies of hard-to-find works—assorted pamphlets with utopian, spiritual, and dietary guidance. Writers of such advice commonly dismissed technocratic experts, worshiped nature, and tended to think in whole systems, not parts. In short, the health food stores offered holistic information that might be called protoecological. (Belasco: 1989)

More and more people turned away from processed foods, while an almost racialized aversion to white bread, white sugar, and white flour took hold too. Some went "back to the land" (often discovering just how hard it is to farm!), but other city folk started food conspiracies in the late 1960s to connect directly to farmers and their produce. Within a decade, urban gardeners were reconnecting to the knowledge gained in the WWII Victory Gardens period to recommence food production in urban areas, in turn linking with growing concerns for food security (E19).

In 1966, women of the San Francisco Diggers began visiting wholesale produce markets to glean overripe fruits and vegetables. They learned canning and preserving to supplement their epic daily free food distributions in the Panhandle. From those early efforts a whole foods movement shaped by a back-to-the-land ethos quickly spread.

An important unsung link in the evolution toward healthier food comes from the farmworkers who were the backbone of California's incredible abundance. Their campaign against DDT was key to shifting public opinion away from chemically soaked foods (and the chemically saturated workforce who were an unavoidable component of the former). The use of DDT in the fields was banned in 1971 after a long struggle and lawsuits brought by the fledgling United Farm Workers (UFW) with the recently formed Environmental Defense Fund (E23).

With the proliferation of weekly neighborhood farmer's markets, San Francisco is awash in abundant, healthy food. At the same time, "food deserts" in poorer neighborhoods and hunger on the streets underscore the sharp class differences that the food renaissance has not addressed. When you're enjoying your dim-sum-to-die-for, or an artisanal arepa, or pampered pupusa, or even just enjoying a stroll through the aisles of nearly pornographically perfect produce at Whole Foods, remember it all began in the 1960s as a revolt against corporate agribusiness by both workers and consumers.

E22: Chinese Shrimping Village

India Basin open space

Hunters Point was home to twelve different shrimp companies, each quite small (504 nets, 16 boats, 53 men working all together), but along with shrimpers on other shores, part of an incredibly productive shrimp fishery in the San Francisco Bay during the 1920s. From 1928 to 1930, more than 7 million pounds of shrimp were harvested from the bay. Here are the twelve companies that worked out of Hunters Point:

1. Leuong Shui Shrimp Company
2. City Shrimp Company
3. Quong Fat Shrimp Company
4. Quong Song Shrimp Company
5. California Shrimp Company
6. Golden West Shrimp Company

7. Yip Fook Shrimp Company
8. See Hop Wo Shrimp Company
9. George Shrimp Company
10. Golden Gate Shrimp Company
11. Wing Hing Wo Shrimp Company
12. Quong Duck Chong Company

The Chinese fishermen sailed their redwood fishing boats to the mudflats. They dropped sail and set the large, triangular nets by staking them into the mud in long lines. The mouths of the nets were set open to the oncoming tide to catch shrimp swept along by the current. As the tide slackened, the fishermen raised nets and dumped the live shrimp into large baskets that were then stored in the boats' hold. The nets were reset in the opposite direction for the next tidal cycle. After two tidal cycles, or about twelve hours, the holds were full and the fishermen returned to camp to process the catch.

In 1939, the U.S. Navy took over the Hunters Point peninsula to expand its ship repair facilities. The Chinese had to go. After being given notice, the San Francisco Health Department organized a controlled burn and destroyed the shacks and piers that had been a source of livelihood for decades.

E23: United Farm Workers against DDT

St. Paul's Church, Church and Valley Streets

Cesar Chavez helped orchestrate the founding of the United Farm Workers Union (UFW) in California's Central Valley in the wake of the 1965 grape pickers strike in Delano. In alliance with Larry Itliong and others, a new alliance of Mexican American and Filipino American farmworkers was finally forged after years of enmity. After the defeat in Delano, Chavez and the fledgling union's leadership chose to launch a table grape boycott that became one of the most successful consumer boycotts in American history. Chavez put together an unprecedented alliance with environmental groups and consumers. The national grape boycott went on for several years before California growers gave in and signed union contracts in 1970–71. What is less remembered from that period was the agitation going on in supermarket parking lots on behalf of the grape boycott that educated middle- and working-class shoppers about the severe problem of pesticides on food. The farmworkers were being contaminated by DDT and similar poisons (made infamous by Rachel Carson's 1962 *Silent Spring*). Historian Robert Gordon summarizes Chavez's new awareness:

> Recognizing the potential appeal of a fight to protect workers, consumers, and the environment, Chavez stated that 'the issue of the health and safety of farm workers in California and throughout the US is the single most important issue facing the United Farm Workers Union. . . . We have come to realize . . . that the issue of pesticide poisoning is more important today than even wages. (Gordon: 1999)

With boycotts and a lawsuit filed in collaboration with the early Environmental Defense Fund (EDF) and California Rural Legal Assistance, the UFW was instrumental in getting DDT banned nationally. Growers began replacing those chemicals with organophosphates (many agricultural pests were developing immunity to DDT by then), but the new pesticides were even more toxic to the workers, albeit quicker to break down in the environment. Because of this, some mainstream environmentalist organizations kept the UFW at arm's length. Nevertheless, the UFW/EDF alliance, though short-lived, was one example of a broad alliance between environmentalists and labor at the start of the 1970s. Emerging out of the battles to pass the Coal Mine Safety and Health Act (1969), the Occupational Safety and Health Act (1970), and the National Environmental Protection Act (1970), rank-and-file workers, along with progressive union and environmental activists, realized that hazardous working conditions, workplace pollution, and the deterioration of the natural environment were closely related.

It's telling that the United Autoworkers, United Steelworkers, United Mineworkers, Oil Chemical and Atomic Workers, and the International Association of Machinists worked closely with the Sierra Club, Friends of the Earth, Environmental Action, and others to pass many new laws during the early 1970s. Little wonder that there was so little opposition expressed in Congress given the broad alliance pushing these changes. Perhaps it is also not surprising that the successful alliance of the time was soon torn asunder by the divergent politics that followed the oil price shock and the severe recession of the mid-1970s.

E24: Food Conspiracies and People's Food System

20th and Alabama Streets

By the late 1960s, dozens of Bay Area households, usually communes or co-ops, formed what became known as food conspiracies. These were buying clubs, a process by which the residents would pool their monies and share the tasks of going and buying food in bulk directly from farmers and occasionally wholesalers. But they were much more than simply buying clubs, too. They were political, consciously set up to contest the supermarkets and corporate agribusiness that dominated food production and distribution. Usually anticapitalist, they were also seeking organic alternatives to the chemically soaked foods sold at large stores.

Jesse Drew describes the basic process:

> The San Francisco Food Conspiracy was a loose federation of autonomous buying clubs based either on neighborhood or political affiliations. Household representatives would meet to discuss and take orders on quantities and varieties of produce and bulk items. If there were 10 households in the buying group, for example, each household might order 10 pounds of brown rice, so an order of a single 100-pound sack of rice could be placed. Or several households could agree to split a case of bananas. The orders were taken, the money exchanged and then the buying club coordinator placed the order. Volunteers picked up the food, brought it back to a central location in the neighborhood, and then members either picked up their order, or had it delivered. (Drew: 1998)

There were hundreds of such clubs in San Francisco by the early 1970s, in the Haight Ashbury, in the Western Addition, Noe Valley, and almost every other neighborhood. For many conspiracy members, it would be the first time they sampled such fare as brown rice, bulgur, garbanzo beans, tofu, and whole grain flours. For many others, it marked the discovery of delicious fresh vegetables, in contrast to the canned or frozen ones they pushed around their plates as children.

Unfortunately, the food conspiracies demanded a lot of volunteer work, so as people grew weary of spending so much time acquiring and distributing food, they also concluded that the model discriminated against working people with children and/or jobs. Clearly the time that was required locked out a number of potential allies. Conversations among members of various conspiracies, and throughout the larger network, led to the idea of opening up storefronts, run on a cooperative basis. Among the first co-op stores were Seeds of Life (Semillas de Vida) on 24th Street in the Mission, Rainbow Grocery on 16th Street in the Mission, the Haight store in the Haight-Ashbury, and Good Life Grocery on Potrero Hill. The stores were run by worker-owned collectives, with workers who rotated jobs within the stores and used some form of profit-sharing for payment (Peirce: 2011).

Most of these new "hippie co-ops" came together as the People's Food System, which at its peak had eleven retail stores, a dry goods warehouse, a dairy distributor, a cheese distributor, two bakeries (one in San Francisco and one in the East Bay), a produce distributor, a refrigerator repair company, a magazine, and, briefly, a day care center (People's Bakery and Uprisings Bakery baked the bread, Merry Milk and Red Star Cheese provided the dairy, Veritable Vegetable provided the vegetables, and People's Warehouse handled the central warehousing aspects.). It was employing hundreds of people and feeding thousands cheap, healthy food. Recently paroled prisoners and refugees from Central America were given priority in hiring at many stores. Given the paranoia of the times (the FBI's COINTELPRO program targeting antiwar activists, the black liberation movement, and radicals in general), most workers operated under their first names only, using the place they worked as a last name, for example, John Warehouse, Sarah Cheeseboard, etc. Ultimately the system unraveled after disputes over accountability and a violent attempt to take over the network in 1978. With all the ex-cons working at various collectives, rival prisoner organizations began to compete for control of the People's Food System.

The final conflict pitted Tribal Thumb prison gang members who worked at Wellsprings Communion Restaurant at Folsom and Langton Streets against other People's Food System representatives. On April 26, 1977, during a break in a long meeting on 3rd Street among collective members, gunfire broke out in the parking lot, leaving ex-San Quentin 6 member Willie Tate critically wounded. Tribal Thumb leader Earl Satcher was shot dead. Within a year, the People's Food System had largely collapsed. Many of the collectives, already less than profitable, found it impossible to continue. Rainbow Grocery (today located at Folsom and Division Streets), which had withdrawn from the People's Food System in 1975, along with Other Avenues Coop on 44th Avenue, are the only two surviving stores from the original People's Food System.

Today's organic farms, farmer's markets, and healthy foods in local stores are all direct products of the People's Food System and other alternative food stores that emerged in the 1970s.

WHATEVER HAPPENED TO THE EIGHT-HOUR DAY?

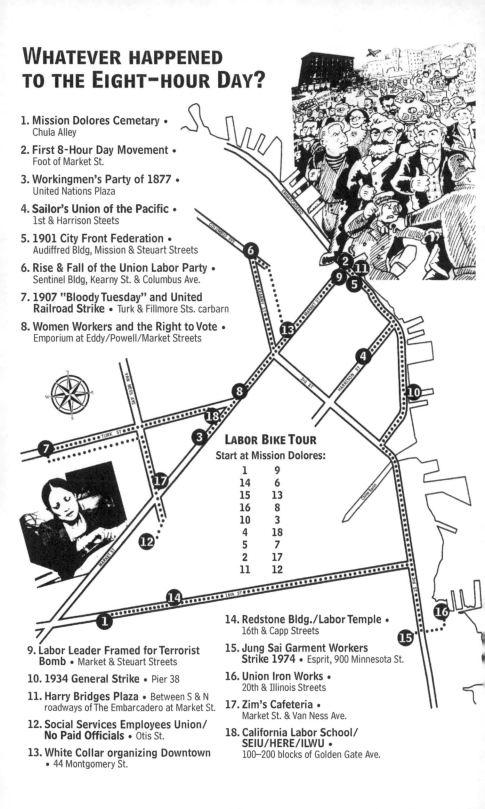

1. **Mission Dolores Cemetary** • Chula Alley

2. **First 8-Hour Day Movement** • Foot of Market St.

3. **Workingmen's Party of 1877** • United Nations Plaza

4. **Sailor's Union of the Pacific** • 1st & Harrison Steets

5. **1901 City Front Federation** • Audiffred Bldg, Mission & Steuart Streets

6. **Rise & Fall of the Union Labor Party** • Sentinel Bldg, Kearny St. & Columbus Ave.

7. **1907 "Bloody Tuesday" and United Railroad Strike** • Turk & Fillmore Sts. carbarn

8. **Women Workers and the Right to Vote** • Emporium at Eddy/Powell/Market Streets

LABOR BIKE TOUR
Start at Mission Dolores:

1	9
14	6
15	13
16	8
10	3
4	18
5	7
2	17
11	12

9. **Labor Leader Framed for Terrorist Bomb** • Market & Steuart Streets

10. **1934 General Strike** • Pier 38

11. **Harry Bridges Plaza** • Between S & N roadways of The Embarcadero at Market St.

12. **Social Services Employees Union/ No Paid Officials** • Otis St.

13. **White Collar organizing Downtown** • 44 Montgomery St.

14. **Redstone Bldg./Labor Temple** • 16th & Capp Streets

15. **Jung Sai Garment Workers Strike 1974** • Esprit, 900 Minnesota St.

16. **Union Iron Works** • 20th & Illinois Streets

17. **Zim's Cafeteria** • Market St. & Van Ness Ave.

18. **California Labor School/ SEIU/HERE/ILWU** • 100–200 blocks of Golden Gate Ave.

III

WHATEVER HAPPENED TO THE EIGHT-HOUR DAY?

Labor history tends to offer a romanticized look at a glorious past of noble workers forming unions. Unions are specific historic and legal entities that have risen at different times in the ebb and flow of class conflict. The unions that we have today all have complicated, often painful histories, including explicit racism and deep sexism. Many people automatically assume that unions are dedicated to the best interests of workers, but too often the interests of unions and workers diverge.

Unions by definition are in the business of selling the labor their members have to offer. But when their politics and alliances are challenged by rank-and-file movements for democracy, or even simply to demand a change in leadership, union leaders have often used the power of their institutions to block these efforts. Corruption of union leaders has happened often enough that the concept of the "pie-card" was invented to describe the everyday business unionism that pits union leaders against everyday workers. If at some point the workers challenge the whole setup, rejecting the system of wage work and capitalism, unions have to choose between siding with the radicalizing workers or the owners with whom they are accustomed to negotiating. When recessions or depressions hit, unions have become institutions committed to protecting the profits and existence of their industry because business union leaders believe that their members share interests with the owners of their industry. This became particularly noticeable during the 1980s when countless unions agreed to concessionary contracts that left their members poorer, if not out of work.

Still, it's clear that workers fare poorly when they remain unorganized, so the unions they *do* have, and the repeated efforts to democratize those institutions—sometimes to radicalize them—are central to labor history.

Labor historians' focus on unions often glosses over the bitter racism that has plagued workers' movements throughout history, and San Francisco's is no exception. In fact, anti-Chinese and anti-black racism dominated the unions in San Francisco well into the twentieth century. Most labor historians also ignore the crucial role played by genocide and slavery in the early economic development of California, in pre-statehood and in its infancy. The labor performed by indentured indigenous people and the African American slaves brought to California, along with the land freed up by a cold-blooded genocide, is fundamental to the establishment of California labor relations.

By the time the Spanish missions were fully secularized by the Mexican government in 1833, it is estimated that the original indigenous population of California had already fallen by two-thirds due to a combination of disease, starvation, and colonial violence (L1). White Americans arrived with the Gold Rush, bringing with them their widely held conviction that all Indians were savages, and proceeded on a campaign of systematic genocide. The U.S. Senate refused to ratify 18 separate treaties negotiated in 1851–52 to create reservations throughout the state, leaving California Indians with no home of their own. The federal government paid out more than $1 million to militias and soldiers who spent more than two decades brutally murdering Indian peoples across the state. Both the *Daily Alta California* and the *Daily Evening Bulletin* of San Francisco openly condoned genocide as late as October 1861, and the slaughter continued into the mid-1870s (Madley: 2016).

The Gold Rush brought with it an enormous land rush as its necessary companion. The wealth that accumulated in San Francisco, derived from mining, agriculture, water monopolization, and railroads, was fundamentally dependent on the rapid seizure of vast swaths of California (and San Francisco) lands through displacement and slaughter of the people who had lived here for millennia. That the Mexican *Californios* were also brutalized and robbed of their holdings only emphasizes the profound hypocrisy of the California histories that have glorified early settlers instead of framing them as the plunderers and murderers they often were.

Slavery was imported right from the beginning of modern California, a generation after abolition by Mexico. Indians were routinely forced into so-called apprenticeships and indentured labor and held for a decade or more in virtual slavery. Children were stolen by the hundreds by marauding whites, often taken after their parents were murdered. State laws passed in 1850 and expanded in 1860 sanctioned the indenture of "any Indian or Indians, whether children or grown persons," including "prisoners of war" and vagrants, which could last a decade or more. Judges were granted the right to bind and apprentice Indian minors without the consent of the parents or guardians. Approximately 20,000 California Indians were held in various forms of servitude from 1850 until 1863, when President Lincoln signed the Emancipation Proclamation. At that point, Governor Leland Stanford had to sign state laws deleting the clauses in the 1850 and 1860 acts that had permitted long-term, unwaged Indian servitude (Madley: 2016).

Black slavery was disallowed in California as part of the federal 1850 Compromise that made California a free state, but as part of that agreement, the Fugitive Slave Act had to be obeyed, which meant hunting down and returning anyone deemed to be property to its rightful owner. Slave owners traveling through California could proceed with their "property" unless they lingered in the state beyond 18 months, whereupon their slaves were automatically free. That first wave of settlers included many southerners who brought slaves with them.

The Underground Railroad had an important terminus in San Francisco (see "Mary Ellen Pleasant"—D15). Free blacks traveled among enslaved African Americans in the gold fields of the southern Sierra, encouraging them to run away. There were many cases in the first years of California of successful escapes, but also regular reports of people being forced back into slavery by California courts. Even after California was granted statehood, several thousand people of African descent were held in slavery with the backing of fugitive slave laws passed by the California legislature and approved by the California supreme court (Smith: 2013).

Both Indian and black children were regularly adopted into white families as state-sanctioned "wards," after which their enslaved labor vanished into patriarchal family structures. Once a ward, a child (and its labor) was under the unchallenged control of the head of family. Widespread enslavement of children through the ward system belies the myth of California's free status in its early years. Still, as the 1850s came to a close, a growing majority of California's white men, the only ones who could vote, were embracing the "free soil" ideology of the antislavery wing of the Democratic Party, a political program motivated by concern for free white labor more than black emancipation.

More people have recently learned that the Thirteenth Amendment banned slavery except in the case of prisoners, but in the nineteenth century, sailors were also subjected to coerced labor, and San Francisco was a hub for this. Sailors were a key sector of the modern nineteenth-century working class because ships were the only means of long-distance transportation of goods and people. They are not a group we normally associate with outright slavery. But decades after the Civil War, in an 1897 U.S. Supreme Court decision, they were deemed exempt from the Thirteenth Amendment's protection against involuntary servitude. Into the twentieth century, the U.S. courts allowed people to be taken onto ships and held there against their will, no matter how brutal or onerous the conditions. It wasn't until the Seamen's Act of 1915 passed in the U.S. Congress that this status was formally rescinded (L4) (Pickelhaupt: 1996).

The specific qualities of the California labor movement were rooted in the mid-nineteenth century, before any kind of self-conscious working class existed. Thousands of men poured into California in 1849–50, most on their way to seek gold in the Sierra Nevada, but many stayed to work in the economy that boomed around the mining rush and the many services it required. The thousands of gold-seekers who rushed to California were themselves imbued with both the white supremacist ideology of Manifest Destiny, and the liberal belief in individualism and personal honor as the foundation of public life. Prior to the Civil War, most white men were committed to a republic of individual producers, either small farmers or self-employed artisans and entrepreneurs. The corporation had not yet risen to the powerful position it would assume within a generation, and while plenty of people took jobs working for wages, few thought of it as anything but a transition on the way to self-sufficiency. The Jeffersonian myth of a nation of small independent farmers and artisans, amplified by Jacksonian frontier populism, still shaped the self-conceptions of most. This was the consciousness of the nascent San Francisco working class in the 1850s before the daily life of wage-labor had become fully normalized.

Those men who arrived were avid proponents of the individual freedom to make contracts—they were free laborers *because* they could make contractual relationships. This idea helped distinguish free labor from slave labor, a system that was pushing hard to expand itself across the south and west. White supremacy was taken for granted by white Americans as they arrived in California even if they were hostile to slavery. Within a short time, the new California legislature passed a "foreign miner's tax" to drive Spanish-speaking miners from Mexico, Chile, and other southern parts out of the mines (of course, those "foreign" Mexicans were in territory that had been Mexico until 1848!). To support this discriminatory tax, white miners insisted that Spanish-speaking miners were not free laborers, but *peons* working for bosses who controlled their output without contracts. The white miners then turned their attention to the competing Chinese miners and adopted the idea of the "coolie," a Chinese worker who worked under slave-like conditions due to oppressive contracts they were forced to sign in China. White workers who had defined their freedom by their ability to sign contracts now confronted a population who had contracted to work in California, but who they defined as noncitizens and enslaved workers. Racism trumped the supposed inviolability of the contract (Smith: 2013).

Thus began a decades-long campaign against so-called "coolie" labor, culminating in the 1870s with violent pogroms across the West against Chinese communities (Pfaelzer: 2007). Within the shifting logic of free labor, white Californians used race as a means of determining rights. By the end of the Civil War, white workers were as hostile to the rights of freedmen as they were to the rights of Chinese. In 1867, California voters were among the nation's first to return to the Democratic Party, sweeping it back into power in California. The Democratic Party had cleverly redefined itself after the Civil War as the party opposed to slavery embodied by the Chinese "coolie" labor that was arriving by the hundreds and thousands at San Francisco's port. Anti-coolie leagues of white workingmen continued to agitate for a ban on Chinese labor, including violent anti-Chinese riots (L3) until finally in 1882, the U.S. Congress passed a California-sponsored bill that became known as the Chinese Exclusion Act (Saxton: 1971).

In this context of xenophobia and racism arose the early union efforts in San Francisco. Living and working in the emerging industrial San Francisco led many white workingmen to band together against exploitative employers. The strength of organized labor rose and fell with the boom-and-bust economic cycle. Workers would gain higher wages and shorter hours when business was good, and employers would succeed at lengthening the working day and imposing wage cuts when times got tougher. To gain strength against this coercive pressure, workers repeatedly came together in dozens of different unions, and these locals joined larger councils or national unions or both. Many of them lasted only a few years or decades. Employers in their turn formed extralegal and illegal associations repeatedly to carry on their side of the class war in San Francisco, usually counting on the San Francisco police department as reliable backup or frontline troops. The particulars of San Francisco's class struggle during its century and a half of development are in many ways a quintessential example of the larger dynamics that have reshaped the world.

With a collapse of shipping and trade during the Civil War, the City enjoyed a thriving economy as everything had to be produced locally, which led to chronic labor shortages for dozens of industries. In 1866, it still took several months to travel from the East to San Francisco, so the labor shortages gave great leverage to the burgeoning working class of the City. San Francisco workers seized the eight-hour day in 1866, before any other places had achieved it (L2). Foregoing any collective bargaining process, groups of organized workers simply announced in newspaper advertisements that they would henceforth work only eight hours a day. But that eight-hour day would disappear a few years later when the first national Great Depression took hold in the 1870s—though efforts to establish an eight-hour workday figure prominently in every labor struggle that followed, right up to and just after WWII.

Twice in San Francisco's history political parties emerged and won elections that broke the two-part duopoly of the Democrats and the Republicans. In the late 1870s, the Workingmen's Party of California swept to power in the wake of violent anti-Chinese riots and what was called "the Great Upheaval" of 1877 (L3). Though the Workingmen's Party seemed to be on its way to a permanent role in city and state politics with one-third of the delegates at the 1880 state Constitutional Convention, the party fractured and the majority who were set on Chinese exclusion returned to the Democrats after 1880. Two decades later, Democratic mayor James Phelan sided with employers in a bitter waterfront strike in 1901, which led to the emergence of the Union Labor Party (L5). The Union Labor Party won the mayoral election of 1901 and again in 1903 and 1905, gaining a huge majority of the Board of Supervisors along the way in spite of united efforts of Republicans and Democrats to defeat them (L6). The great earthquake and fire of 1906 scrambled everything, though, and in the disaster's wake, a graft and corruption scandal was uncovered that brought the Union Labor Party down. Though they briefly regained the mayoralty in 1909, the ULP was unable to sustain its presence in City politics after that.

In the first half of the 1910s, union power among building trades, and in manufacturing and along the waterfront, still held strong. Women gained the right to vote in state elections in 1911, largely thanks to working-women in San Francisco who backed an aggressive and modern electoral effort (L8). On "Preparedness Day," July 22, 1916, a terrorist bomb blew up in the middle of a parade, killing ten and injuring dozens more. Labor leaders were framed for the crime (L9); though the union movement rallied in their defense, Tom Mooney and Warren Billings went to jail until the late 1930s.

A major turning point in San Francisco labor history came in 1934 when in the depths of the Depression, dockworkers and seamen banded together up and down the Pacific Coast in a strike that helped usher in the New Deal and the ensuing accommodation between capital and labor that gave rise to eight-hour days, weekends, and the much-vaunted American "middle class" in the post-WWII era (L10). Few know that before WWII San Francisco was a union town where nearly everyone from the many blue-collar industrial workers to the women in the department stores to the waitresses and busboys at the local lunch counter all proudly belonged to unions and enjoyed an unusual amount of power over the conditions of their everyday lives.

A growing self-awareness and a working-class talent for wildcat strikes in the late 1930s shook San Francisco's controlling class to the core. Business planners in San Francisco faced an entrenched, self-confident, smart, historically savvy working class in pre-WWII San Francisco. Workers enthusiastically took more power in worksites all over town, utilizing innovative tactics from sit-downs and occupations to costumed picket lines, theatrical demonstrations, and clever grassroots informational campaigns. After enduring hundreds of these short strikes, employers naturally began to look at the bigger picture. How could the chokehold of organized labor be bypassed, if not defeated? How to eliminate those pesky neighborhoods full of memories, full of class consciousness, short of mass murder or war?

The elite responded with a decades-long process to regain the upper hand in the balance of power. The forces unleashed by the Depression-era upheavals on the waterfront made San Francisco's local class struggle a crucial staging area for reshaping ruling-class response. Ultimately, this long-term counteroffensive changed life, both at work and at home. The massive expansion of industrial production for WWII began the regional reorganization of the economy, which local planners endorsed and extended in the postwar era. Ultimately, they succeeded in moving shipping to Oakland, heavy industry to the North and East Bay, and in spawning hi-tech industries around university enclaves, and so on. What began as an effort to circumvent organized workers in San Francisco by moving unionized industries out of San Francisco to other parts of the region became a model for the globalization that has swept the world in the past half century. San Francisco has been an important test site for improving and extending the control of capitalism.

As the blue-collar employment base of the city was systematically moved out, so too were the neighborhoods most connected to the living legacy of the Big Strike: South of Market (home to thousands of retired longshoremen) and the Fillmore (the African American cultural center during the '40s and '50s due to the great wave of southern blacks that came to build ships in WWII). The San Francisco Redevelopment Agency (SFRDA), the municipal planning and building agency answerable only to itself, pursued a slum clearance approach to these two venerable, lively, and neighborly areas. These reservoirs of local working-class knowledge and history were systematically razed, the inhabitants largely dispersed. The Italian North Beach neighborhood, centered on the old Produce Market area north of Market and near the waterfront, was decimated when the Produce Market was moved south in 1959 to make way for the Golden Gateway Apartments, off-ramps for the then-new Embarcadero Freeway, and eventually the Embarcadero Center high-rises.

The International Longshore and Warehouse Union (ILWU) was at the forefront of radical unionism in the United States after West Coast dockworkers set up their own union in 1936 (L11). Workers enjoyed a quarter-century golden era, controlling their labor process, and with a high degree of control over their own work lives thanks to the Hiring Hall. That golden era came to a close after 1960 when the ILWU signed the unprecedented Mechanization & Modernization Agreement (M&M), which set the Bay Area's shipping industry rapidly on the path to the use of containers and what is clumsily called "intermodal surface transportation." This reorganization of global shipping allowed manufacturing to be moved overseas to sites of cheap labor and natural resources, or as ILWU Local 10's Herb Mills put it, "the container has been the technological means of exploiting cheap labor throughout the world" (Mills: 1996). The M&M agreement was not designed to kill the Port of San Francisco, but it was its death knell. It also accelerated the deindustrialization of San Francisco, a process that had already begun after WWII. Shipping to and from the bayshore of San Francisco peaked in the early 1960s after more than a century of being the most important business here. As the port shriveled, blue-collar manufacturing disappeared from the City, leading to the closure of dozens of factories producing nationally familiar brands such as Del Monte Foods, Hills Brothers and MJB and Folger's Coffees, Hellman's Mayonnaise, Hamm's Beer, Pepsi-Cola, Hostess Twinkies, and many more. With them went their predominantly unionized workforces.

As social movements evolved through the upheavals of the 1960s and against the background of the permanent (Cold) war, organized labor became an aggressive agent of the capitalist order. Unions supported anything that seemed to create jobs, leading the charge for San Francisco's absurd and finally truncated freeway plans, as well as lending uncritical support for Manhattanization and redevelopment of its own residential neighborhoods. Ultimately this short-sighted economism led to the rapid decline of trade unionism as a political and economic force, even if various efforts were made to create independent rank-and-file-led unions, for example in the welfare bureaucracy in the late 1960s (L12) and among restaurant workers in the late 1970s (L17). Decades passed before labor activists began to see how post-WWII, mid-century prosperity was not permanent, and that resistance would have to face the global reach of the modern economy. But union power had become so weak that a new strategy of working-class resistance would be required, one that outflanked capitalism's globalism with goals and tactics completely outside the logic of capitalism's occasionally stubborn partner, trade unionism.

Since the 1970s, San Francisco has seen a rapid expansion of medical, financial, legal, and technology work. At the end of second decade of the twenty-first century, clerical workers, programmers, technical writers, nurses and doctors, analysts, corporate managers, financial planners, artists, musicians, and more all join together to produce a daily crescendo of digital signals. San Francisco is still one of the most popular tourist destinations in the world, and the tourist and convention industries employ the most people in the local economy, in restaurants, hotels, taxis, and all the "services" that underpin the endless stream of visitors coming here. The medical sector, supported by government-guaranteed profits, has expanded its place in San Francisco and the national economy unlike anywhere else in the world, with several major hospital chains and the University of California all building huge new hospitals in the past decade.

Unions in the private sector shrank steadily after Ronald Reagan became president and inaugurated his tenure with a refusal to negotiate with the Professional Air Traffic Controllers in 1981, choosing to fire them all instead. Shortly before the PATCO strike, San Francisco's Blue Shield insurance company finally settled a lengthy strike with its white-collar employees by agreeing to a three-year contract with substantial wage increases but only taking back 150 of the original 1,100 workers who went on strike in early 1980. Takeaways, givebacks, and decertification battles became the norm in the withering 1980s. The Greyhound Strike in 1991 was a dismal defeat. The two-month newspaper strike in late 1994 ended in something of a draw, but ultimately as a win for management's efforts to reduce employment. (The dramatic shrinkage of newsrooms and professional journalism in the twenty-first century was wholly unexpected as recently as the mid-1990s.)

After languishing semi-abandoned for more than a decade, the old warehouses and factories of South of Market and North Mission sprang back to life in the early 1990s after the 1989 Loma Prieta earthquake. The quake damaged enough buildings—mostly in former swamp or wetland areas and areas of bay fill—to kickstart a mini building boom that began with the live/work lawyer lofts that were trending in the early 1990s. Later, massive condominium projects and, by the early 2000s, the doubling of downtown to South of Market, would fully vanquish any memory of the industrial past that held its own there for over 100 years.

During the past few decades, San Francisco has seen an unprecedented and incomprehensible property boom of new construction (largely offices and luxury condominiums), fueled by unchecked inflation in prices and rents. This has produced an extreme housing crisis that confronts even the well-paid, while the poor are locked out and left to fend for themselves on the streets. Living on San Francisco's major boulevards and crowded into forgotten corners of the City are thousands of destitute residents, more than 70 percent of whom once had a roof over their heads here, and nearly all of whom work in various capacities in the margins of the city's economy (sfist.com: 2016). Few people, whether longtime residents or recent arrivals, can really make sense of this juxtaposition.

Confronted by the full arsenal of ruling-class power over the last six decades, San Francisco's once-vaunted labor movement in the first decades of the twenty-first century has been reduced to whispering where it once roared. The local outcome of this old dance with capital is a restructured city economy. Since the beginning of the twenty-first century, the so-called New Economy based on tech and the Internet has moved to the forefront, bringing with it attendant booms and busts. Organizing and agitational efforts among white-collar workers in the 1970s–90s have not yet found a contemporary echo (L13). San Francisco trade unions were buoyed by the convincing victory of the hotel workers in their 1994 strike and again in a successful months-long strike in 2018. Local 2 of the Hotel and Culinary Workers Union continues to maintain union shops in most of the large hotels as well as a few restaurants in town. But the gourmet ghettoes and restaurant rows in the neighborhoods remain alien territory as far as Local 2 is concerned. Union campaigns have succeeded mostly in hospitals and universities and among city employees, all occupations that cannot easily be moved elsewhere. Public worker and teacher unions are the remnants of a once powerful union movement in San Francisco, along with the hotel workers. Smaller unions continue to thrive among convention services, building trades, and elsewhere, but without the political clout once taken for granted.

The working class, rarely identified as such anymore, is fragmented along racial and status lines, and increasingly stratified at work. New categories of white-collar technicians and professionals— highly paid wage workers—are far removed from the gritty industrial working class of the mid-twentieth century and earlier. San Francisco has a much different working population now, doing different work than it did half a century ago.

Remarkably, the twenty-first century workers of San Francisco are routinely working ten or more hours a day, frequently six days a week. The long-sought workday of eight hours has been largely forgotten. Thanks to deep structural changes in the world economy, many of which were pioneered by the business elite of the Bay Area, both the well-paid and the underpaid are working longer and harder, and organized pressure to reduce work is a historic glimmer. San Francisco, as much as any city in the United States, has seen the original stark class divisions of the nineteenth-century Gilded Age reproduced in the twenty-first-century New Economy during the much-vaunted tech booms.

How will San Francisco's long history of labor militancy open a new chapter in the class conflicts to come? It's a history yet to be written.

L1: MISSION DOLORES CEMETERY

Chula Alley

After having passed by the Golden Gate for decades, the Spanish finally arrived at the bay in 1776, the same year that the United States declared its independence from England in the 13 colonies along the eastern seaboard. The Spaniards unconsciously encountered a well-maintained food paradise. The annual fires set on local hills and plains by the original peoples maintained a deliberately cultivated landscape of oaks, edible plants, and open meadows. The open spaces they created were ideal for hunting game, while the shorelines provided abundant sources of food. Like the rich alluvial wetlands of early civilization in Mesopotamia, the bay sustained a dense and diverse population in hundreds of small settlements, surrounded by an abundant environment from which it was easy to live. The first peoples of the Bay Area spoke dozens of languages and lived in dispersed communities in all parts of the area. They traded necessities and treasures back and forth, but in terms of measurable economic activity, they lived without money, markets, or private property, and yet lacked for nothing while living in sophisticated societies of dense exchange.

But the Spanish colonizers did not believe they were meeting civilization(s) with knowledge from which they could learn. On the contrary, the Spanish colonists and soldiers decided that the existing people here were extremely primitive and proceeded, through religious conversion and forced labor, to "civilize" generations of people and erase connection to their own land. Later anthropologists pejoratively categorized the California tribal peoples as "diggers," observing the practice of foraging for roots as one food staple, and decided the lack of fixed towns and sedentary agriculture was evidence of a lack of civilization (Castillo: 1994).

Chula Alley off Dolores Street provides a view of the last cemetery still extant inside San Francisco city limits. It is the original cemetery located at Mission Dolores, built in 1791, and home to a number of prominent early San Franciscans whose names still grace the city's streets, such as Noe, Guerrero, De Haro, and Liedesdorff. The thousands of Indians who perished in the early mission system were buried elsewhere, probably under today's intersection of Dolores and 16th Streets and to its north. And perish they did, because the Spanish missions were based on the brutal exploitation of Indian labor in what can only be called slavery (Sandos: 1997).

What began as an effort to extend and defend the northernmost claims of the Spanish empire in Alta California eventually gave way to a highly romanticized Californio culture based on vast cattle ranches. The church's initial intention to convert local indigenous people into Spanish Catholic peasants (to whom they assigned the label "neophytes") gave way to the imperative of pressing the same population into the workforce needed to run the ranches with their hundreds of thousands of cattle, sheep, pigs, and horses. As whalers and others came to the bay to resupply and repair their ships, a growing trade in hide and tallow took hold, fueling further the extension of the rancho economy in the decades after Mexico gained its independence from Spain. Livestock ranching was the primary activity on land from 1776 to the mid-1840s, an economy fully dependent on a workforce of local Indian laborers.

By the time historian Ira Cross was writing a history of California labor in 1935, he could unselfconsciously write:

> With secularization came the legal emancipation of the neophytes; but the change proved most unfortunate in not a few respects. Many of the Indians continued to suffer the lot of serfs, being treated as such by ranchers and others who had work to be done. Moreover, they refused to work either under the padres or for them, insisting that they had been freed from all connections with the missions. The greater number of them wandered off and returned to their old ways of living. Frequently they took with them the horses, cattle, and sheep of the missions, and in other ways helped themselves freely to the padres' wealth and stores. Protest and supplication by the mission fathers were in vain. Their sixty years of patient effort and sacrifice in christianizing and in teaching the Indians the more rudimentary of the useful arts were as so much wasted labor. (Cross: 1935)

The prevailing myth of the primitivism of the original inhabitants still informs most people's ideas about what they were like: so ignorant and helpless that their extermination was inevitable. Worse, it is commonly believed that their extermination was effectively accomplished in the nineteenth century, obliterating the twenty-first century reality of a resurgent

Native California claiming its own history and reminding the rest of us that its legacy is very much alive today.

L2: The First Eight-Hour Day Movement

Foot of Market Street

Right after the Civil War in 1867, thousands of San Francisco workers informed their employers that the eight-hour workday would replace the ten- or twelve-hour days that until then were the norm, at the same pay. The most common practice was for a union to meet and adopt resolutions fixing a certain date after which its members would work but eight hours a day. This was not achieved through collective bargaining but by placing announcements in the newspaper. By June 2, 1867, the *Morning Call* wrote: "the eight-hour system is more in vogue in this city than in any other part of the world, although there are no laws to enforce it."

On June 3, a march of over 2,000 workingmen swamped Market Street. They marched in order of trade or job based on the dates upon which their union had adopted the eight-hour day. The ship and steamboat joiners led, followed by plasterers, bricklayers, hodcarriers, stonecutters, lathers, riggers, gas fitters, house carpenters and painters, to name just some of the dozens of occupations then extant (Cross: 1935).

(Interestingly, in the midst of this unprecedented shortening of the working day, San Francisco workers renewed their enthusiasm for baseball, and the sport boomed. The last organized games had been played in 1861, but by early 1866 there were a half dozen teams playing, enough to create a Pacific Base Ball Convention, and games were held regularly in the Mission District and other locations throughout the City.) (MacFarlane: 2017).

But in 1869, a technological coup arrived in San Francisco in the form of the first Transcontinental Railroad. Celebrations erupted in San Francisco as in the East. Few could see that the railroad would radically alter the labor market in San Francisco. Thousands of unemployed men came to the City, unions were broken, wages slashed, and hours extended.

By the mid-1870s, a Great Depression was gripping the United States, the eight-hour day was gone, and a new labor militancy was beginning to appear among the 30–40 percent unemployed workers.

The 1870s was a decade marked by militant uprisings. The Paris Commune that erupted in March 1871 sent shock waves around the world as the first-ever working-class seizure of power in a major world city set a powerful example, albeit short-lived. Also, Sioux Indians led by Sitting Bull and Crazy Horse impeded the progress of building the Northern Pacific transcontinental railroad, which led to the bankruptcy of Jay Cooke and Company, its major financier, one of the precipitating events of the Panic of 1873 that led to the Depression. Mechanics and farmers in the United States were already organizing themselves into powerful combines. In the vast farming regions, railroad monopolies spurred farmers and small businessmen to band together to confront that concentrated power, notably in the Grange movement founded in 1867. The Knights of Labor, the first national labor organization to articulate the needs and demands of newly industrialized mechanics, railway workers, and many other skilled craft workers confronted the same railroads, as well as the emerging corporations in coal mining, steelmaking, shipbuilding, and many other industries.

L3: WORKINGMEN'S PARTY OF 1877

UN Plaza, 7th and Market Streets

When workers struck against a sudden wage reduction in late June 1877 along the Baltimore & Ohio railroad, the movement spread rapidly, and within days federal troops were shooting at strikers to suppress the unprecedented strike wave. On July 23, 1877, the nascent Workingmen's Party of the United States held a rally to support the rail strikers in the sandlots alongside the construction site of the new San Francisco City Hall (today, the Main Library sits on this site). Several thousand workers listened for several hours to speeches decrying the power of the capitalists and robber barons and demanding work, wage hikes, social insurance, women's suffrage, and the eight-hour day. Toward the end of the afternoon, a march of the Anti-Coolie League arrived at the edges of the rally, and their vitriolic calls for the violent expulsion of Chinese labor from San Francisco was embraced by many young, unemployed men in the crowd. A riot spilled out from the area, and during that first night a number of Chinese laundries, and factories employing Chinese labor, were attacked and some were burned down.

The next morning, July 24, 1877, William Coleman and other wealthy businessmen called for a new Committee of Safety (a Vigilante Committee similar to what Coleman and others had used to control mobs two decades

1877 "anti-coolie" riots erupt near the new City Hall, then under construction. (Courtesy Kevin Mullen)

earlier in 1851 and 1856) and quickly enrolled several thousand men to combat the marauding rioters. Later known as the Pick-handle Brigade for their use of the wooden clubs, they also resorted to heavier arms. The Pacific Mail Steamship Company at the Beale Street Wharf southeast of Rincon Hill was a prime target of the rioters, due to its role in providing transport for immigrant Chinese labor to San Francisco. A platoon of Naval Marines was placed around the docks with Gatling guns and cannon full of grapeshot to repel any possible attack. In fact, rioters did set fire to a lumberyard nearby and for a while prevented efforts to extinguish the fire, but ultimately it petered out. By the end of three days of rioting, there were four dead and fourteen wounded. Several factories employing Chinese workers as cigar makers or in boot manufacturing had fired their workforces and replaced them with white workers, though in a couple of cases they hired children to maintain the low wages they were accustomed to paying their Chinese workers (Ovetz: 2018).

After this uprising, an Irish self-employed drayman named Denis Kearney founded the Workingmen's Party of California (he had been rejected by the Workingmen's Party of the United States because he was known to be self-aggrandizing and having a contemptuous attitude toward the working class). His incendiary speeches based on the slogan "The Chinese Must Go" quickly gained thousands of followers and after a January 1878 convention, the party gained electoral success in San Francisco and other towns in the state. It was during this same era that the union bug was invented, its first appearance being a label wrapped around cigars to proclaim they were "made by WHITE MEN!"

Republicans and Democrats joined together to resist the rise of the Workingmen's Party of California (WPC) as delegate elections for a new state Constitutional Convention were taking place. Ultimately the WPC gained one-third of the delegates, and though a number of their planks were very progressive for their time (including the eight-hour day, women's suffrage, progressive taxation to prevent accumulation of wealth, breaking up of monopolies, and against convict labor), the only result of their participation in the California Constitutional Convention was a plank demanding that Chinese immigration be stopped (and in 1882, a California-sponsored bill passed into federal law establishing the Chinese Exclusion Act). In 1880, the Workingmen's Party of California fractured, as half their members returned to the Democratic Party and the other half dispersed into local factions mostly focused on carrying out racist attacks on Chinese (Saxton: 1971).

L4: Sailor's Union of the Pacific

1st and Harrison Streets

In the mid-1880s, sailors were the mobile industrial workforce that made the local and global economy possible. The Port of San Francisco was by far the largest on the West Coast, and many more ships called at its docks than anywhere else. The men who sailed the seas and the coastal trade were indispensable, and supplying sailors to ships was a thriving business. A peculiar system sprung up to combat the perpetual shortage of able-bodied seamen available to ship out, run by boardinghouse and brothel owners known as "crimps." As ships pulled into harbor, the sailors on board would be inundated by offers of places to stay, free drinks and meals, and promises of sexual delights. After months at sea, most seamen were ready to let loose, and the local businessmen knew how to take full advantage of them. Often the sailors became so inebriated so quickly that by the time they woke up from their binge drinking they were again at sea, having lost their wages to the boardinghouse and the crimps who handed them over to the next captain.

Along with returning sailors, sometimes San Francisco's visitors or bank clerks or draymen might have found themselves out along the Pacific Avenue Barbary Coast seeking pleasure and a stiff drink, only to wake up the next day at sea. Lack of experience or skills was less important than being simply alive and mobile, because once you were at sea you had no rights. You had been "shanghaied." Someone had signed a document in your name, usually the bar or hotel owner or crimp, in exchange for payment of whatever bill you may have run up in their establishment (calculated, of course, at exorbitant rates), plus a bonus.

The labor historian Ira B. Cross, in his article "First Coast Seamen's Unions" published in 1908, declared "it is impossible to do justice to the brutality shown to the sailors in those days." Along with the reign of cruel "bucko" mates and masters, the seamen were afflicted with a legal status that made them virtual slaves. At sea, seamen were under the complete control of the ship captain, a system that was upheld in an 1897 U.S. Supreme Court decision, *Robertson v. Baldwin*:

> The court excluded civilian sailors on merchant ships from the 13th Amendment's protection against involuntary servitude [i.e., slavery] with the extraordinary rationale that Seamen are . . . deficient in that full and intelligent responsibility for their acts that is accredited to ordinary adults, and therefore must be protected from themselves in the same sense in which minors and wards are entitled to the protection of their parents and guardians. (Pickelhaupt: 1996)

In the face of this system, seamen began to organize their first union, the Coast Seamen's Union. Burnette Haskell was one of the early organizers, a fascinating radical lawyer who had attended the International Workingmen's Association convention and returned to organize a local committee of the organization. Exhorting sailors from a soapbox along the waterfront between Howard and Harrison Streets, Haskell helped to attract a couple of thousand sailors to launch the union. The Coast Seamen's Union was founded on March 6, 1885, with a call for labor organization—the Sailors' Declaration of Independence—from a lumber pile on the Folsom

Street Wharf in San Francisco. The dour Norwegian Andrew Furuseth became its early leader, and after merging with the Steamship Sailors a few years later it was renamed the Sailor's Union of the Pacific in 1890 and remains active today (Schwartz: 1986).

It was Furuseth's tireless efforts to change the legal environment that finally led to the federal Seamen's Act of 1915 becoming law, which put an end to the routine violence on ships, and granted new rights to sailors in port, too. Shanghaiing was not made illegal until a federal prohibition was signed by President Teddy Roosevelt in 1906, and then didn't fully disappear until after the LaFollette Act of 1915 imposed new regulations on maritime employment and commercial sailing vessels.

Just a few years later, though, soon after WWI, an employer counterattack virtually broke the union in 1921. A California Sedition Act made any association with radical ideas (this just after the Russian Revolution) subject to fines and imprisonment for union leaders, which prompted Furuseth to lead an aggressive purge of his own union, firing all radicals associated with either the anarchistic Industrial Workers of the World or pro-Soviet Union Bolshevism. After a decade under the thumb of "fink halls" and the bluebook company unions (employer-controlled hiring halls and unions), the seamen joined together with the longshoremen in 1934 to stage the epic waterfront strike that shifted labor relations in San Francisco for good and reestablished the Sailor's Union of the Pacific as the legitimate representative of the sailors, as it has remained to the present.

L5: 1901 City Front Federation

Audiffred Building, Mission and Steuart Streets

At the end of 1900, workers were unionizing in many industries in San Francisco, notably workers along the waterfront and the men who moved cargo from the docks to nearby warehouses on horse-drawn wagons, the Teamsters. At the end of 1900, the Teamsters signed an agreement with the Draymen's Association, while the Sailor's Union and four different longshore unions made their own alliance. This set the stage for broader cooperation, when in early 1901, a federation of all onshore and offshore waterfront unions, including the Teamsters, was formed. Called the City Front Federation, by the summer of 1901 it included 14 unions, approximately 15,000 members, and a treasury of $250,000. The Federation was anchored by the Sailors, the Teamsters, and four longshoremen's unions, but also included a number of smaller unions, such as the marine firemen, porters, packers and warehousemen, ship repair craftsmen, and harbor workers. Together they had enormous leverage over transportation and commerce and could choke off the City's economic life as needed.

Nowadays we refer to the shoreline as the "waterfront," but at the turn of the twentieth century it was commonly referred to as the "city front." The difference was one of perspective: at that time nearly everyone came and went from the City through the piers along the shore, and most experienced seeing the City first from the water. Few arrive by water anymore, and most of us experience the shore from land, hence, the waterfront.

The apparent stability achieved was a false dawn before the coming conflict. What the newly organizing workers didn't realize was that the owners were also banding together in a semi-secretive group, the Employers' Association. The Employers' Association was determined to break the union movement, and especially to ensure that no closed union shops would prevail among the key industries of the City. With over 300 major businesses joining, they quickly developed a well-endowed war chest of a half million dollars to use for strikebreaking.

In July, a religious convention arrived in town, and the Teamsters refused to move their luggage by way of a nonunion drayage firm. The previously cooperative Draymen's Association, with the full backing and encouragement of the Employers' Association (who were determined to take advantage of their recent defeats of thousands of restaurant and metal workers), decided to lock out union Teamsters. By late July, 2,000 Teamsters were on the picket lines, and more than half of the City's 600 police were assigned to patrolling (and attacking) the strikers (Shoup: 2010).

By the end of July 1901, the entire City Front Federation authorized a strike on the waterfront. The Employers' Association tried to break the strike with hundreds of scab workers brought in from afar, but the strikers held their lines and talked many scabs out of breaking the strike. Violent attacks by special police and scabs were met with the same by strikers in many skirmishes around town in August and September. In late September, a gun battle erupted between police and strikers on Kearny Street north of Market Street at 1 a.m. Finally, California governor Henry Gage intervened, and after threatening to put the city under martial law, he held negotiations with all the unions and employer groups *except* the Employers'

Association. In one day, a settlement was reached returning things to the status quo ante, with union recognition the norm, and this led the Employers' Association to quickly unravel since its main raison d'etre had been to break the unions. By the end of the strike, there were five dead and over 300 injured.

L6: Rise and Fall of the Union Labor Party

Sentinel Building at Kearny Street and Columbus Avenue

Democratic Mayor James Phelan ordered the police to help the Employers' Association by protecting and even escorting scabs to and from work during the course of the City Front Federation strike. As a result, the Democratic Party lost working-class support, which became apparent that fall when a new working-class party, the Union Labor Party, rolled to victory in the mayoral election in November 1901, electing Musician Union leader Eugene Schmitz.

Schmitz narrowly won the election and began the period of so-called union rule in San Francisco politics. Analysis of voting patterns during 1901–12, when the ULP won many elections, showed consistent working-class electoral strength underpinning the ULP's success. Middle-class support was also substantial, with the remainder split between Democrats and Republicans. A convincing majority of San Francisco felt more comfortable with elected leaders who pledged to protect the interests of the working man against big business and its well-known corruption. Schmitz's personal attorney, former Republican operative Abe Ruef, became the "power behind the throne" of the new regime. His ability to gain the support of several thousand bartenders and tavern owners was instrumental in the electoral victory (Tygiel: 1983).

Ruef was unpaid by the mayor's office, but he wrote most of the mayor's official papers and conducted an ongoing series of meetings with Mayor Schmitz, city commissioners, officials, seekers of favors or jobs, and so on, all from his offices at California and Kearny Streets. He developed a system whereby retainers would be delivered to his office (often in cash) to ensure that the Board of Supervisors and mayor would grant franchises for streetcar lines, electric lights, telephone service, and real estate development deals to the company making the payment. Ruef would divide his fees between himself and the head of the supervisors who would dole

Sentinel building, aka the Columbus Tower. (Chris Carlsson)

out individual payments to each of the supervisors who were party to this pay-to-play system. Participants included PG&E, Pacific Telephone and Telegraph, Home Telephone, Parkside Realty Co., and United Railroads (URR). URR, owned by Patrick Calhoun (grandson of Confederate leader

John C. Calhoun), employed the state attorney general, Tirey L. Ford, to make its payments to Ruef (T10) (Bean: 1952).

After several years of slowly building this system up, much to everyone's surprise, the ULP, in spite of major opposition in the daily press, defeated a fusion ticket of Democrats and Republicans in the 1905 municipal elections and swept to complete control of the Board of Supervisors and reelected Schmitz. After the 1906 earthquake and fire devastated the city, Rudolph Spreckels, James Phelan, and a group of wealthy businessmen constituted themselves as a Committee of Fifty, with a number of subcommittees to carry out the rapid rebuilding of the City. Under pressure in the disaster, Mayor Schmitz authorized the Committee of Fifty but found his authority usurped by the insurgent businessmen. Spreckels was head of the Camps Department that created the much-loved little green earthquake shacks, some of which still nestle in various hillside and other locales around the City, often with larger buildings built on and around them. Phelan, who had failed repeatedly to regain power after his 1901 defeat, used his new parallel power as head of the Committee of Fifty's Finance Committee to prioritize supporting business and rebuilding his own fortune (Fradkin: 2005).

To guarantee that the elected ULP leaders would never regain their power, Rudolph Spreckels financed an investigation of the corrupt practices of the city government. It was easy enough to expose, given the extensive system of bribes and payoffs that Ruef was running under the guise of "legal fees" in his capacity as close advisor to the mayor. A lengthy and scandal-ridden public campaign, which included the mysterious death of the police chief on the bay, and the shooting of the graft prosecutor in the courtroom, eventually led to only one conviction out of over 380 indictments, that of Ruef himself. None of the many business leaders who had personally participated in knowingly paying bribes were ever brought to trial. On taking office in 1909, new district attorney Charles Fickert dismissed all pending charges related to the graft prosecution, bringing that chapter of San Francisco history to a close.

The beautiful building at the corner of Columbus Avenue and Kearny Street, originally known as the Sentinel Building, was under construction when the 1906 earthquake and fire struck. Delayed for some years after that, it was finally completed in 1912. The original developer and owner was Abe Ruef. Today, the Sentinel Building is owned by filmmaker Francis Ford Coppola.

L7: Bloody Tuesday and United Railroads Strike

Turk and Fillmore Streets carbarn

Streetcar workers known as carmen voted on May 4, 1907, to strike against the United Railroads Company (the fifth strike since 1902). On May 6, hundreds of strikers surrounded the carbarns where the idle streetcars sat, but also where strikebreakers were being housed in preparation to break the strike. On May 7, violence broke out and earned the day the historic designation Bloody Tuesday. When six streetcars bristling with armed guards departed a surrounded carbarn, the strikers and their supporters launched a cascade of rocks and bricks. Gunfire erupted between armed guards and men shooting from nearby vacant lots. Strikebreakers opened fire on the crowd from inside the carbarns too, and at the end of the day two were dead and 20 wounded.

With over 10,000 streetcar men, metalworkers, laundry workers, and telephone operators on strike in May 1907, militant socialist unionists distributed handbills urging workers to "Tie Up The Town."

United Railroads Company owner Patrick Calhoun became a hero to the local elite for standing up to the union and the municipal graft prosecution simultaneously. The National Association of Manufacturers wired him enthusiastic support and promised millions of dollars to destroy labor's power in San Francisco, amid local calls for a new vigilance committee; but by June the ardently pro-business *Argonaut* was lamenting the "jellyfish of our capitalistic and mercantile community" for its tepid engagement in the class war under way.

At the end of May, the Metal Trades agreed to an eight-hour day to be phased in between December 1908 and June 1910. This forced one-third of the striking metalworkers to relinquish the eight-hour day they had already achieved prior to the strike! Another compromise was reached in the laundry strike—a 51-hour week immediately, with a 48-hour week by June 1, 1910.

The streetcar strike dragged on for months in the face of Calhoun's intransigence. Boycotts, sabotage, and small riots characterized the summer and early autumn, but the United Railroads Company gradually hired a full complement of permanent replacements. On Labor Day, a streetcar was attacked, and a building worker shot to death in the skirmish. The strike was officially called off (and lost) in March 1908. Six men died and over

250 were seriously injured. Accidents during the strike increased dramatically and killed another 25 and injured over 900. The labor movement lost over $300,000 in strike funds, and the Carmen's Union turned in its charter in late 1908, conceding their termination (Knight: 1960).

L8: Women Workers and the Right to Vote

Emporium at Eddy/Powell/Market Streets

From the failed 1896 suffrage campaign to the ultimately successful effort in 1911, women's role in the daily life of San Francisco noticeably changed. Whereas in 1896 no woman could comfortably walk down the street without a male escort lest she be considered immoral, after the 1906 earthquake and fire a deeper change in urban life was well under way. In particular, an influx of young, single women began to work for wages and live independently in city apartment buildings. The rebuilding City saw a great expansion of downtown offices to manage far-flung trade networks and new retail apparel outlets, which took over the adjacent Union Square area from the prostitution and vice that had been thriving in that area before the earthquake. Many of the young women who found jobs in this new economy moved into nearby, respectable residential hotels in the Tenderloin. The second block of Turk Street had a concentration of young women in its residential hotels, the 1909 census showing a 70 percent female population in two establishments there. Overall, about 30 percent of hotel and lodging house occupants in the Tenderloin were female during this era (Sewell: 2011).

Many of these new workingwomen embraced the growing (white) union movement in the City; for example, the Waitresses Union was launched in San Francisco in 1908. It was inspired by the return home of Maud Younger, the "Millionaire Waitress," who had grown up wealthy in San Francisco in the 1870s. On her way through New York in the 1890s to tour Europe, she visited a tenement on the Lower East Side of Manhattan and was so moved by the poverty and resilience of the local women there, she stayed for years. During that time she participated in early organizing campaigns and strikes among the immigrant women in New York who began the Waitresses Union there. On her return to San Francisco she launched Local 48 for white women waitresses only, with offices at 440 Ellis Street in the Tenderloin. Before long she was not only the head of the dynamic new union, but also a lead organizer of the campaign to get women the right to vote (Cobble: 1991).

In 1911, California women won the right to vote after decades of campaigning (a watershed year in California politics that brought in many progressive reforms, including the popular initiative). Early efforts during the post-Civil War Reconstruction period to gain women's suffrage made little progress, and a major push in the middle of the 1890s also fell short. The new urban workingwomen were productive participants in society, and they were increasingly assertive about their political rights. The 1911 women's suffrage campaign was markedly different than previous efforts. Instead of relying on middle- and upper-class leaders, unionized workingwomen formed the Wage Earners' Suffrage League and asserted themselves in door-to-door campaigning, reaching out to voters (all men, after all) where they were, in bars and restaurants, on streetcars and in the streets (Englander: 1992). The right to vote for women passed with only a 3,500-vote majority (out of a quarter-million male-only votes in California). When workingwomen campaigned in bars, they convinced enough of their union brothers that they would not use their new voting power to ban alcohol, which may have tipped the balance. They also used new technology, notably the automobile, to engage in mobile, highly visible public campaigning. The campaign was headquartered in a donated office in the Emporium building, just across Market Street from the Tenderloin gateway intersection of Eddy and Powell Streets (today's cable car turnaround at Hallidie Plaza).

L9: LABOR LEADERS FRAMED FOR TERRORIST BOMB

Market and Steuart Streets

On July 22, 1916, a large parade up San Francisco's Market Street had been organized by the Chamber of Commerce and the conservative business establishment to drum up patriotism and support for U.S. entry into WWI. Inspired by a similar effort earlier in New York City, they called it Preparedness Day. At 2:06 p.m., as marchers were entering Market Street from Steuart Street a bomb exploded, killing 10 and critically injuring 40 more.

In addition to the raging World War I in Europe, U.S. troops were already gathering at Nogales to invade Mexico in pursuit of Pancho Villa, Irish ex-pats were busy raising money and arms to support Irish

Preparedness Day bombing scene, Market and Steuart Streets, July 22, 1916. (Courtesy OpenSFHistory.org wnp30.0004 [Emiliano Echeverria/Randolph Brandt Collection])

independence just three months after the unsuccessful Easter Rebellion in Ireland, and a bloody strike on San Francisco's waterfront had killed a man and left dozens injured only a month earlier. Blame for the bombing could be attributed to many potential actors.

The next morning, July 23, Martin Swanson was appointed as special investigator by District Attorney Charles Fickert. Swanson, a detective with a long involvement in strikes and various labor confrontations in San Francisco, did contract work for PG&E, the Pacific Telephone and Telegraph Co. (later PacBell), United Railroads, and other companies. Swanson wasted no time in announcing that militant San Francisco labor leader Tom Mooney, his wife Rena, a radical worker named Warren K. Billings, and two others were responsible for the crime. Mooney had been a major actor in numerous strikes and organizing campaigns. By the end of 1915, he'd become a thorn in the side of the San Francisco Labor Council as much as the Chamber of Commerce with his radical calls for industrial unionism. Power towers providing electricity to the United Railroads

Company streetcars had been blown up in June on San Bruno Mountain, casting suspicion on a campaign to reestablish a union among carmen led by local radical Tom Mooney.

Over the next two years, it was gradually revealed that Swanson was the man primarily responsible for finding and coaching false witnesses against Mooney and Billings. Photographic evidence exonerating Mooney, which showed him on the roof of the Eiler's Building at 712 Market Street at the time of the bombing, was held by the prosecution but never shown to the defense. Mooney was tried first, and based on false testimony and suppression of evidence, convicted of first-degree murder and given the death sentence. Sometime later Billings was tried, and though some of the testimony had already been discredited, he too was convicted of first-degree murder but given a life sentence. The three other alleged co-conspirators were tried later and all acquitted as the fraudulent case against them had collapsed by then (Gentry: 1967).

Demonstrations sprung up across California and the world (including in wartime Belgium and Sweden) calling for justice for Tom Mooney and Warren Billings. President Woodrow Wilson, feeling the international pressure, asked California's governor to intervene. Mooney had his death sentence commuted to life in prison by California's governor in 1917. For many more years, the California labor movement and radical organizers demanded a new trial for Mooney in what became a major cause celebre, but it was not to happen. It took another 22 and a half years before Mooney was granted an unconditional pardon by newly elected liberal Democratic governor Culbert Olson in January 1939. Billings would receive his release from prison later in 1939.

L10: 1934 General Strike

Pier 38

The dramatic events of 1934 were preceded by over a decade of labor repression. After a brutally violent waterfront lockout in 1919, the longshore unions were broken and replaced by a "gang boss" union referred to as the blue book union (for the membership booklet one was required to maintain). To get work during the 1920s heyday of "the American Plan" (a nationwide propaganda campaign against unions and in favor of open shops), workers were required to "shape up" at the docks each morning at

Strikers march along waterfront in early June 1934. (International Longshore and Warehouse Union archives)

dawn and hope to be picked for work. The best way to assure being chosen was to bribe the gang boss with kickbacks from the day's wages. As the Depression took hold after 1929, resentment over the corrupt shape-up fed the clandestine organizing efforts that came to a head in the 1934 General Strike, in which the workers lost the battle but put a lethal dagger into the heart of 15 years of anti-union propaganda and open shop conditions.

Longshoremen from the entire West Coast held a convention in San Francisco in February 1934. The workers met for ten days but excluded paid union officials as delegates. While they elected old International Longshoremen's Association (ILA) officials to coordinate the West Coast organizing campaign and to plan for a coastwide strike, they also resolved that no agreement could be valid unless approved by a rank-and-file vote. They also put forth five demands: companies' full recognition of the union, union-controlled hiring halls to replace the shape-up, a raise in pay from $.85 to $1.30/hr., a 30-hour week, and a coast-wide agreement covering all U.S. ports and expiring at the same time. They also passed three important resolutions that strengthened their new power and self-confidence: a call for a waterfront confederation of all marine workers, including Teamsters; rank-and-file gang committees to handle grievances instead of business agents; and opposition to arbitration since it always led to defeat (Selvin: 1996; Schwartz: 2000; Quinn: 1949).

The strike by longshoremen and seamen, after some delays, finally began on May 9, 1934. After nearly two months of losing $100,000 a day, and after the repudiation of a deal signed by union president Joseph Ryan without rank-and-file approval (Ryan was booed off the stage in San Francisco after he presented the "deal"), the owners, with the support of Mayor Angelo Rossi and the S.F. Police, decided to open the port. At noon on July 3, 1934, the Industrial Association tried to transport goods from the docks to a warehouse. State-owned Belt Line Railway freight cars were placed at Pier 38 to protect a caravan of police cars that escorted trucks loaded with scab cargo to the warehouse. Strikers who tried to stop the caravan were attacked by police with clubs, guns, and tear gas, and the strikers retaliated with bricks and railroad spikes. All afternoon the fighting continued.

After a holiday truce on July 4 (during which California governor Frank Merriam ordered the National Guard to stand by), police charged 2,000 strikers who were picketing Pier 38 and drove them away after an hour and a half of fighting. The fight continued later in the afternoon in the Battle of Rincon Hill, where 5,000 strikers and supporters overlooked the waterfront and the Belt Line Railway. Vomit gas and tear gas were used extensively (salesmen from competing firms were handing out free samples to the police), along with the usual guns and clubs, and strikers responded with anything they could get their hands on.

As rumors flew that the National Guard were arriving in the evening, the workers made a last desperate push to seize the railway only to be repelled by police. On this Bloody Thursday, July 5, 1934, over 100 people were wounded, and police bullets killed strikers Nicholas Bordoise and Howard Sperry.

The corner of Steuart and Mission Streets, where the two strikers were killed, was adorned with flowers and chalked with the inscription: "Two men killed here, murdered by police." The governor sent in 1,700 National Guardsmen, who installed barbed wire and machine-gun nests along the Embarcadero. Troops were ordered to shoot to kill.

Freight was moved through this phalanx of protection but languished at the warehouse since the Teamsters continued to refuse to move it. The strike held on, 250 ships lay idle between San Diego and Seattle, and the companies were now losing $1 million a day.

After Bloody Thursday, popular opinion, previously divided, quickly swung to the strikers' side. A spontaneous general strike began across the

Bay Area. On Monday, July 9, a crowd of 40,000 people solemnly filled Market Street in a funeral procession for the slain strikers. Mike Quin gives an eloquent description:

> Slowly—barely creeping—the trucks moved out into Market Street. With slow, rhythmic steps, the giant procession followed. Faces were hard and serious. Hats were held proudly across chests. Slow-pouring like thick liquid, the great mass flowed out onto Market Street. Streetcarmen stopped their cars along the line of march and stood silently, holding their uniform caps across their chests, holding heads high and firm. Not one smile in the endless blocks of marching men. Crowds on the sidewalk, for the most part, stood with heads erect and hats removed. Other watched the procession with fear and alarm. Here and there well-dressed businessmen from Montgomery Street stood amazed and impressed, but with their hats still on their heads. Sharp voices shot out of the line of march: "Take off your hat!" The tone of voice was extraordinary. The reaction was immediate. With quick, nervous gestures, the businessmen obeyed. Hours went by, but still the marchers poured onto Market Street, until the whole length of the street, from the Ferry Building to Valencia, was filled with silent, marching men, women, and children. Not a policeman was in sight throughout the whole enormous area. Longshoremen wearing blue armbands directed traffic and presided with an air of authority. No police badge or whistle ever received such instant respect and obedience as the calm, authoritative voices of the dock workers. Labor was burying its own. (Quin: 1949)

The joint marine strike committee called for a general strike. Fourteen unions voted to support the call the next day, and the Teamsters voted to go out on July 12 if the strike remained unsettled. Over the next week, momentum for a general strike snowballed. The Central Labor Council, which had denounced the maritime strike leaders as communists in late May, scrambled to head off the general strike by creating a Strike Strategy Meeting, an effort characterized by Communist Party organizer Sam Darcy as an effort "to kill the strike, not to organize it" (Selvin: 1996).

Between July 11 and 14, over 30,000 workers went out on strike, including Teamsters, butchers, laundry workers, and more; by July 12, 21 unions had voted to strike, most of them unanimously. At 8 a.m. on Monday, July 16, the San Francisco General Strike officially began, involving around 150,000 workers around the bay. But it had already been rolling along for a few days by then.

During the strike, President Roosevelt officially stayed aloof; his labor secretary Francis Perkins cabled him that the General Strike Committee of Twenty-Five "represents conservative leadership." Sure enough, the General Strike began to weaken almost as soon as it began. On top of the violent attacks by vigilantes throughout the City, the conservative Central Labor Council's Strike Committee authorized so many exceptions that they dramatically undercut the general strike. On the first day, they allowed streetcar operators to return to work, ostensibly because their civil service status might be jeopardized. (Notably, the Chairman of the Labor Council was president of the streetcar workers Edward Vandeleur, who had opposed the strike from the beginning.) The ferryboatmen, the printing trades, electricians, and telephone and telegraph workers were never brought into the strike. Typographical workers and reporters continued to work on newspapers that spewed forth anti-strike propaganda.

The newspapers coordinated a vitriolic attack on the strike. *The Examiner* ran a front-page piece on July 16 with the headline "General Strike in England Crushed When Government Took Control of Situation" next to a front-page editorial "A Lesson from England." The *Los Angeles Times* picked up the theme and wrote "The situation in San Francisco is not correctly described by the phrase 'general strike.' What is actually in progress there is an insurrection, a Communist-inspired and led revolt against organized government. . . ."

On July 19, the fourth day of the general strike, the General Strike Committee voted narrowly to end it. On July 20, the Teamsters voted to return to work, fearing that the Mayor's Committee of 500 and the Industrial Association would put strikebreakers on all the trucks in San Francisco and leave the Teamsters without jobs.

This was the end for the longshoremen and seamen's strikes along the waterfront. Reversing their February pledge, they submitted to arbitration. Ultimately, they won partial victories on wages and hours, but the key issue of union control over hiring halls seemed lost to a formula that allowed for joint management of hiring halls with the shipping companies. But the unions got to pick the dispatchers, so they enjoyed control in fact, if not by contract. And the strength of the maritime workers was far from broken. During the period from January 1, 1937, to August 1, 1938, more than 350 small strikes and work stoppages occurred along the Pacific Coast. Daily life changed dramatically after 1934. In spite of a desultory and ambiguous conclusion to the 1934 upheaval, the strike still led to an extended period of worker activism, unionization, and a profound shift in power relations in most of the City's workplaces, creating and reinforcing a broad sense of camaraderie and solidarity among the working class. The Waitresses Union took off again. By 1941, the union card was in the front window of the vast majority of restaurants in San Francisco—culinary workers had successfully unionized nearly 98 percent of the City's eating establishments. Workers across most occupations discovered the power of strikes, and by the late 1930s, unions were becoming entrenched in most parts of San Francisco's economy (Cobble: 1991).

The ILWU, which was founded in August 1937 as an independent union, pursued an organizing strategy it called the March Inland. Warehouse workers were ready to join. Joe Lynch told interviewer Harvey Schwartz:

> You had commercial warehouses strung along the waterfront from the Hyde Street pier over to Islais Creek; then you had cold storage warehouses; behind those you had mills, feed, flour, and grain; behind those you had grocery—big grocery, with 1500 people—and that's the way they organized. Gee, it was terrific. Then came hardware, paper, and the patent drug industry, and the coffee, tea, and spice in '37. Liquor and wine came in '38. Then it was a mopping up operation after that. By World War II, the union had under contract, either wholly or partially organized, 46 different industries in warehouse, distribution, production and processing. (Schwartz: 1995)

L11: HARRY BRIDGES PLAZA

Between south and northbound roadways of the Embarcadero, foot of Market Street

Naming the plaza in front of the Ferry Building in the late 1990s for Harry Bridges was claimed by labor activists as a great victory for the working class. Plans are still out there to erect a monument to the man, but have

Harry Bridges speaking in Civic Center, 1946. (International Longshore and Warehouse Union archives)

so far not come to fruition. If the Bridges statue is ever erected, it may ironically serve to underline how his life demonstrated the power of capital to absorb moments of radical opposition, using the energy of the working class against itself.

When Harry Bridges departed this world in March 1990, he left behind a unique institution, the International Longshore and Warehouse Union (ILWU). His legacy, and the meaning of the union's history, is still being discovered. From its origins in the 1934 Big Strike, the ILWU helped transform the lives of countless men who worked the waterfront, but more crucially, the ILWU helped tip the balance of power in San Francisco's class struggle decisively toward the working class during its glorious and glorified early history in the 1930s and '40s.

Bridges himself rose to lead the rank-and-file movement for union recognition, democracy, and a hiring hall. These achievements in the mid-1930s were crucial victories in the hard-fought battles of the Depression-era class war. Bridges famously defended the rights of everyday workers to control their own fate, and he also led the vital effort to integrate African American workers into the longshore union. Strike after strike in San Francisco had been broken by using nonunion African American workers, who for the most part could only get hired as strikebreakers, as they were systematically excluded from the racist white unions.

After WWII, Harry Bridges was repeatedly put on trial by the federal government as part of its larger effort to weaken organized labor and root out perceived communists and communist influence. Thanks to grassroots organizing by rank-and-file longshoremen and other workers, combined with skillful legal defense by Vincent Hallinan and others, Bridges was able to defeat most of the cases against him, although he was saved more than once by appeal courts overturning guilty verdicts of lower courts (Larrowe: 1972).

The technological linchpin of the world economy is the shipping container, without which production could not have been exported to the far reaches of the planet. In 1960, Bridges and the leadership of the ILWU presided over a bitter fight in the union that led to the Mechanization and Modernization Agreement (M&M), which allowed for the containerization of shipping and the division of the longshoring workforce into tiers (known as A, B, and casual, followed six years later by the rise of the "steady men" to operate the new high-tech cranes) (Weir: 1967). In making this agreement, the ILWU was the first trade union in the United States to agree formally to trade control of technology, work rules, and the pace of work for money and pensions. In so doing, they struck a favorable financial deal for the workers then employed, but also ushered in a process that has radically expanded the power of capital at the expense of workers worldwide.

Bridges went further than making a trade union agreement that benefited his own workers at the expense of the working class more broadly. Recognized as a labor statesman in the wake of the M&M agreement, he was named to the Port Commission, while a number of other ILWU officials took positions with the Redevelopment and Planning Commissions. In the mid-1960s, local real estate magnate Ben Swig targeted hotels and apartments on 3rd and 4th Streets in the South of Market for redevelopment. These were precisely where longshoremen and seamen who had been part of the 1930s' class upsurge had retired and were living in dense but comfortable housing. A decade-long fight over what is now the Yerba Buena Gardens, spearheaded by retired communist waterfront workers like Peter Mendelsohn and George Woolf, created a number of low-income senior apartments in the area, and also defeated Swig's plans for a 70,000-seat football stadium and a dozen 50-story office towers (giving us instead the gardens, museums, and amenities we have there now). During this bitter fight, Bridges and the union sided consistently with the local business elite and its government planners AGAINST the very men who had originally created the union and gave it its fiercely democratic nature (Hartman: 2002).

In 1971, a 109-day rank-and-file strike against renewing the West Coast longshore contract (due to the steady men provision) was channeled by Bridges and his allies into a small wage increase and weak rules on union jurisdiction over stuffing (i.e., packing) the containers (Mills: 1996). Nearly a half century later, the rank and file still has the right to elect its leaders, but as with many formal democracies, it has become an increasingly empty ritual. The much-praised union democracy has fallen pretty far, with a bare 20 percent of the ILWU's members bothering to participate in recent union elections.

A monument for Harry Bridges, if it is ever built, would further solidify an amnesiac and glorified understanding of a complicated past. On the other hand, if we challenge the unspoken assumptions and explore the lost history surrounding Bridges, the ILWU, and San Francisco's endless class war, perhaps we can use this proposed monument to reveal much more than is intended.

L12: Social Services Employees Union
No Paid Officials

Otis Street

The Social Service Employees Union (SSEU) of San Francisco appeared at the Department of Social Services, San Francisco's welfare bureaucracy, in 1966, just as a widespread revolt was sweeping the country. The SSEU aspired to be completely democratic. Its activities were carried on by the workers themselves, on their own time and sometimes on work time. Decisions about union activities were made collectively by both union and nonunion members. During its entire existence (between approximately 1966 and 1976) it had no paid officials and signed no contracts with the Welfare Department management.

The 200+ workers involved in SSEU at its peak evolved a unique strategy for improving their own conditions as workers and for challenging the basic authoritarian relations that prevailed (and still prevail) around them. This strategy depended on the diverse and wide-open media they created, consisting of uncensored newspapers and leaflets. It was also based on a dialogue/confrontation process between the workers and their managers, welfare administrators and government officials.

In San Francisco, long a city with a bohemian underground and strong oppositional currents, for many people, dropping out of the establishment meant a rejection of regular work. Still faced with the inflexible demands of a money economy, however, these dropouts often turned to the welfare system for survival. As counterculturists came into regular contact with the social workers of the welfare bureaucracy, the two groups began sharing ideas and perspectives.

Very soon most welfare workers stopped seeing themselves as representatives of the state and the welfare system. Instead, they counseled welfare recipients on how to best take advantage of "the system." But more importantly, they spoke out for themselves as workers trying to be creative in their work and helpful to people in need. They went along with the widely held notion within the SSEU that it was part of a broader movement for fundamental social change.

The SSEU slowly dissolved in the 1970s, like other small independent unions that grew out of the rebellious '60s. The last official SSEU meeting was in 1976. By some accounts the dissolution process began as early as 1970, although regular publication of their newsletter continued until 1975.

L13: White-Collar Organizing Downtown

44 Montgomery Street

The first radicals to promote worker organizing in the Financial District published a newspaper called *Second Page*, but it didn't last much beyond the 1972–73 period. Attempts to organize bank workers were made by a group calling itself Bankworkers United in the early 1980s, but by 1986 they had vanished in the shakeup that preceded Crocker Bank's merger with Wells Fargo Bank. Also in the early 1980s, traditional unions were trying to gain a foothold through organizations like Women Organized for Employment, Service Employees International Union (SEIU) national

Local 925 (its creation and name inspired in part by a hit movie starring Jane Fonda, Dolly Parton, and Lily Tomlin), and the more left-wing Union WAGE. Existing union shops at Blue Shield/Blue Cross (then a nonprofit health-care insurance system) and in various union offices around the area were mostly under the aegis of the Office and Professional Employees International Union (OPEIU). City government employees, along with health-care workers and teachers, unionized during the 1970s, but with little impact on the growing Financial District.

In 1980, the OPEIU Local 3 sent 1,100 Blue Shield data processing workers out on a strike that ultimately lost badly, resulting in only 150 returning to work. SEIU is the largest union in San Francisco. It represents city workers in dozens of jobs as well as some private-sector janitors, hospital workers, and other white-collar workers.

A different approach was pursued by a group of radicals (of whom I was one) who launched *Processed World* magazine in 1981 in the Haight-Ashbury. We were a small group of dissidents, mostly in our twenties, who found each other while working in San Francisco's Financial District and using our only marketable skill after years of university education: handling information. In spite of being employed in offices as "temps," few really thought of themselves as office workers. More common was the hopeful assertion that we were photographers, writers, artists, dancers, historians, or philosophers. Beyond these creative ambitions, the choice to work as a temp was also a refusal to join the rush toward business/yuppie professionalism. Instead of 40–70-hour workweeks and thankless corporate career climbing, we sought more free time to pursue our own interests. Thus, from the start, *Processed World*'s expressed purpose was twofold: to serve as a contact point and forum for malcontent office workers (and wage workers in general) and to provide a creative outlet for people whose talents were blocked by what they were doing for money.

Processed World never had a specific goal in creating a community, beyond hoping for a movement to erupt independently of the magazine. Many people came to the magazine and its gatherings (regularly at Spec's bar in North Beach, as well as collating parties for each issue) looking for answers, for some kind of organizational structure, or at least for an idea about what to do the next day at work. The magazine collective did not seek to become an organization or union itself and had no clear-cut plan of action in which to incorporate people, let alone an actual organizational presence in offices.

Not that the organizing-oriented and programmatic groups had a great deal more success. Attempts to organize office workers by traditional bureaucratic service-worker unions like the SEIU and OPEIU were largely a flop. Indeed, these unions, like most others during the early 1980s, actually lost a lot of members to decertification elections and runaway shops, which began to afflict the clerical workforce in much the same way as they had been already battering industrial and transportation workers for several years. More promising efforts, like the underground independent proto-unions Bankworkers United and IBM Workers United, fizzled out in the heavy rain of repression under Reagan. As the 1980s progressed, and people became more atomized than they were even at the start of the decade, expectations of a political movement based on office workers evaporated.

L14: Labor Temple, Redstone Building

16th and Capp Streets

The elegant if decaying building at 16th and Capp Streets, today's Redstone Building, was built in 1914 to serve as the Labor Temple for the City's burgeoning union movement. The *Labor Clarion*, the voice of the San Francisco Labor Council, was published here for decades, and 54 union locals maintained offices in the building during its decades-long role as the Labor Temple: the bakers and bakery wagon drivers, the bindery women, blacksmiths, butchers, carriage and wagon workers, cigar makers, coopers, horseshoers, ice and milk wagon drivers, janitors, sailmakers, and tailors. But after 1968, most of the labor movement vacated the building. Since then, it has been home to small organizations, artists, photographers, and several art and theater groups; the latter have made good use of the various gallery and theater spaces that the building still holds, where Theatre Rhinoceros, the Lab, and others have flourished.

In the lobby and the mezzanine, the artists of the Clarion Alley Mural Project (D11) painted a number of labor history murals, dramatizing the big strike of 1934, the 1938 Chinese Lady Garment Workers strike, the Emporium and department store union campaigns of the 1930s and '40s, and the shocking assassination of Painters Union Local 4 leader Dow Wilson in 1966.

In 1965, Dow Wilson was an up-and-coming local union leader. He was neck-deep in a struggle for union democracy against the old guard in the Painters Union. He was also challenging corrupt practices in the San Francisco Housing Authority and fighting for tenants' rights, an early example of social justice unionism. In July 1965, painters went on strike across the Bay Area, beginning with a firm commitment to settle as a group and not undercut each other. But after several weeks, three small locals broke ranks and settled, one of which was led by Wilson's archenemy in the Bay Area Painters Union, Ben Rasnick, but Wilson organized thousands of painters to reinforce the picket lines, which continued. A short time later, the Painters Union agreed to the best contract in the country, covering 7,000 workers. After defeating the employers and corrupt union officials, Wilson announced plans to run for vice president of the International Union. The International mounted their own attack on Wilson, putting him on trial for "slander," a trial that was soon abandoned due to a Supreme Court decision invalidating such charges.

On April 5, 1966, Dow Wilson was murdered in his own home. A few weeks later, another dissident Painters Union official, Lloyd Green, was also killed by a shotgun blast through his window. Two men were convicted of the murder, when one, trying to escape a death sentence, turned on the man who ordered the murders: Ben Rasnick. The fight for control of the union had led to the murders of Wilson and Green. Rasnick was sent to jail, but the murders stymied the movement for union democracy—by the 1970s, the Painters Union was in sharp decline, like most blue-collar unions in the Bay Area (Benson: 1997).

L15: JUNG SAI GARMENT WORKERS STRIKE 1974

900 Minnesota Street

The Esprit Clothing Company in the 1970s and 1980s used to have its main showroom and warehouse in Dogpatch at 20th and Minnesota Streets, while it owned over 90 percent of the Great American Sewing Company (Jung Sai) in Chinatown. Esprit was then owned by Doug and Susie Tompkins (he had originally founded North Face clothing), and was enjoying a booming business in the fashion trade. Across 20th Street, the company built a private park for its employees, but today that park is part of the City's Recreation & Park Department and is open to the public.

Over 100 garment workers—all but two women of Chinese heritage—went on strike in 1974 against the Jung Sai Garment Factory in Chinatown, located at 646 Washington Street. At one point, striking Chinese women were arrested at the Esprit showroom and warehouse. In the early 1970s, this area was still predominantly African American, and black neighbors came out to support the Chinese strikers as they were being manhandled by the San Francisco police. After almost a year of strike activities, 64 arrests, and court injunctions, these immigrant workers, mainly Chinese immigrant women with two men, inspired popular support throughout the San Francisco Bay area. Hundreds of Asian American activists and supporters cut their teeth during this campaign. Writing in *The Nation* in May 1994, Laurie Udesky reported:

> According to the National Labor Relations Board, Esprit threatened, harassed and intimidated the workers, and then shut down the would-be union plant. The NLRB—which awarded back pay, ordered Esprit to negotiate with workers and recommended that the factory be reopened—wrote a scathing criticism of Doug Tompkins's "thread of paternalism," lambasting him for shutting down his plant in response to "perceived ingratitude." The NLRB says Tompkins's paternalism was also apparent in his description of the factory his insistence, for example, that the shop was a "distinctive experiment," a "sort of model sewing shop in the social sense of the words." Esprit vigorously challenged the NLRB's decision in appellate court, which upheld the board and ordered payment of back wages. More than ten years after the plant closed, Esprit paid $1.2 million to those of the former workers who could be tracked down. There have been no successful organizing efforts since at Esprit.

Doug Tompkins left Esprit in 1989, selling his half of the company to his by-then ex-wife Susie Tompkins. We'll never know how the bruising union battle at Jung Sai affected him, but thanks to the profits he banked from his business life he could pursue his passion for conservation. He helped launch the Foundation for Deep Ecology and fund a number of ecological initiatives. Doug Tompkins was a ruthless capitalist in the 1970s–80s and made millions by exploiting Chinese immigrant garment workers, even while he was an avid hiker, kayaker, and conservationist. When he died in a kayaking accident in 2015, he deeded his holdings of over 2 million acres of wilderness in Southern Chile to the Chilean government to become a new national park (Enders and Franklin: 2015).

L16: Union Iron Works

20th and Illinois Streets

The Union Iron Works under the ownership of Irving M. Scott moved to Potrero Point in the early 1880s, later known as Pier 70 under the Port of San Francisco. The oldest industrial building west of the Mississippi River sits along 20th Street east of Illinois Street, once the site of the Pacific Rolling Mills. Facing it from the north side of 20th Street are the red brick headquarters of the Union Iron Works until its bankruptcy and sale in 1901 to Bethlehem Steel, the former powerhouse for the area, and at the corner of 20th and Illinois Streets sits an elegant white office building that was the headquarters of Bethlehem Steel and Shipbuilding Corporation during its half century of ownership. All of these historic buildings are being refurbished as part of a massive rebuilding and repurposing of the old Pier 70 into a modern mixed-use development of offices, restaurants, and galleries.

The Union Iron Works was part of the earliest tech boom in San Francisco, and after a generation of business near 1st and Mission Streets, they moved to occupy what became San Francisco's largest industrial facility for many decades. It was here that owner Scott reoriented the company's focus from serving the needs of the mining industry (winding down after the gold and silver booms and the 1884 Sawyer decision banning hydraulic mining) to building warships for the U.S. Navy and any other buyers (including the Japanese Imperial Navy in 1900). A great number of ships of the so-called Great White Fleet that toured the world in 1907–09 were built here, demonstrating quite literally President Teddy Roosevelt's policy to "Speak Softly and Carry a Big Stick." The myth that the streets of nearby Potrero Hill were named after warships built at the Union Iron Works has been debunked. The naming of streets took place largely in the 1850s, decades before the establishment of the Union Iron Works at Potrero Point, and thus could not have been following the ships' names.

L17: Zim's Cafeteria

Market Street and Van Ness Avenue

After a long, slow decline through the 1960s, unionization of restaurants was waning and Local 2 of the Hotel and Restaurant Workers Union was under the control of Joe Belardi, a very typical old-boy union boss who ran the local as his personal fiefdom. With rank-and-file revolts in favor of union democracy popping up all over the country during the mid-1970s, Local 2 had its own insurgent campaign, the Alliance for the Rank and File (ARF), that took it by storm in 1977–78. After an intense and bitter campaign in 1978, the ARF candidates won Local 2's election, only to have the new president and several new board members make an alliance with the old guard as soon as they took office. Only one new vice president remained true to ARF, demoralizing but not defeating the insurgency (Churchill: 1999).

In 1980, the Zim's cafeteria chain was targeted by ARF activists who were determined to bring the locally owned chain under union control. There were several around San Francisco, but the most prominent one sat at the corner of Market Street and Van Ness Avenue (a Walgreen's occupies the same spot now). Cleverly, the union organizers got workers and supporters to stage coffee-in's, basically occupations of the lunch counters with every patron ordering one cup of coffee and then sitting there nursing it for hours, preventing other customers from coming in. A few weeks of this brought the owners to the table, but Zim's was doomed in the new union-busting Reagan era. By the middle of the decade, the company went bankrupt and the coffeehouses closed; at roughly the same time the new-style coffeehouse was spreading across the City. Espresso bars with nonunion baristas brought fancy new gourmet coffee drinks to every neighborhood after years when the only place in town you could get an espresso was in Italian North Beach. After another few years, Starbucks hit the area; and before long Berkeley's Peet's had turned into an international chain; and after 2010, San Francisco's own Philz was franchised too, all with nonunion workers.

L18: California Labor School SEIU/UNITE HERE/ILWU

100–200 blocks of Golden Gate Avenue

Clustered along two blocks of Golden Gate Avenue at the edge of the Tenderloin is an unsung epicenter of labor organizing and left-wing politics, going back to the middle of the twentieth century. Founded nearby in 1942, the California Labor School was launched to be an independent school for workers and others to develop a wide range of skills, including art, photography, writing, and liberal arts, in addition to mastering the growing body of labor law and the collective bargaining lessons of the era. After rapid growth during the mid-1940s, it moved to the building at 240 Golden Gate, and from 1947 to 1951 the school came under severe persecution because many teachers and students were associated with the Communist Party USA. (A block east, at 150 Golden Gate Avenue, the International Longshore and Warehouse Union had its headquarters during the same era—the ILWU was rejected from the CIO during the merger of the AFL and CIO in 1955, accused of being a communist-dominated union.) The Federal Congress decreed that the Labor School was a communist-front organization under the language of the Internal Security Act (the McCarran Act) of 1950. The IRS revoked its tax-exempt status, and it also lost the ability to accept returning soldiers using GI Bill benefits to cover tuition. By 1957, the school had lost most of its enrollment and was under severe pressure to pay disputed back taxes and thus declared bankruptcy and went out of business (California Labor School: 1957).

For the past few decades, 240 Golden Gate has been home to the Service Employees International Union (SEIU). SEIU has become one of the largest unions in the United States, and its Local 1021 covers thousands of workers in San Francisco and Northern California (Local 1021 was formed when then-International president Andy Stern ordered ten locals in the Bay Area and Northern California to merge after an internal political struggle). 240 Golden Gate continues to serve the union even though its main offices are across town.

Across the street at 209 Golden Gate Avenue is the hiring hall of Local 2 of the restaurant and hotel workers union. (They called themselves UNITE HERE after a merger in the early 2000s of the United Needle Trades Union—UNITE—with the Hotel Employee and Restaurant Employee Union—HERE; the combination was dissolved in 2009 after bitter internecine warfare among the formerly collegial union leaders.) Local 2 has had its own tumultuous history on this block, with a massive rank-and-file revolt in 1978–80 that led to the ouster of the old-guard leadership under Joseph Belardi and the emergence of a new militant leadership (L17). Co-optation and conflict quickly ensued after the election, and the subsequent turmoil led the union's International to put Local 2 into trusteeship, where it stayed for a number of years. After it regained its independence, Local 2 has been at the heart of a number of major labor battles in San Francisco, primarily focused on the large hotel chains that dominate the tourist industry. In 2006, UNITE HERE won a major victory over the industry and gained large wage increases and good contracts going forward.

Once again, in 2018, a 61-day strike against the Marriott chain in San Francisco (coinciding with a wider effort in seven other cities, all of which settled before San Francisco) led to retroactive pay raises, improved safety and health care, and a resounding victory for the largely immigrant workforce in the city's hotels (Bacon: 2017).

TRAILS, SAILS, RAILS & WHEELS

1. **Mission Plank Road** • 3rd & Mission Streets

2. **Wind-Powered Transportation... Back Then** • Hyde Street Pier

3. **The Heyday of Horsecars** • Mission Creek east of 3rd Street bridge

4. **Carville-By-The-Sea** • 48th Avenue & Judah Street

5. **Steamships** • Pier 40

6. **Cable Cars** • Cable Car museum, Mason & Washington Streets

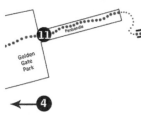

TRANSIT BIKE TOUR
Start at Pier 7:

9
5
3
1
6
12
7
10
14
8
11
4
(skip airport)

7. **19th Century Bicycling: Rubber was the Dark Secret** • Market & 6th Streets

8. **MUNI: Public Streetcars and Buses** • 15th & Church Streets mural

9. **Ferries on the Bay** • Piers 5–7

10. **Automobiles Take Over San Francisco Streets** • Market Street & Van Ness Avenue

11. **Freeway Revolt** • Panhandle Park, west end

12. **BART** • Stockton/Powell Street Station

13. **San Francisco Airport** • SFO

14. **Bicycling's Rebirth to Critical Mass** • Duboce Avenue between Market & Church Streets

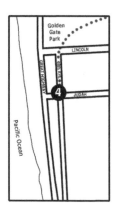

IV

TRAILS, SAILS, RAILS, AND WHEELS

Walking, riding, sailing, driving—how people made their way to San Francisco, and once here, how they moved around—is the focus of this transit history. Looking at transportation through time reveals San Franciscans continually reshaping the landscape and the shoreline to accommodate deep-water sailing ships, flat-bottomed scow schooners, horse-drawn carriages, cable cars, electric trolleys, railroads, trucks, cars, buses, and even bicycles. Together labor and nature shape and are shaped by decisions made about moving people and goods. At the beginning of San Francisco's urban history, no one could know how completely the peninsula's hills and swamps would be reorganized, how rail travel would go from horses to steam to cables and electricity and eventually give way to gasoline-powered cars and trucks. No one could imagine that improvements in roads would be demanded by bicycle riders, only to be overrun themselves a decade later by the sudden and dramatic rise of the private automobile.

Most of the eastern end of the City is deeply layered with transit history, from freight and passenger vessels that once clogged the waterfront to the wagons, trains, streetcars, trucks, and taxis that serviced the docks. Rendering the City suitable for a fixed urban street grid, and of course as a port, unleashed a rapacious and single-minded process that leveled hills and filled waterways and shorelines. San Francisco has lived through 150 years of rapid and radical change in how people get around, commute to and from work, and move goods in and out of the City. Beyond the dramatic reshaping of ecology and landscape, the history of transportation is also the history of the people who built the systems, ran them, and rode on them, filling lost chapters of class struggle and violent strife that frequently accompanied changes in ownership and control of our local transit systems. The history presented here is not, however, a transit fanatic's close history of materials, technical details, or rolling stock.

The twenty-first-century Bay Area is covered in asphalt, highways, and bridges. The inexorable expansion of car ownership and car dependency for over a century has produced the paradoxical reality that the personal autonomy and mobility promised by the privately owned car has been overwhelmed by the impossibility of using enough land for roads and parking to make using autos convenient, speedy, or comfortable. San Francisco shares a predicament with the rest of the nation: the supposed popular preference for cars disguises a puzzling and paralyzing chokehold on public policy and resources by the automobile, oil, and rubber industries. How did a region that was once crisscrossed by interurban trains and intraurban electric streetcars, along with a booming ferry service reaching all parts of the Bay Area—providing transportation to more than 90 percent of the local population—come to this strange dysfunctional impasse? Not surprisingly, it didn't happen all at once.

Had you been one of those settlers at the far edges of the Spanish empire in the eighteenth century, you might have been in the caravan that slowly made its way up from Monterey in 1769, crossing the dense redwood forests along the San Mateo hills to suddenly catch a glimpse of one of the world's great harbors. Funny to think that a site so rich in maritime history now, once surrounded by the most abundant natural supplies of seafood imaginable, was essentially stumbled upon by European settlers who were traveling extremely slowly on foot and horseback, with a herd of cattle for their sustenance.

Spanish settlers established permanent structures in what is now San Francisco in 1776, at the Presidio, and at Mission Dolores. To go from the Presidio to the Mission or vice versa was mostly done on foot or by horseback. In the mists of San Francisco's prehistory before the Spanish arrived, local indigenous people had worn paths that made up a rough triangle between areas familiar to us as the Presidio, the Mission, and North Beach, places they spent part of every year. The Spanish used these clearly well-worn paths, and one of them, leaving the Presidio toward the Mission, became known as Lover's Lane, presumably so named because lonely soldiers had to walk along it to the Mission to court the few eligible young women in the area.

The diagonal geologic formations of Franciscan bedrock and upthrust chert beneath San Francisco were not yet well understood, but what was plainly apparent from the beginning was the endless sea of sand that covered the peninsula, running from the Pacific Ocean all the way to the bay at Yerba Buena Cove. Dunes had formed over thousands of years, and much of what we now experience as the relatively flat parts of San Francisco were themselves once dominated by 80- to 200-foot-tall sand dunes, with swamps and wetlands occupying the low areas between them. In its original state, the full eight blocks south from Market Street to Townsend Street were dry land only from 2nd Street to 3rd Street. Sand hills 80 feet high stood at 2nd and Howard Street, 3rd and Market, and 2nd and Market. A salt marsh interrupted 4th and 5th Streets near Folsom and continued northwest almost to Market. Half of today's South of Market lay under regular tidal flows of water or seasonal freshwater wetlands.

The route between the early city at Yerba Buena Cove and the old Franciscan Mission Dolores several miles to the southwest was so sandy that even a load of hay from the Mission's fields was hard to deliver by horse and cart into the town, and usually came by water via Mission Creek and Mission Bay. The Mission Plank Toll Road was built in 1851 from Kearny Street to 3rd Street, and out Mission Street to Mission Dolores (T1). The City's first public transit opened in 1852 along the plank road. The service was the Yellow Line's omnibuses, an 18-passenger horsecar, an expanded version of the stagecoach (T3). Walkers and horse riders finally had a reliable way through the relentlessly shifting sands, the ubiquitous marshes, and the deep mud that would plague the City during the rainy season.

Before they could walk up and down the sand dunes of San Francisco, people had to arrive, which most did by sailing ship. Dozens of the earliest ships to arrive in Yerba Buena Cove were abandoned as sailors bolted to try their luck in the Gold Rush. Many of those ships, dragged into the shallow mudflats, were converted into warehouses, piers, hotels, and even a jail. A process of filling in the shallows and extending the piers into the deeper waters of the bay began a long process of remaking the City Front. After decades of crisscrossing wooden piers extending out from multiple streets, a seawall began to be built. Between its origins in the 1870s and the final shape created in 1912, the San Francisco port was a chaotic mishmash of dilapidated wooden structures subject to rot and collapse.

The sudden development of San Francisco as a world port thanks to the Gold Rush gave a huge boost to the sailing ships of the era. Clipper ships, towering three-masted sailing ships with dozens of sails, were developed to meet the radically increased demand for goods and passenger service between the East Coast, San Francisco, and Asia. They were enormously profitable for their owners, dominating world trade during the mid-nineteenth century. Prior to the railroads, they were the fastest way to travel for individuals. Sailing ships crossed the Pacific Ocean from China, the Philippines, Chile, and Australia, while the French, Germans, English, and Americans made their way by sail around the Cape Horn in terrifying journeys that often ended in shipwreck and death (T2).

The sailing ships rounding the Horn were quickly joined by a growing fleet of early steamships (T5). Once they were in the Pacific, steamships dominated the business of bringing passengers who had crossed the Panamanian isthmus to California. Soon steamships were crossing the Pacific connecting San Francisco to Hawaii, the Philippines, China, and Japan. The steamship companies enjoyed a century of profitable commercial activity before they finally were superseded by automobile and jet travel in the post-WWII era.

When the Golden Spike was driven home in Promontory, Utah, in 1869, it connected the first Transcontinental Railroad, and for the first time, provided an overland journey that took weeks instead of months (when it wasn't disabled by weather or bad repair). As more lines opened, the transcontinentals also began to integrate the West Coast with the rest of the United States socially and economically, and opened up human travel and migration as well as expanding trade across the continent. The arrival of the Transcontinental Railroad brought workers from the East who within a few short years deeply altered the relationship between capital and labor on the West Coast.

The trains were built with huge land grant subsidies by the federal government (a subsidy from the taxpaying public, i.e., workers); the nineteenth-century history of railroads and robber barons is well documented (White: 2011). Moreover, the trains introduced entirely new patterns of urban growth, farming, real estate speculation, and market relations. This accelerated the industrialization of the western economy, putting relentless pressure on small producers and workers living in urban and rural communities. (And, crucially, the transcontinental railroads accelerated the destruction of Plains Indians cultures as the vast buffalo herds they depended on were decimated by a mechanized slaughter.) Transcontinental rail brought so many new workers in the first few years that San Francisco's tight labor market was soon flooded with willing workers, giving employers the leverage to once again extend working hours and end the short-lived eight-hour day in San Francisco (L2).

The Great Uprising of 1877, a near national general strike that summer, nearly paralyzed the newly industrializing United States. Prompted by a walkout of rail workers in the B&O railyards of Baltimore, it soon spread throughout most major cities of the East and Midwest. San Francisco, too, had a brief work stoppage at the Southern Pacific terminal at 3rd and King Streets, while railway workers sabotaged trains in the vicinity of Sacramento in solidarity with the strikers back east (a cross-continental solidarity hard to imagine before the building of the Transcontinental Railroad). The 1870s is the same decade in which the cable car was invented (T6), allowing San Francisco's elite to move from their mansions on Rincon Hill over to Nob Hill, where the earliest cable car lines ran to the top. (Back on Rincon Hill, the 2nd Street Cut to facilitate commerce for the businesses south of Rincon Hill had plunged the once tony neighborhood into a downward spiral (E13).) Multiple competing firms began getting franchises from the City to lay track, and soon San Francisco was crisscrossed by a number of privately owned cable car systems competing with the horse-drawn trolley cars that had been the first urban rail systems.

In the last decade of the nineteenth century, the bicycle took San Francisco by storm, and dozens of bicycling clubs sprang up (T7). The bicycle contributed to a long process of eroding the monopoly power of railroads by pioneering a self-propelled form of individualized transportation. The bicycle was enthusiastically embraced by people from many classes, notably middle-class women who found an unprecedented freedom from oppressive social norms in bicycling. Bicycle riding liberated women suffering from hysteria, vapors, and nerves brought on by stiflingly tight corsets and harsh patriarchal social manners. But the bicycle did more than provide a new degree of personal freedom. What we can only recognize now, in long hindsight, is the way the bicycle set the stage for the automobile, which came along in the early decades of the twentieth century. It is a curious irony that in the summer of 1896 more than 5,000 bicyclists rode together on Market Street demanding good roads and asphalt! Sometimes demands are met but things turn out very differently than expected.

The Ferry Building was once a bustling port of entry with up to 30 million people a year passing through it. Dozens of ferries crisscrossed the bay providing service to cities all around its shores (T9). Additionally, ferry service was one of the primary means of transportation to the interior of California, with regular stops at delta towns and riverside cities up and down the Central Valley. When ferry traffic collapsed after the Bay Bridge opened, the iconic Ferry Building fell into disuse; in the late 1950s, it was "blindfolded" by the double-deck Embarcadero Freeway built in front of it. Neglected and languishing for years, the historic gateway to the City resumed its symbolic role after the 1989 earthquake fatally damaged the freeway, leading quickly to its long-sought demolition. Now overlooking a new waterfront and revived bay ferries, the Ferry Building no longer opens on a gritty industrial city. A clean, modern, "fun-filled urban destination," San Francisco's twenty-first-century waterfront is a popular public promenade lined with imported $70,000-each Canary palm trees overlooking the lumbering streetcars spruced up to evoke an imaginary past. Similarly, the piers that stretch along the waterfront in either direction from the Ferry Building (with their Spanish Revival façades), crowded with dockworkers and cargo for a half century, have been repurposed into offices, museums, parking lots, and storage facilities.

San Francisco's hodgepodge of streetcar and cable car franchises were gradually merged into the Market Street Railway Company, owned by Southern Pacific (SP, also headquartered in San Francisco). But SP did not invest in city rail, and in 1903 they sold their interests to a new company, the United Railroads (URR), owned by Patrick Calhoun. The URR modernized the system, selling off old horsecars and obsolete streetcars, some of which ended up near the beach in Carville-by-the-Sea (T4). A political dispute pitted leading citizens opposing overhead trolley lines against the URR in the first years of the twentieth century. Determined to put power lines underground, papers were filed to establish a publicly owned Municipal Railway the day before the 1906 earthquake and fire. Bitter and violent strikes by URR workers, especially in 1907, galvanized public opposition to the privately owned streetcar company. By 1912, the first publicly owned line was running on Geary Street, and the City engineer was soon building public streetcar tunnels to the western "outside lands." The "roar of the four" competing streetcar lines on Market Street entered the City's lore, along with the class divisions once denoted by the moniker "south of the slot" (in reference to the cable car slot running down Market Street), working classes to the south, middle and upper classes to the north. With the advent of the internal combustion engine fueled by petroleum oil, private car sales soared, while the URR received no public subsidies and could not raise fares due to competition from the publicly owned and more modern MUNI. By the mid-1920s, intraurban trolleys were no longer profitable. Popular support for "progressive" politics favored public owner-ship of utilities, including public transportation. But it wasn't until 1944, after a brief wartime boom in passengers and revenue, that all transit was finally merged into San Francisco's MUNI (T8).

Meanwhile, taxpayers were also paying for the new infrastructure of asphalted roads. Ford and the other automakers—along with oil, rubber, and steel companies—enjoyed booming sales and enormous profits as Americans embraced the car (T10). Profits in these industries were si-phoned off the top, with the "true" costs of building and maintaining a huge infrastructure of roads and highways absorbed by the working public (not to mention medical and funeral costs from the increasing rate of fatal collisions associated with transportation). At the same time, in-dividual workers privately accepted a huge cost burden of the transit system by embracing private ownership (with its associated maintenance and fuel bills) of the vehicles by which they would get to work and do their shopping.

In the 1960s, San Franciscans blocked a massive freeway building program designed by the California Department of Highways, and for many years, it was this "Freeway Revolt" that was blamed for the City's notoriously bad traffic (T11). But already in 1947, regional transit studies predicted insurmountable traffic congestion and proposed a new regional train system as a necessary complement to highways and bridges. The East Bay's efficient and extensive Key System carried commuters across the lower deck of the Bay Bridge into the Transbay Terminal, but the Key suc-cumbed to the General Motors–Standard Oil-led conspiracy to dismantle urban rail and replace it with buses. When a new Bay Area Rapid Transit District was granted authority over transbay rail service in the late 1950s, they thwarted efforts to preserve rail on the Bay Bridge to make way for what would eventually be the BART system. BART ran its first trains in 1972 and began using its new tube under the bay in 1974 (T12). By the early twenty-first century, BART had finished several extensions, reaching the Livermore Valley, Antioch, both San Francisco and Oakland Airports, and will soon reach San Jose. Development booms near BART stations have urbanized formerly distant suburbs and agricultural lands, while helping clear the way for downtowns in San Francisco and Oakland to expand upward and outward.

As San Francisco became both a corporate headquarters for Pacific Rim multinational companies and one of the world's most desirable tourist destinations, the commercial airline business expanded dramatically. The city's airport, built on tidal wetlands along the San Mateo County bayshore in the early 1930s, grew to be one of the nation's busiest airports by 2000. Efforts to build new runways to accommodate the traffic increase at the dawn of the twenty-first century failed when local politicians, environmentalists, and regional regulators blocked then-mayor Willie Brown's development agenda. But a new BART station, an Airtrain, and expanded terminals supported the airlines that bring millions of tourists and their billions of dollars every year (T13).

Unexpectedly, thousands of San Franciscans decided to start bicycling in the early 1990s. Embracing the bicycle as a "quiet statement against oil wars," or as a simple gesture of ecological sanity, or maybe just as a preferable alternative to carmageddon and overcrowded, endlessly delayed public transit, dozens, then hundreds, and eventually tens of thousands began using the bicycle as everyday transportation. This choice found dramatic public representation in the phenomenon of Critical Mass, which began in San Francisco in September 1992, and spread contagiously to over 400 cities on all the continents of the world in the following years. A century after the first mass bike rides in San Francisco demanding asphalt and good roads, a different kind of mass bike ride erupted, inventing a new kind of transit-oriented political expression, an unprecedented mobile public space, and a jolt to the popular imagination of what cities could be (T14).

Over the decades, in San Francisco and around the world, it has become clear that no amount of highway building or road expansion will ever solve traffic congestion. San Franciscans figured this out earlier than most and decades ago adopted a "transit first" public policy that ostensibly favored public transit, walking, and bicycling over the automobile. Expanded efforts to improve public transit with Bus Rapid Transit lanes on major boulevards and extensions of streetcar lines in several key areas have embodied the City's commitment to "transit first." But endless public disputes over curbside parking, parking lots, parking in new developments, priority lanes for buses, dedicated bikeways, and other forms of traffic calming for pedestrians and bicyclists, etc., show that the deep bias in favor of the private car holds sway in San Francisco as much as anywhere in the United States, public policy notwithstanding. San Francisco is more choked with cars today than it has ever been (a recent study by the San Francisco County Transportation Authority showed that gig economy car services like Uber and Lyft have added 62 percent to local traffic congestion over the past six years (Swan: 2019)). As the twenty-first century rolls on, we are increasingly stuck in traffic. Everyone knows transportation is broken, and no one is sure whom to blame. Taking a stroll through the long history of transportation's evolution in the Bay Area may prompt ideas about where we go from here.

T1: Mission Plank Road

3rd and Mission Streets

Standing at today's 3rd and Mission, it's difficult to imagine what it looked like in 1851. To the south and southwest, where the Yerba Buena Gardens is now, was the edge of marshes, and in the distance were sand ridges undulating across the landscape. To the southeast was a sand dune towering over 100 feet tall, blocking the view of Rincon Hill behind it. Looking north up 3rd Street (notice how it climbs approximately 25 feet to Market Street, a hint of the former landscape beneath), you would have seen a large sand dune blocking the way until excavators cut a passage through to connect Kearny Street to 3rd Street to build Mission Plank Road.

Mission Plank Road was financed in 1851 by the entrepreneur Colonel Charles Wilson. It follows closely the route of today's Mission Street, and its early history tells a surprising story of the terrain that we now blithely ignore as just another old city street. First of all, Mission Plank Road was devised to connect the City's new center at Portsmouth Square overlooking Yerba Buena Cove with the old Mission, miles to the southwest across nearly impassable sand dunes and swamplands. Other than an hourslong effort on horseback across shifting sands and dangerous bogs, one reached the Mission by boat through the sprawling Mission Bay and into the deep channel that ran from approximately today's 8th and Townsend to the tidal inlet around today's 17th-18th Streets and Shotwell/Folsom Streets.

First the road had to break through the 80-foot sand dune that covered the area that is today's intersection of 3rd/Market/Kearny/Geary. A path was cut through from north (Kearny Street) to south (3rd Street), and wooden planks were laid down as the roadbed. The planks were made of

Oregon fir, each one four inches thick. The original route went down 3rd Street and then right (west) on Mission, following the same path of today's street all the way to its curve southward around 12th Street, and to what was originally Center Street and now is known as 16th Street. The problem was at approximately 7th Street, where a deep bog extending from Mission Bay through the dunes northwesterly blocked the route. Few understood then that a major upwelling of fresh water from the aquifer under the peninsula created a brackish wetland where fresh water and tidal saltwater met to create a remarkably fertile zone of swampy mud— considered an unfortunate impediment and obstacle to be removed by road builders at the time. Across the bog, planners tried to erect a bridge built on pilings,

> but that plan had to be abandoned, to the astonishment and dismay of the contractor; the first pile, forty feet long, at the first blow of the pile driver sank out of sight, indicating that there was no bottom within forty feet to support a bridge. One pile having disappeared, the contractor hoisted another immediately over the first and in two blows drove the second down beyond the reach of the hammer . . . there was no foundation within eighty feet . . . pilings were abandoned, and cribs of logs were laid upon the turf so as to get a wider base than offered by piles. The bridge made thus always shook when crossed by heavy teams and gradually settled till it was in the middle about five feet below the original level.
>
> —J. S. Hittell, *History of the City of San Francisco and Incidentally of the State of California* (cited in Olmsted: 1986)

Built as a toll road with an eight-year franchise granted by the City, it opened after repeated repairs to the 7th Street crossing finally stabilized the thoroughfare. Tolls ranged from 25 cents for a single horse and rider to one dollar for a four-horse team. Wilson's company saw returns of up to 10 percent per month on the investment when traffic boomed on the new road. Its success also increased property values and developments around the Mission, a pattern that was to be repeated for decades to follow with every streetcar line and road built by private developers in San Francisco.

The tollhouse was on the west side of 3rd Street at Stevenson Street. "In those days," recalled one resident 20 years later, "when you had turned the corner of Third Street to Mission, going west, you were pretty well out of town" (Olmsted: 1986).

T2: Wind-Powered Transportation . . . Back Then

Hyde Street Pier

Nearly everyone who came to San Francisco in its first decades traveled by sailing ship. It was the main option until the first transcontinental railroad opened in 1869, and ship transit continued as a common experience until well into the twentieth century, though sails were steadily replaced by steam engines as the source of power. It really wasn't until after World War II that transoceanic travel left the seas in favor of the skies.

There had already been a steady oceangoing trade across the Pacific for two centuries before the San Francisco Bay became a participant. Manila galleons carried goods between Mexico and the Philippines, both Spanish colonies during the 1500s and 1600s (it's a little-known fact that Filipinos were among the first to arrive in California, long before the Gold Rush). By the time Mission Dolores was being founded in the Spanish territory of Alta California, and the United States won its independence from England, American merchants were aggressively entering the world shipping business. Ships flying the Stars and Stripes were soon calling at ports in the West Indies, Africa, China, and India, not to mention leading the industrial exploitation of the largest mammals in the sea, the whales.

The mission economy, based primarily on trade in cow hides and tallow, was supplemented by the first great slaughter on the West Coast that decimated the native sea otter population between the late 1700s and the 1840s. Richard Henry Dana was a sailor in that era, and colorfully describes his experience in the San Francisco Bay in 1835 in his classic *Two Years before the Mast*:

> Here, at anchor, and the only vessel, was a brig under Russian colors, from Sitka, in Russian America, which had come down to winter, and to take in a supply of tallow and grain, great quantities of which latter article are raised in the missions at the head of the bay. The second day after our arrival, we went on board the brig, it being Sunday, as a matter of curiosity; and

there was enough there to gratify it. Though no larger than the *Pilgrim*, she had five or six officers, and a crew of between twenty and thirty; and such a stupid and greasy-looking set, I certainly never saw before. Although it was quite comfortable weather, and we had nothing on but straw hats, shirts, and duck trowsers, and were barefooted, they had, every man of them, doublesoled boots, coming up to the knees, and well greased; thick woolen trowsers, frocks, waistcoats, pea-jackets, woolen caps, and everything in true Nova Zembla rig; and in the warmest days they made no change. The clothing of one of these men would weigh nearly as much as that of half our crew. They had brutish faces, looked like the antipodes of sailors, and apparently dealt in nothing but grease. They lived upon grease; ate it, drank it, slept in the midst of it, and their clothes were covered with it. To a Russian, grease is the greatest luxury. They looked with greedy eyes upon the tallow-bags as they were taken into the vessel, and, no doubt, would have eaten one up whole, had not the officer kept watch over it. The grease seemed actually coming through their pores, and out in their hair, and on their faces. It seems as if it were this saturation which makes them stand cold and rain so well. If they were to go into a warm climate, they would all die of the scurvy. (Dana: 1840)

Starting with the 1848 Gold Rush, thousands of people arrived in San Francisco from across the seas. The new port was soon a forest of masts as sailors and passengers alike abandoned ship and took off for the gold country. This in turn gave rise to an industry of labor "recruiting" in San Francisco known as "crimping," which gained the better-known moniker for those who were thus recruited of being "shanghaied." Finding sailors for ships through trickery, bribery, and force was a thriving business in San Francisco all the way into the twentieth century (L4).

Sail power made oceangoing travel possible. Passengers leaving New York or Boston on clipper ships hoped for a quick journey around the southern tip of South America, meaning they would make it safely to the far-off port of San Francisco in four months or less. The clippers employed a dizzying array of sails that made up as much as an acre and a half of canvas, known as spanker sails, spencer sails, jibs, topsails, skysails, royal studdingsails, moonsails, and more. Thanks to rapidly advancing hull designs, they were able to shorten travel time between the northeast and San

Francisco to less than 100 days, while carrying heavy equipment, machinery, houses, large quantities of furniture, and bulk merchandise. In the first year of use, a typical clipper would make up to $50,000 above their building cost, and a speedy captain could make $3,000 for a trip, with a bonus up to $5,000 if he made it in under 100 days.

Water-based travel had many decades to go before giving way fully to rail, and then truck and automobile. But the lore of the sea still holds our imaginations, romantically for some, horrifying for others. Herman Melville's incredible classic *Moby Dick* is imposed on many of us in our high school years, and that's a pity because it's a book better digested at an older age. In it he describes a remarkable multiracial onboard culture of sailing life, the hellish brutality and barbarism of life at sea, and the conditions of the sailors (workers) on the floating industrial processing plants that were whaling ships in the nineteenth century. There's a rich lore of stories that imbue waterfront dives and creaking timbers with salty memories that today we can only consume vicariously. The questions of historiography, how we know what we know about the past, are raised by the largely anecdotal accounts of sea passage from that long-ago era.

In her essay "About That Blood in the Scuppers" (Brook, et al: 1998), Georgia Smith offers a compelling example:

> One afternoon in the 1890s, Hiram Bailey and his friend Ben (neither one a sailor) went into a dive down on the waterfront:
>
> > "Looking round we found ourselves in a rather coarse, and certainly common Battery Point saloon, kept by one Calico Jim, a Chilean as I subsequently learned. (This same gentleman some years later shanghaied six San Francisco policemen sent to arrest him; and was eventually relentlessly followed and shot dead by one of them on the streets of Callao in Chile, South America.) We were about to return outside, not liking the general atmosphere of the place, when a tallish, high-cheeked, square-jawed, adder-eyed, raw type of man arrested us with his silvery-toned voice:
> >
> > *Say, yoo two, ef yer want a lonesome conversassy, jest vamoos inter thet er room there. (He indicated a door at*

the opposite end.) Yooll sure be all possum in there . . .
out of the bar-room heat and thet. . . . Jest ring fur yer
poisons.

Did someone really dupe (or dope) six cops, all at once, put them on a ship, and get away with it? Was the man who spoke to Bailey really high-cheeked, square-jawed, and adder-eyed? A rich vein of unreliable history is mined by guys sitting around getting drunk, telling each other lies—which, however, are slathered onto a base of truth. Calico Jim figures in shanghaiing lore, and though his authenticity is disputed, his profession was real: He was a crimp, one who made a living by delivering men—via persuasion, trickery, or force—to sailing ships in need of crew.

We try to understand what the conditions of life were in different historical periods, when the possibilities and conditions people faced were radically different than what we know in our world. Basing our understanding on anecdotal tales lends itself to nostalgic fantasies as much as to exaggerated and overheated imaginings. Scholarly efforts to untangle the truth from the stories is an ongoing project. But we know that thousands of people went to sea for centuries, and depended on rickety wooden vessels powered by vast expanses of canvas sails. It's difficult to imagine working on ships for years at a time, climbing masts in gale force winds, prying at ropes and sails caked in thick ice, while trying not to fall to your death in violent seas. But people did it—almost routinely— for decades. Those who survived those perilous journeys often stayed and became the early Californians who shaped the culture at the edge of the continent, freed from the expectations and burdens and cultural norms that they'd left behind, for better and worse.

T3: The Heyday of Horsecars

Mission Creek east of 3rd Street bridge

After walking through the mud and sand of early San Francisco, locals were ready for other kinds of transportation. A brisk business began as soon as roads could be laid out, relying on horse-drawn omnibuses and hacks (stagecoaches and carriages). The breakthrough came quickly when

Horsecar on Howard Street (now South Van Ness) near 25th Street, 1884. House with witch's-hat tower is 1336 South Van Ness, still standing in 2019. (Courtesy OpenSFHistory .org wnp26.1094 Photographer Unknown [Courtesy of a Private Collector])

the horsecar made it to San Francisco after sweeping the market in eastern cities in the late 1840s.

Unlike an omnibus ride, the horsecar was smoother and went a reliable six mph on its steel rails, making regular stops and providing straps for standing passengers to hang onto. As the horsecar regularized urban inner-city transit, it helped usher in zoned fare systems and ringing bells for passengers to signal a stop. It wasn't accepted without resistance.

In the 1956 book *Trolley Car Treasury,* Frank Rowsome Jr. describes the attitude that confronted the horsecar advocates:

> Iron-track cars were radically new and very probably dangerous to the established order. The metal strips in the streets would likely cause carriages to turn over. It was felt that property value along such streets would be injured, trade in stores would fall off, and car-riding would cause the lower social orders to become still more contentious.

It helped horsecars gain acceptance that local merchants usually had a big increase in trade after the start of a new horsecar line on the street in front of their establishments. Not that it was an altogether pleasing experience. The smell tended to stick in your mind. Rowsome describes a "special horsecar smell, blending the odors of smoky coal-oil lamps, sweating horses, and the pungency that came when the straw on the floor was dampened with many a dollop of tobacco juice." In San Francisco, horsecar lines were crisscrossing the City by the 1860s. One of the early lines ran up Market on its way to Woodward's Gardens at Valencia and 14th.

In the 1880 Census, there were 233,959 San Franciscans and an estimated 23,000 horses. Just a few years later, the horsecar peaked in 1886 when there were 525 horse railways in 300 cities in the United States. One hundred thousand horses provided the "horse power" to make those carriages go. By then, a generation had adapted to their use, and urban development patterns had already begun to change. Instead of having to find housing in dark and dingy tenements next to a factory, a workman could commute five or more miles a day on a horsecar, which allowed a growing dispersion and separation of residential from commercial land uses.

Of course, horses need fuel too. A typical streetcar horse ate 30 pounds of grain and hay a day, meaning in 1880 there was demand for about 350 tons a DAY of hay and feed in San Francisco. A booming business brought hay to San Francisco along Channel Street, not far from today's ballpark. In the nineteenth century, Mission Creek was a bustling industrial port handling tons of hay, lumber, and other goods every week.

The thousands of horses not only ate tons of hay but produced tons of "exhaust," too. Like all late-nineteenth-century cities, San Francisco faced an ongoing issue: how to manage all the horseshit falling on city streets and in the horsecar company stables? San Francisco was lucky. From the mid-1870s, as much horseshit as possible was deposited on the sand dunes that became Golden Gate Park. Park designers William Hammond Hall and John McLaren discovered that barley sprouts in horseshit were an excellent starter to stabilize sand dunes and begin to create soils suitable for a more European biota. Within a decade the park's trees, bushes, and lawns were coming to life thanks to the helpful beginnings in tons of horseshit.

And what became of the animals after years of dutiful car-pulling? According to Rowsome:

> The most crucial decision was when to sell off horses in services. (The tannery or glue factory was only a last resort, and meant

that someone had miscalculated; most ex-streetcar horses returned to farm life for their last few years.) Horsecar horses led highly regulated lives. They were stabled for nineteen or twenty hours a day, in stalls specified by industry standards as not less than 4 feet wide and 9 feet long. Their workdays were measured in miles, not hours (they were expected to make it 12–15 miles a day). (Rowsome: 1956)

Like transit systems right up to the present day, social struggles erupted on the horsecars too. On April 17, 1863, Charlotte L. Brown was ordered off an omnibus railroad car by the conductor because she wasn't white. Unwilling to acquiesce to this blatant racism, she sued the company for $200. The company argued in court—in the middle of the Civil War—that they were protecting white women and children, but the judge rejected their argument and decided for Charlotte Brown.

Her success in court, though, did not immediately translate into change. Within days of the judgment, another streetcar conductor forced Brown and her father from a car. The tenacious Brown brought another lawsuit. And in October 1864, District Court Judge C. C. Pratt ruled that San Francisco streetcar segregation was illegal. He stated:

It has been already quite too long tolerated by the dominant race to see with indifference the negro or mulatto treated as a brute, insulted, wronged, enslaved, made to wear a yoke, to tremble before white men, to serve him as a tool, to hold property and life at his will, to surrender to him his intellect and conscience, and to seal his lips and belie his thought through dread of the white man's power. (Elinson and Yogi: 2013)

Unfortunately the local transit systems, often privately owned and operating on solely a few blocks along one route, continued to refuse service to African Americans. Three years later, in 1866, Mary Ellen Pleasant filed another suit, this time against the North Beach Municipal Railroad. She, like Brown, was an independent African American woman, and determined to gain her rights; they were also both well-known activists in the Abolition movement, Pleasant having been instrumental in establishing the West Coast terminus of the Underground Railroad in the 1850s. She won her case and was awarded $500, though the award was overturned by a State Supreme Court appeal even while they affirmed the illegality of enforcing segregation on transit systems. It wasn't until 1893 that the State of California passed a statewide prohibition on transit segregation.

The last horse-drawn streetcar in San Francisco rolled up Market Street in 1913, but mostly horsecars had been abandoned by the turn of the century. In San Francisco, an aggressive capitalist consolidator and modernizer named Patrick Calhoun purchased every independent streetcar line in 1901 and merged them into his United Railroads, which led to the abandonment of the last four miles of horsecars that had been the backbone of transportation just a generation earlier. Southern Pacific's Market Street Railway Company had already sought in the 1890s to regularize the rolling stock and track gauges, and began selling off horsecars in the mid-1890s to anyone who wanted one. Famously, a number of them ended up in the sand dunes near the beach just south of Golden Gate Park in an odd village that came to be known as Carville-by-the-Sea.

T4: CARVILLE-BY-THE-SEA

48th Avenue and Judah Street

In 1895, the Market Street Railway Company, San Francisco's dominant street transportation company (owned by the Southern Pacific Railroad Corporation), faced a capital shortfall and a surplus of obsolete horsecars,

Carville c. 1905, array of residences and commercial buildings built of old streetcar bodies; looking northeasterly toward Golden Gate Park and Fort Miley. (Courtesy OpenSFHistory .org wnp4.1663a Photographer Unknown [Courtesy of a Private Collector])

that is, horse-drawn streetcars that were being phased out in favor of the new electric streetcars. The company's manager hit upon the clever idea of selling the surplus horsecars, many of which were finely made wooden structures suitable for other uses such as clubhouses, stores, even homes. Ads in local papers advertised the abandoned vehicles for "$20 with seats, $10 without." By 1900, more than 100 of these cars had been bought and towed to the far western end of San Francisco, just south of Golden Gate Park, where they sat in the sand dunes. Mayor Adolph Sutro, who owned the land, encouraged the arrival and development of Carville, as it quickly became known, as a way to collect temporary rents on his property (LaBounty: 2009).

Charles Dailey, self-professed Civil War veteran, was the first to set up a coffee shop in a streetcar, and it soon attracted many more people. Another early tenant was a women's bicycling club known as the Falcons. San Francisco was pulsating with bicycle fever in the last years of the nineteenth century, and the Falcons soon filled several abandoned cars and added a lean-to for bike parking. They built a table that could seat 28 and enjoyed a ride to their beachside clubhouse every weekend where they could swim in the ocean "when no one was looking," play cards, and hold court with artists and writers and others frequenting Carville including Ambrose Bierce, Mayor Sutro, and Collis Huntington.

In the early 1900s, a group of musicians called their car "La Boheme" after the popular new opera, and in 1908, when Metropolitan Opera cast members visited, they claimed it was the best stop on their trip. Carville was soon home to a few hundred people. After the 1906 earthquake and fire, refugees streamed into Carville. Many people stayed and the neighborhood became more formalized. The Oceanside Improvement Club managed to establish electric, gas, and water service for residents by 1910, as well as graded and paved streets. Bigger plans for a sewer line were still in the future. In 1928, the Municipal Railway extended the Judah streetcar line to the beach, and that connected the long-isolated sandy village to the rest of the City. Stucco houses, apartments, and motels soon replaced the dozens of streetcars still standing. A few houses around 48th Avenue and Irving Street still have old streetcars inside their modernized structures, but without an invitation to visit, it's difficult to find or see them.

T5: Steamships

Pier 40

The 1850s was the era in which steamships were emerging to supplant the long dependence on wind and sail, which was lucky for San Francisco-bound travelers. Many early arrivals made their way on East Coast steamships or a panoply of forgotten vehicles—scows, schooners, whaleboats, and other floating craft—along the coast into the Caribbean and to New Orleans. From there they proceeded to the port city of Aspinwall (now Colón), for the difficult trans-isthmus journey through Panama (then part of Colombia, or as it was known at the time, the Republic of New Granada). A railroad across the isthmus was under construction already in 1850 in response to the surge of demand to travel to California for the Gold Rush. But after disembarking at the port, travelers depended mostly on native dugout boats to take them up the wild Chagres River; and then—if they did not fall ill to tropical disease—after crossing the Continental Divide, they finished the journey on foot or by mule for the last 20 miles over old, decrepit Spanish trails.

Steamships shaped transportation to and from San Francisco from its urban beginnings, being used to navigate the inland empire of major rivers in California for decades, as well as serving the coastal trade for passengers, lumber, and more. The Pacific Mail Steamship Company was founded in 1848 and was immediately granted lucrative federal contracts to move U.S. mail. Its first steamer, the *California*, arrived at the end of February 1849. Though the ship left New York before the Gold Rush was announced, by the time it was heading north it found dozens of gold seekers in Panama who had rushed to cross the isthmus on their way to San Francisco. The Pacific Mail Steamship Company was historically lucky, having a ship in the right place at the right time. Soon it was doing a booming business.

Knocked-down steamboats were being shipped to San Francisco from the East right from the start. A thriving business to reassemble the ships started off the shores of Rincon Point and spread steadily southward along South Beach to what became known as Steamboat Point (between today's 2nd and 3rd Streets along Townsend). Historian Nancy Olmsted describes one successful steamship builder:

John G. North established his boatyard at Steamboat Point about 1854 "on the south side of Townsend, between Third and Fourth." The noblest vessel ever to be launched from Steamboat Point, the sidewheeler *Chrysopolis*, came from North's yard in 1860, before he moved to the Potrero. She was the biggest steamer ever built at San Francisco up to that date, the grandest of the floating palaces of the California river trades and the all-time speed queen of the Sacramento riverboats. North is said to have built 53 steamboats and 220 vessels of other types, including the first three-masted schooner on the Pacific Coast, the *Susan and Kate Dellin*, launched at Steamboat Point in 1854. (Olmsted: 1986)

In 1867, the Pacific Mail Steamship Company launched the world's first regular trans-Pacific steamship service linking the United States with Asia, assured of profits by another federal contract to carry the mail. Pacific Mail also became the principal means of transport to California in the nineteenth century for Chinese and Japanese immigrants. Both migrations vastly enriched California's economy and culture, providing the backbone for the rapid expansion of agriculture, vineyards, and mining—Chinese labor was instrumental in building the transcontinental railroad, and also in draining and shaping the Sacramento-San Joaquin River delta and helping turn it into rich agricultural islands.

The Pacific Mail Steamship Company played a dominating role in shipping goods to and from San Francisco. But it was, according to historian Richard White, a "lazy and corrupt corporation." It made easy money from mail carrying, and also bringing fruit and coffee from Central America to San Francisco. It carried back rice, lumber, flour, and manufactured goods (but not wheat, which was sent by the famous clipper sailing ships). When the first transcontinental railroads opened for business, they desperately needed to fill their cars with freight. But the prices they charged were well above what Pacific Mail charged to ship goods and send them by rail across the Central American isthmus to a waiting steamship on the Caribbean side that could bring the goods to New Orleans and the East Coast as fast and cheaper than the new railroads (White: 2011).

So the Central Pacific and later the Southern Pacific railroads offered to pay what amounted to a subsidy to Pacific Mail to ensure that it would raise its rates. Pacific Mail went along with the scheme, which lasted from

1870 until the late 1890s; after an 1880 dispute the monthly subsidy rose from $25,000 to $110,000. For decades after their construction, San Francisco and California businesses did not really need the railroads to connect to the East and the rest of the world. As exports rose in the late 1880s—mostly sugar and fruit (canned, dried, and green)—the railroads began to show some advantage, especially with the invention of refrigerated cars for green fruit.

Steamship services began to decline in the face of rising competition from railroads and eventually motorized vehicles. Until WWII, steamship service up and down the California coast served all the major coastal cities, but the postwar boom in freeway construction, suburban expansion, and adoption of private cars killed travel by steamship.

The Pacific Mail Steamship Company transitioned into Dollar Line, also San Francisco-based, and in 1938, Dollar Line's name was changed to American President Lines (today's APL, a global container-shipping company).

T6: San Francisco's Cable Cars

Cable Car Museum, Mason and Washington Streets

In the 1870s, horsepower was the primary means of terrestrial locomotion, but the higher slopes and summits of San Francisco's steep hills were out of reach. A technology born in the silver mines of Nevada's Comstock Lode made it possible for the City's hilltops to become home to some of the wealthiest robber barons of the Gilded Age. San Francisco's first "tech boom" was driven by mining but came to shape the City itself. A young Englishman named Andrew Hallidie made his name by inventing the cable car, the diminutive vehicle that conquered San Francisco's steepest hills.

Hallidie was luckier than a lot of the men who settled in San Francisco during its first decade. He came from a family of inventors and machinists, and his father had several patents on wire rope developed between 1835 and 1849. Father and son decided to travel to San Francisco and arrived in 1852. Andrew went on to study engineering and surveyed water ditches and roads, worked in machine shops, and sharpened and repaired tools for the miners in mountain communities before returning to San Francisco in 1857. He started a small wire rope factory at Mason and Chestnut Streets, using all the old horseshoes he could find as raw material.

The invention of cable cars by Andrew Hallidie is an oft-told saga, with a perhaps apocryphal point of origin on a rainy winter day in 1869 when he saw a team of horses pulling a horsecar up a steep grade on Jackson Street between Kearny and Stockton Streets. One horse slipped, the conductor slammed on his brake but it broke, and the horses and streetcar ended up at the bottom of the hill in a mangled, mutilated mess. Andrew Hallidie wrote that he wanted to construct a public transit system that would alleviate the "great cruelty and hardship to the horses engaged in that work."

Hallidie's new cable car was built on Clay Street and had its maiden voyage on August 2, 1873. There were several technological alternatives to the particular designs of his system, but his was the first to get up and running over the top of Nob Hill, in spite of his difficulties in acquiring the capital he needed to begin. Once he did, the new cable car proved to be a big success (Bonnett: 1997).

Within a few years, the Sutter Street Railroad opened using a slightly altered cable car design (they avoided paying Hallidie royalties when the U.S. Circuit Court held that Hallidie's system had not yet been perfected and was thus experimental, and could not claim patent infringement), and within the first year they attracted almost a million passengers. By the mid-1880s the Sutter Street Railroad had expanded its cable car lines across Market Street to Mission Street and on to Brannan Street, and out Pacific Avenue all the way to Divisadero Street. Big powerhouses were needed by each system to keep the endless ropeways turning underground.

Leland Stanford took up the challenge by 1878, opening the California Street Cable Railroad. Mark Hopkins and other railroad barons began building their mansions at the top of Nob Hill in this era, and all invested in the new cable car railroad that made ascending the hill a pleasure. It attracted 11,000 passengers on its first day and eventually was extended westward all the way to Presidio Street at the edge of the City's four large cemeteries covering nearby Lone Mountain. The Presidio Street terminus became a hub for connections by steam railroad out to the beach and Cliff House, or to other lines that ran to Golden Gate Park.

Several competing companies were opening lines as fast as they could in the late 1870s and early 1880s. Charles Crocker's Geary Street, Park & Ocean Railroad ran from Market Street to Central Avenue along Geary Street. At Central, the line connected with a steam dummy running further west on Geary before turning south to terminate at the small wooden station at Fulton Street and Fifth Avenue, still standing at the edge of Golden Gate Park today. Cemetery trips were a major source of revenue for all the lines that passed near the big burial grounds where today's Inner Richmond is.

In 1883, Charles Crocker, Collis P. Huntington, and Leland Stanford of the Southern Pacific Railroad opened a new cable car line on Market Street that became the largest in the City and the fourth largest in the United States. The cable car slot down the middle of Market also gave rise to a quick denotation of class in nineteenth-century San Francisco: if you lived "south of the Slot," everyone knew you were working class. If you were north of it, by contrast, you were probably middle or upper class. With the spread of cable car lines across the City to the west and south, workers could build homes on the distant hillsides and still get to work in a timely manner. The process of urban sprawl would continue from the cable car-induced boom of the early 1880s, through various ups and downs, all the way to the present era, now turning distant valleys and hills miles to the north, east, and south of San Francisco into endless suburbs. BART has an analogous role to that of the cable car back in nineteenth-century San Francisco, fueling intensive urbanization along its lines.

The cable car was in turn supplanted by the rise of electric streetcars in the 1890s. But a romantic attachment kept them going long beyond the era when they were the cutting edge of modernity. Immediately after WWII, the City planned to take out all the remaining cable car lines and replace them with the new, modern diesel buses that auto, tire, and oil interests were pushing. The buses arrived, but Friedel Klussman, a Pacific Heights matron, led a vigorous campaign to save the cable cars. It became a popular cause, and a 77 percent vote in November 1947 saved the much-loved vehicles on their remaining lines.

In 1979, the safety and reliability of the cable cars came under scrutiny, and the system was closed for major repairs. In 1982, the cable car system was closed again for a complete rebuild. This involved the complete replacement of 69 city blocks' worth of tracks and cable channels, the demolition and rebuilding of the car barn and powerhouse, new propulsion equipment, and the repair or rebuilding of 37 cable cars. The system finally reopened on June 21, 1984.

Today the cable cars are a tourist attraction and the kernel of the now-expanded historic streetcars that run on the F- and E-lines on Market Street and the Embarcadero. Together they provide a glimpse into an earlier era of public transportation, and remarkably, still serve as public transportation for the many San Franciscans who live along the surviving routes. They also serve as crucial props in the "Disneyfication" of San Francisco—the ongoing preservation of historical facades and sites that carry the nostalgic essence of a San Francisco that was mostly obliterated long ago.

T7: Nineteenth-Century Bicycling: Rubber Was the Dark Secret

Market and 6th Streets

The bicycle came to San Francisco during the last quarter of the nineteenth century. Like other places, it first developed based on wooden wheels, similar to those that were bearing stagecoaches and being drawn by horses. Horse-drawn streetcars were the predominant mode of transit in the 1870s, peaking in the 1880s, at a time when the individual horse was also still a major source of personal transportation.

The "boneshakers" were aptly named, running over heavily rutted streets on solid wooden wheels, eventually improved by coating them in solid rubber. The bicycle was not a transit option at that early stage but a novelty, and a device that attracted the adventurous few who were ready to break with the limits of human-powered locomotion. In "The Winged Heel" column in the *San Francisco Chronicle* of January 25, 1879, the writer fully grasps the possibilities:

> The bicycle ranks among those gifts of science to man, by which he is enabled to supplement his own puny powers with the exhaustic forces around him. He sits in the saddle, and all nature is but a four-footed beast to do his bidding. Why should he go a foot, while he can ride a mustang of steel, who knows his rider and never needs a lasso? The exhilaration of bicycling must be felt to be appreciated. With the wind singing in your ears, and the mind as well as body in a higher plane, there is an ecstasy of triumph over inertia, gravitation, and the other lazy ties that bind us. You are traveling! Not being traveled.

The second club nationally, and the first on the West Coast, was the San Francisco Bicycle Club, founded on December 13, 1876. Members petitioned the Park Commission for permission to ride their newfangled devices in Golden Gate Park. Overcoming their astonishment that there was actually a club for wheelmen, the park commissioners allowed them to "enter Golden Gate Park at the Stanyan Street entrance to the South Drive before 7 a.m. only." Intensive self-policing kept the wheelmen within the bounds of the concession, and before too long the "privileges were extended" (Howard: 1905). But it was in the next decade that bicycling began its precipitous takeoff:

> The Bay City Wheelmen [founded in 1884] was the first competition for the SF Bicycle Club. It raised enthusiasm to the highest pitch. Each man was eager to find opportunities for the keenest rivalry, for the honor of his club was at stake, and in those days wheeling was a clean sport. Sport for the true love of sport. There were none of the sordid motives which follow in the train of professionalism. To become a professional was to place one's self outside of the social pale. (Howard: 1905)

The explosion of bicycling is easily traced in the production statistics over a scant ten years, from 1885 to 1895. Where six factories produced about 11,000 bicycles in 1885, there were 126 factories in the United States producing a half million bikes ten years later (*San Francisco Chronicle*, May 12, 1895).

The bike clubs organized century rides around the Bay Area and annual "Bike Meets" where the fastest cyclists would compete against each other before large audiences. One of the biggest ever was during the 4th of July weekend in 1893 when an estimated 20,000 spectators jammed a special track built at Central Park just south of City Hall to watch the scorchers as they hurtled around the loop.

Generally absent from most accounts of the bicycling boom in the 1890s is a closer look at the key ingredient that made it possible: rubber. Rubber was the magic ingredient that altered the transportation landscape, but not before it had already become an essential ingredient to much of the newly industrializing world. Bicycling technology was evolving fast, with inventors in Europe, Japan, and the United States all striving to make the device easier and more popular. Over 7 million bicycles were in use by

1895, thanks to the air-filled rubber tire that was being mass-produced by Dunlop in Birmingham, England; Michelin in Clermont-Ferrand, France and Pirelli in Milan, Italy; and Goodrich and Goodyear in the United States. Along with steel frames, ball bearings, new gears, and chains, the machine had become much more pleasant to ride as well as easier to use.

But where did this rubber come from? Two major regions of the world were permanently altered in the frenzied pursuit of rubber supplies: Amazonia and the Congo. In both cases, an extreme brutality was used, mutilating and murdering literally millions of people to produce the precious rubber, the whole process lashed by the rising demand in the United States, Europe, and Japan created by the bicycling boom (Jackson: 2008).

Meanwhile, bicycling was being embraced by women in unprecedented numbers, as many saw the device as their best means for at least a partial self-emancipation. Women's clothing was changing, and social mores were too. In "Thousands Ride the Noiseless Bicycle," in the *San Francisco Chronicle* (May 19, 1895), the shift is described:

> In the Park the other day, out of forty wheelmen, thirty-five were appropriately dressed in knickerbockers of some sort, short coats and caps. It is the same way with women. The long skirt is being pretty generally discarded, and if a woman cannot wear either bloomers or a short skirt she might as well keep off the wheel. . . . People used to ride only for pleasure. Now they ride instead of taking the cars, and own wheels instead of feeding horses and washing carriages. Doctors use the silent and inexpensive steed very extensively in making professional calls. For night calls it is always ready, and there is a considerable saving in hack hire, livery stable fees and coachman's wages. The keepers of livery stables say the bicycle has cut into their business far more seriously than electric cars ever did.
>
> A well-known riding teacher says that most of his women pupils take their first lessons in skirts on a woman's wheel. They go out on the road this way from three to ten times. They then come back to him in bloomers, learn to mount and dismount from a man's wheel, which is a great deal harder than the other way, and never again can be induced to ride a woman's wheel. Girls who ride for pleasure like to ride with men, of course, and the

only way to do it is to keep the pace they set. It cannot be done in skirts on a woman's wheel, and a man, even a polite escort, cannot be expected to ride slow forever, and so it happens that men's wheels grow more popular with women every day, and after awhile when people stop talking about it and the small boy stop hooting it will all be very charming and agreeable.

The mass of cyclists in San Francisco were not narrowly focused on bicycling alone. They became the backbone of a broad movement for improved streets and Good Roads. On July 25, 1896, thousands of cyclists filled the streets in the largest demonstration seen in the City's history, watched by perhaps as many as 100,000 spectators. The streets were dusty or muddy, and piles of horseshit were deposited everywhere. Streetcar tracks laid by private entrepreneurs often created barriers 18″ or more above the surface of the street, or left slippery and treacherous cable car slots in the middle of many streets. Roads were far from the uniform surface we are used to today.

A five-year bicyclist named McGuire, speaking for the South Side Improvement Club, stated: "The purpose for the march is three-fold; to show our strength, to celebrate the paving of Folsom Street and to protest against the conditions of San Francisco pavement in general and of Market Street in particular. If the united press of this city decides that Market Street must be repaved, it will be done in a year" (*SF Chronicle*: May 19, 1895).

It would take the devastating damage of the 1906 earthquake and fire before the City's streets were systematically improved. What bicyclists could not have known during the mid-1890s agitation was that their effort to improve streets would be taken advantage of not by thousands of new cyclists, but instead by the emergence of the private automobile, which also depended on some of the same technologies that had brought the boom in bicycling, rubber air-filled tires for smooth riding being a key example.

T8: MUNI: PUBLIC STREETCARS AND BUSES

Church and 15th Streets, Market Street Railway Mural

Prior to the twentieth century, two distinct public transportation systems existed in San Francisco. The first, the Market Street Railway Company, was privately owned by Southern Pacific Railroad Corporation in the

San Francisco 1940: the "Roar of the Four" still filled Market Street with streetcars.
(Author's collection, photographer unknown)

1890s and was the product of the earliest consolidation of numerous smaller privately owned horsecars, cable cars, and streetcars in the City. The other consolidation was created in 1892 by the voters of San Francisco, who incorporated a publicly owned transit system into their new city charter. The new system did not actually begin operation until December 28th, 1912, but it was the seed for the present-day MUNI.

When Eastern investors, led by Patrick Calhoun (grandson of a former Confederate leader), took over the jumble of San Francisco streetcar lines in 1901, they inherited a system that had 234 miles of track, 56 miles of cable, 166 miles of overhead trolley, four miles of horse cars, and eight miles of ancient steam railroad. Each had a different gauge of track, with a rolling stock consisting of 376 cable cars, 414 trolleys, 65 steam dummy cars, and ten horsecars. About half of the lines had been converted to overhead trolleys by 1900 (Matoff: 1999).

In 1902, United Railroads (URR) began making regular, secret payments to Union Labor Party fixer Abe Ruef as a special consulting attorney to the Union Labor Party mayor. URR wanted to extend their streetcar lines throughout the City and also ensure they could continue to place overhead trolley lines wherever their streetcars ran. These payments were made by Tirey L. Ford, who at the time was also the attorney general of the State of California, a position he continued to hold for several more years while he was also general counsel to URR (Bean: 1952).

By the time the Union Labor Party swept to reelection in 1905, city luminaries Rudolph Spreckels and James Phelan were trying to block URR over the issue of overhead trolley lines along Sutter Street, where both men owned property. They insisted on much more expensive and less unsightly underground conduits. Rudolph Spreckels and his father Claus filed incorporation papers for the Municipal Street Railways of San Francisco on April 17, 1906, in order to prove that underground conduits were economical and superior, and to pressure Calhoun to give up his resistance to undergrounding the electrical lines.

During these same years, the workers on URR, the streetcar men, went on strike nearly every year, culminating in a very violent and protracted strike in 1907 that led to dozens of deaths and hundreds of injuries before the intransigence of the Calhoun ownership finally broke the union. A decade later, another violent strike on the streetcars reestablished the union, but the bitterness between workers and management on the privately owned URR was part of what fueled the public enthusiasm for the now-expanding Municipal Railway, known today as MUNI. On December 30, 1909, with a turnout of over 42,000 voters, two propositions for the City's own streetcar service obtained majorities over 70 percent. The number of voters made it the largest turnout for any special or primary election in San Francisco up to that time (Matoff: 1999). The vote was a strong repudiation of Calhoun's URR and its harsh treatment of its workers. In 1921, URR reorganized itself out of financial difficulties and renamed itself the Market Street Railway Company, taking the name from the nineteenth-century firm.

After James "Sunny Jim" Rolph was elected mayor in 1912, he appointed M. M. O'Shaughnessy as the City's chief engineer, thus inaugurating a decades-long relationship that completely reshaped San Francisco's publicly owned Municipal Railway. In April 1913, when a "Lower Market Street Agreement" allowed the city-owned system to use the outside tracks on Market Street and the Ferry Building turnaround, streetcars often clogged the street and gave rise to the expression "Roar of the Four." Under O'Shaughnessy's guidance, the Municipal Railway extended its streetcar lines across the city, and crucially, built several tunnels to facilitate better service. In December 1914, the 911-foot-long Stockton Tunnel was opened to streetcar service, designed to bring people to the 1915 Panama-Pacific International Exposition. The 12,000-foot Twin Peaks Tunnel opened in 1917 for the K-line streetcar (joined later by the L- and M-lines, both of which started as local west-side lines before entering the tunnel later), and was the longest streetcar tunnel built up to the time. In October 1928, N Judah service began from the Ferry Building to the beach (and through the 4,232-foot Sunset Tunnel), the last of the new streetcar lines until the end of the twentieth century.

The intersection of 3rd and Market Streets was a key transit hub in those days, with lines running south down 3rd Street to the Southern Pacific Depot at Townsend Street, while the first MUNI line, the B-car, ran out Geary Boulevard to the Richmond District. Nearly all the streets South of Market and in the Mission District, as well as most commercial district corridors, had streetcar lines on them, the majority of which were converted to bus lines (often using the same numbers that once denoted the streetcars), starting in the 1930s and accelerating through the modernization efforts of the 1940s and 1950s.

Streetcars were big business, but they had to deal with city bureaucracy as well. Cities trying to get a handle on the streetcar barons (as they were then called) severely regulated service and fares as well as dictated technical issues. By the middle of the twentieth century, most streetcar companies were already bankrupt from competition with autos and buses running on heavily subsidized roads. Additional competitive pressure came from the City's own streetcar lines, run by MUNI.

MUNI built its own lines with taxpayer dollars, voted in by bonds, and could secure the best routes for itself in competition with URR. The City could afford to dig the massive tunnels that connect the east and west. In January 1939, both MUNI and the Market Street Railway began providing service to the Transbay Terminal at 1st and Mission Streets. The Bay Bridge had been open just a year, and rail service began on the lower deck of the bridge in 1939. The Key System, the Sacramento Northern Railway, and the Southern Pacific's Interurban Electric Railway provided the train service on the bridge, although the Sacramento Northern and the Southern Pacific abandoned their bridge service after only a few months. (From January 1939 until August 1940, Sacramento Northern electric interurbans could be taken from the terminal to the city of Chico, 183 miles away.)

The Key System was a suburban electric streetcar system built throughout Berkeley and Oakland in the first decades of the twentieth century to facilitate suburbanization and real estate development, running down many of the wide boulevards of those growing towns (such as San Pablo, Sacramento, Shattuck, Telegraph, Broadway, East 14th, Foothill, and MacArthur). After years of connecting to the Southern Pacific ferries, when the Bay Bridge opened, the Key System ran across it until 1958 when it was discontinued (T12).

Between the great earthquake and fire of 1906 and the absorption of Market Street Railway into MUNI in September 1944, the City was covered by railway lines. By the time Market Street Railway disappeared, its own tracks and cars were in such poor repair that MUNI decided to scrap them all and replace them with buses. The only lines that continued to be served by rail were the MUNI lines: J-Church, K-Ingleside, L-Taraval, M-Ocean View, and N-Judah. Until the 1970s, all of these lines converged on Market Street and terminated in the Financial District.

With the coming of BART and the MUNI subway (which was paid for by BART as compensation for running only one line through San

Francisco and not serving as a proper metro as had been promised), street-cars ceased to run on Market Street except for the antiques that were run on special occasions, such as the Trolley Parades. In 1990, work began on the F-line, which used restored PCC cars from Philadelphia and other cities, and decorated the cars in the colors of the many different city lines that once used them. The F-line was the first "new" line built by MUNI in many years. It was also the first streetcar route in memory to replace a bus (the 8 Castro), and now the F-line runs the length of Market Street and north along the Embarcadero to Fisherman's Wharf; the more recently adopted E-line runs the historic PCC cars along the waterfront from Fisherman's Wharf to the Giants ballpark at 3rd and King Streets. A new subway connecting the T-line to Chinatown runs underground into a tunnel at 4th and Brannan Streets and continues past the Moscone Convention Center, Union Square, and into Chinatown.

Because the City gets its power cheaply from its own dam at Hetch Hetchy, most of MUNI's buses and all of its streetcars are powered by publicly owned electricity. When first adopted in the mid-twentieth century, the fleet depended on diesel fuel. Nowadays, MUNI has also led the way in the adoption of hybrid biofuel/electric buses in place of diesel.

T9: Ferries on the Bay

Ferry Terminal behind Ferry Building

Thousands of people use ferries on the San Francisco Bay these days, so it's hard to remember that ferry service died out for several decades after the construction of the Bay Bridge and the Golden Gate Bridge. Of course, the long history of Bay Area mobility is a story of water travel. Whether moving hay into the City to feed the thousands of horses pulling wagons and omnibuses, or bringing the lumber in to build the wooden City, or taking big loads of grain or canned fruit and vegetables to far-flung ports, everything came and went by ship for a long time. But it was also true that most people wanting to go from one part of the Bay Area to another would find ferry travel the most convenient and appropriate means to make their trip.

In 1850, just a year since the beginning of urbanization, the first ferry service was established between San Francisco and Oakland, running across sand bars to San Antonio Creek, better known now as the Oakland

Estuary. Ferries were the main transportation choice for travelers between San Francisco and Sacramento, and points in between, and continued to be well into the twentieth century. Back in 1862, the San Francisco and Oakland Railroad Company built a three-quarter-mile pier from West Oakland into the Bay. Thus began a decades-long concentration of cross-bay ferry traffic between West Oakland and San Francisco's Ferry Building. After the Civil War in 1868, real estate promoters laid out streets and docks in Sausalito and began providing North Bay ferry service. When the first transcontinental railroads spanned the country, the original terminal was in Sacramento, where passengers transferred to fast ferries to finish their trip to San Francisco and the coast. Before long the new railroad barons had acquired the local ferry services, and by 1881 they extended the wharves well into the Bay on what became known as the Oakland Mole, where trains and ferries met in the bay all the way to 1957 (Bonnett: 1997).

John Leale was a San Francisco ferryboat captain for four decades spanning the last quarter of the nineteenth century until just before WWI. He lived long enough to see the opening of the Bay Bridge that would nearly destroy ferry service in the Bay Area. His memoir, *Recollections of a Tule Sailor*, captures a San Francisco and waterborne life that is long-forgotten now.

On his arrival in San Francisco in 1864, he docked at the Folsom Street Wharf and from there took a horse-drawn omnibus to the 3rd Street Wharf, then jutting into Mission Bay:

> A whitehall boatman rowed us over to the Potrero to the home of a relative, at a point which later became the Union Iron Works [Today's 3rd Street and 20th Street]. Third Street at that time ended at about Townsend Street or Steamboat Point. Between there and the Potrero was a large bay at the head of which was San Francisco's first Butchertown [close to Costco at 10th and Bryant Streets]. I later learned that it was a long way by land from the Potrero to Third Street with its mud and unpaved road. . . . The morning after my arrival, I meandered to the top of a nearby hill, and after surveying the beautiful bay and mountains before me I realized that I was indeed in California.
>
> My first job in California was cook of the Schooner *Emma Adelia* of which Captain Andrew Nelson was captain and owner. My work was not cooking alone but also tending the jib sheet and

working cargo. During the summer we ran in the fruit trade [up and down the Sacramento River]. The passengers who got on board well up river had a whole day's entertainment plus looking for a cool spot, for a summer day on the Sacramento is "heap hot." Rio Vista was usually the last landing and the boys would turn in for about five hours, to be called when Angel Island was reached, for we must have coffee before beginning to discharge. This would be perhaps three or four o'clock in the morning, and if it happened to be low water with the corresponding steep gangway plank, it was a tough job. At about 11:30 AM we would leave the city again for the next trip. So it will be seen that the life of a deckhand on the river in those days was a bit strenuous. (Leale: 1939)

Over the last century and a half, over two dozen major cross-bay ferry lines existed, serving 29 destinations. The golden era of ferry transit stretched from the 1870s to its peak in the 1930s. Ten million passengers went through the Ferry Building in the first decade of the twentieth century, and just 30 years later there were 60 million annual bay crossings, along with 6 million autos. A quarter of a million daily commuters traveled through the Ferry Building to work or other destinations. Ferries made approximately 170 landings a day at this time, and the Ferry Building was served by trolley lines that left every 20 seconds for city destinations. The ferry was as deeply rooted in the daily lives of San Franciscans as cars and planes are now. When Tom Mooney was finally pardoned from jail in 1939 (where he served 22 and a half years for the bombing of the July 22, 1916, Preparedness Day March—a crime he demonstrably did not commit; see L9), he left San Quentin Prison by ferry and went to Sacramento to receive his pardon from Governor Culbert Olson. After the pardon and press conference, he took the train to Oakland and ferried across to San Francisco, where he was greeted by 10,000 well-wishers as he emerged from the Ferry Building into Market Street.

By the end of the 1930s, the two great bridges were complete and the patterns of urban life and cross-bay travel were altered forever. The great urban theorist Lewis Mumford had no trouble in 1963 describing what the Bay Bridge had done to ferry travel:

The Bay Bridge, between San Francisco and Oakland, brought far greater damage than benefits to both cities: it pumped up a once unnecessary volume of private traffic between them, at a great expense in expressway building and at a great waste in time and tension spent crawling through rush-hour congestion. This traffic eventually wiped out, by impoverishment, the excellent rapid transit that had been installed on the Bay Bridge (the Key System) a form of transportation that the citizens of San Francisco have now repentantly voted to restore [the BART system], at an expense far greater than the cost of the original system. The ferry ride across the bay from Oakland was one of the region's greatest recreational resources—an incomparable experience, so exhilarating, at almost any time of the day, that one often sought an excuse for making the journey. It was not a long ride—not more than twenty-five minutes or so, and certainly not longer than the present depressing rush-hour crawl over the bridge. (Mumford: 1963)

A similar story follows the ever-popular Golden Gate Bridge, which opened in May 1937. Flourishing ferry service between Sausalito and San Francisco rapidly declined after the bridge opened, stopping entirely by 1941. For the next 29 years, the only way to get from San Francisco to Marin County and points north was by driving across the Golden Gate Bridge. During those same three decades, motor traffic on the Golden Gate Bridge went from 3.3 million trips at the beginning to 28.3 million by the late 1960s (and is now hovering around 40 million per year). Local traffic planners and highway engineers proposed new bridges to cross the bay from Telegraph Hill to Angel Island and Tiburon, but these ideas never got off the drawing boards.

Instead, the indomitable ferry came back into the picture. In August 1970, a newly minted Golden Gate Ferry (GGF) service began from Sausalito to San Francisco. By the end of December 1976, the Larkspur Ferry began its service. It was another year and a half before the familiar Golden Gate Ferry terminal behind the Ferry Building was dedicated in summer 1978. Golden Gate Transit provides a decent history of itself, as well as this overview of its current service:

GGF operates two commute passenger ferry routes across the San Francisco Bay that connect Marin County and the City and County of San Francisco: (1) Larkspur/San Francisco, and (2) Sausalito/San Francisco. Today, GGF runs 50 crossings on the

Larkspur-San Francisco route and 30 crossings on the Sausalito/ San Francisco route. Since March 31, 2000, dedicated San Francisco Giants Baseball Ferry Service has been provided between Larkspur and the waterfront ball park located at Mission Creek. (goldengateferry.org/researchlibrary/history.php)

One of the untold stories of the current GGF service is that at least two of the daily runs between Sausalito and San Francisco keep running thanks to the revenue provided by bicycle-renting tourists who ride across the Golden Gate Bridge and return by ferry!

The Vallejo Ferry Service started in 1986, initially as a commercial operation of the Red & White Fleet in San Francisco to shuttle midday visitors north to the newly opened Marine World in Vallejo, and commuters back and forth in morning and evening runs. The commuter runs proved unprofitable, and within a few years the city of Vallejo had to take over the service under strong pressure from its ferry-riding citizens.

The bay ferry operations all got a big boost when the 1989 Loma Prieta earthquake knocked out the Bay Bridge for several months. State transportation money was made available to excursion and tour boats while also bolstering existing public ferry services. The network of ferries established under pressure from clogged freeways and a basically dysfunctional automobile-based transit system seemed to finally solidify with a new public awareness of their indispensability. After a weeklong BART strike in 1997, ferry passengers surged again, and as of a few years ago, the Vallejo Baylink service was running three daily ferries back and forth.

The ferry's future is bright. Waterborne transportation is likely to enjoy a considerable expansion whether due to high oil prices, impassable traffic jams, or just an embrace of a more civilized way to move across our beautiful bay.

T10: AUTOMOBILES TAKE OVER SF STREETS

Market Street and Van Ness Avenue

"Whose Streets? OUR Streets!" yell rowdy demonstrators when they surge off the sidewalk and into thoroughfares. True enough, the streets are our public commons—what's left of it (along with libraries and our diminishing public schools)—but most of the time these public avenues are dedicated to the movement of vehicles, predominantly privately owned autos. Other uses are frowned upon, discouraged by laws and regulations and what have become our customary expectations. Ask any driver who is impeded by anything other than a "normal" traffic jam and they'll be quick to denounce the inappropriate use or blockage of the street.

For decades, over 30,000 people have died each year in car crashes on the streets of the United States. This daily carnage is utterly normalized to the point that few of us think about it at all. If we do, it's like the weather, just a regular part of our environment. But it wasn't always this way. Back when the private automobile was first beginning to appear on public streets, a large majority of the population, including politicians, police, and business leaders, agreed that cars were interlopers and ought to be regulated and subordinated to pedestrians and streetcars.

Motorists and their political representatives argue that the norms of mid-twentieth-century American life can be extended indefinitely into the future. But there is a lost history that has been illuminated by Peter D. Norton in his book *Fighting Traffic: The Dawn of the Motor Age in the American City.* He skillfully excavates the shift that was engineered in public opinion during the 1920s by the organized forces of what called itself "Motordom." Their efforts turned pedestrians into scofflaws known as "jaywalkers," shifted the burden of public safety from speeding motorists to their victims, and reorganized American urban design around providing more roads and more space for private cars.

It's almost impossible to imagine the speed with which conditions on urban streets changed at the dawn of the motorized era. The California Automobile Association's *Motorland* magazine in August 1927 described the rapid growth in car ownership: "In 1895 there were four cars registered, in 1905 there were 77,400 in use, in 1915 the total had risen to 2,309,000, and in 1925 there were 17,512,000 passenger automobiles on the highways, and the total is now in excess of 20,000,000" (Norton: 2008).

With death and injury tolls rising, cities took various measures to address the problem. Crosswalks were invented but often ignored. The common usage of the streets by all was considered sacrosanct, and attempts by Motordom and/or police to regulate people's use of the streets was widely resisted. By 1920, "jaywalking" had become a crime in San Francisco. That year, during a safety campaign, San Francisco pedestrians found themselves in pretend courtrooms in public locations. Crowds watched as San Franciscans were lectured on the perils of jaywalking.

Traditional use of the streets by pedestrians was being criminalized by new traffic codes. A young graduate student named Miller McClintock, who had become the nation's preeminent traffic researcher thanks to his 1925 thesis *Street Traffic Control*, put forth a new Uniform Traffic Ordinance. It was quickly adopted by San Francisco's Board of Supervisors, and was intended to "legislate jaywalkers off the streets," crowed a *Motorland* editorial. In 1915, Ford already had a factory at Twenty-First and Harrison Streets in the Mission making Model-T's, and by the mid-1920s, the new car business was fully ensconced along Van Ness Avenue in San Francisco.

As the 1920s continued, more and more cars were being sold, and the streets were both crowded and contested. (From 1914 to 1928, the number of autos registered in San Francisco grew tenfold, from 12,081 to 122,808.) Streetcar operators blamed cars for clogging thoroughfares and slowing down their lines, causing late runs and generally inconveniencing passengers. Motorists parked everywhere, jamming curbsides two-deep when they weren't weaving through chaotic urban streets. Attempts to regulate and standardize traffic patterns began during this era, with lanes, crosswalks, traffic signals, and parking regulations slowly emerging as "solutions" to the problems created by tens of thousands of private cars filling the streets.

When sales slumped in late 1923 and into 1924, analysts speculated that the market for cars was saturated (at about seven Americans per car at the time). The car industry consisted of dozens of companies that went bankrupt or merged during this first contraction in sales. The industry reorganized its public relations and launched concerted efforts to redefine saturation: "There was no 'buying-power saturation,' [*Motordom*] said. The real bridle on the demand for automobiles was not the consumer's wallet, but street capacity. Traffic congestion deterred the would-be urban car buyer, and congestion was saturation of streets" (Norton: 2008).

Miller McClintock's career is a window into the process of private corruption of public interests that riddles American history up to the present:

In his graduate thesis the old McClintock had maintained that widening streets would merely attract more vehicles to them, leaving traffic as congested as before. The automobile, he wrote, was a waster of space compared to the streetcar, noting that "the greater economy of the latter is marked." "It seems desirable," McClintock wrote, "to give trolley cars the right of way under general conditions, and to place restrictions on motor vehicles in their relations with street cars." He described the automobile as a "menace to human life" and "the greatest public destroyer of human life." (Norton: 2008)

In 1925, McClintock opposed elevated streets as expensive and impractical, but by 1927 he reversed himself and supported them. He had been hired by Studebaker's vice president to head up the new Albert Russel Erskine Bureau for Street Traffic Research, which was first placed in Los Angeles where McClintock was teaching at UC, but a year later moved by Studebaker to Harvard University, where the car company continued to fund the ostensibly "independent" institute. As the years went by, McClintock became one of the foremost authorities on traffic planning.

McClintock came to San Francisco early in his career. In the August 1927 *Motorland* magazine, he penned an article summarizing his research, "Curing the Ills of San Francisco Traffic": "It is recognized that an ultimate requirement for the solution of street and highway congestion is to be found in the creation of more ample street area." And sure enough, it was in this exact period that San Francisco embarked on a series of street widenings throughout the City, including, for example, Capp Street and Army Street in the Mission District. McClintock's traffic study shows the predominant car-free life of San Franciscans at the time.

Incredibly, streetcars were used by 70 percent of the people depending on some kind of transportation to get downtown, while only a quarter used passenger cars; but the latter made up 61 percent of vehicular traffic as compared to 11 percent for the streetcars! (Norton: 2008).

What has been poorly understood in the triumphant narrative of the private automobile is how cars benefited from enormous public expenditures, even when they were being used by a relatively small minority of the population. New infrastructure to accommodate motorists far outstripped any public investment in public streetcar service, let alone any subsidies for the privately owned lines. Meanwhile, electric streetcar companies were slowly going bankrupt, with their fares publicly restricted through regulation and the public streets on which they operated slowly being taken over by private vehicles.

At the 1939 Golden Gate International Exposition, United States Steel displayed its vision of San Francisco in 1999, with wider streets, cloverleaf intersections, and an elevated highway:

> Artist Donald McLoughlin had prepared a dioramic view of San Francisco in 1999 for the US Steel exhibit in the Hall of Mines, Metals and Machinery. This prognostic nightmare showed the city stripped of every vestige of 1939 except Coit Tower, the bridges and Chinatown. All maritime activity had disappeared from the Embarcadero. Shipping was concentrated at a super-pier at the foot of 16th Street.
>
> North of Market Street every block contained a single, identical high-rise apartment house. South of Market, sixty-story office towers of steel and glass alternated with block-square plazas in a vast checkerboard pattern. Elevated freeways ran through the geometric landscape. (Reinhardt: 1973)

McLoughlin correctly anticipated the removal of maritime activity from San Francisco's waterfront, though his massive modern pier is actually spread along the Oakland bayshore. Visions like this informed the post-WWII population as it fled cities for the suburbs. Those who remained, though, had a different idea of what our cities would become, and thanks to their stopping the highway builders in their tracks in the late 1950s and early 1960s, San Francisco took a different path (T12).

It is interesting to recall that while tens of thousands of citizens were mobilized to stop freeway building in San Francisco (the very same elevated, pedestrian-free streets McClintock had come to endorse as an industry flack), thousands more, mostly African American and white youth, staged a vigorous civil rights campaign along auto row, demanding that blacks be given equal treatment in hiring by auto dealers, especially Don Lee's Cadillac dealership (D6).

Contrary to the certainty of today's motorists, streets have not always been the domain of cars. Clever marketing prior to the Depression led to radical redesign of both the physical streets and our assumptions about how public streets should be used.

T11: THE FREEWAY REVOLT

Panhandle Park, west end, at Shrader Street

In honor of the leader in the citizen revolt that led to the city government blocking many planned elevated freeways crisscrossing the City, Sue Bierman Park sits on the former site of the on- and off-ramps of the Embarcadero Freeway at Clay and Washington Streets that dominated the waterfront from its construction in 1953 to its destruction in 1993. But it was the Panhandle in the Haight Ashbury that was really saved by Bierman's organizing work. In the 1950s, the California Department of Highways had a plan to extend freeways across San Francisco. At that time, the freeway reigned supreme in California, but San Francisco harbored the seeds of an incipient revolt that ultimately saved several neighborhoods from the wrecking ball and also put up the first serious opposition to the post-WWII consensus on automobiles, freeways, and suburbanization.

After the *San Francisco Chronicle* published a map in 1956 showing freeway routes crisscrossing the City proposed by the California Department

Embarcadero Freeway. c. 1958. (Author's collection, photographer unknown)

of Highways, committees of citizens emerged in many neighborhoods to oppose the plans. By 1959, over 70,000 citizens had signed petitions objecting to various segments of planned elevated freeways, and the city's Board of Supervisors voted to block most of them. But the California Department of Highways engineers, all men, were not impressed by the female-led opposition in San Francisco. The middle-class women in Glen Park who led the effort to block plans to run a freeway through Glen Canyon, today one of San Francisco's most beloved open spaces and parks, were derogatorily dismissed by traffic engineers as the "Blue Gum Girls." But they prevailed. One bucolic neighborhood, Potrero Hill, was cut off by freeways on both sides, first its west side by the central freeway in the mid-1950s, and then Interstate 280 on its east flank. Neighbors were incensed and flooded City Hall and local press with complaints. Interstate 280 was built over the old Islais Creek watershed from Daly City to the former marshes east of Bernal Heights. The City fought bitterly against the engineers who wanted to run I-280 along the shores of San Francisco's drinking supply at the Crystal Springs reservoirs down the peninsula, and eventually forced the freeway builders to reroute I-280 on the ridge line above the reservoirs. All along, traffic planners assumed their mandate was to connect the Bay Bridge to the Golden Gate Bridge with freeways, and both bridges to freeways running south out of San Francisco on both west and east sides. But San Franciscans didn't accept this vision and put up an extraordinary fight.

Sue Bierman helped found the Haight Ashbury Neighborhood Council to oppose the Panhandle/Golden Gate Park Freeway that was meant to connect the Golden Gate Bridge to the Central Freeway. In May 1964, a mass rally was held at Kezar Stadium in the southeast corner of Golden Gate Park, featuring folksinger Malvina Reynolds singing her anti-freeway anthem. The Central Freeway was stopped not far from City Hall with off-ramps at Fell and Oak and others at Franklin and Gough at Turk (where they stood until the 1989 Loma Prieta earthquake). Over nearly a decade from 1956 to 1964, thousands of activated citizens pressured city leaders until a climactic vote was taken in 1964. First-ever African American Supervisor Terry Francois (an NAACP lawyer who then-mayor Jack Shelley appointed as a reliable vote for his pro-labor majority on the Board) gave an epic speech analyzing the pros and cons of the Panhandle-Golden Gate Park Freeway from the point of view of being a black man living in an integrated part of the Haight Ashbury while the Redevelopment

Agency was demolishing the largely black Fillmore just to the north. Five votes were already against the freeway, and five votes were in favor. Francois shocked the City and the nation when he cast his vote "no." Never before had a City refused to allow a freeway to be built. For another year, Mayor Shelley and his supporters tried to convince a majority to vote for the Panhandle Freeway, or at least for the Golden Gateway Freeway that had been truncated on the waterfront at Broadway. But in 1965, both projects were finally defeated for good by 6–5 votes, Supervisor William Blake from the Sunset being a surprise last-minute conversion to the "no" campaign. Interstate 280 was authorized and completed in the early 1970s, but it too was eventually truncated and redesigned to end where it does today at 5th and King Streets (Germain: 2016; Issel: 1999).

Just to the south of Mission Creek runs a waterfront road named Terry Francois Boulevard. To this day, San Francisco has never allowed a connecting freeway to be built across the City.

The 1989 Loma Prieta earthquake helped advance the (then) stalled cause of freeway removal by hopelessly damaging the Embarcadero Freeway and Central Freeway. As a result, they were removed and re-placed by today's much-admired boulevards along the Embarcadero and Octavia Boulevard, where today the old freeway corridors are filled with new apartment buildings and a surface roadway. The complaints of Chinatown merchants over the demise of the Embarcadero Freeway led to the construction of the new subway that is nearing completion as this is being written. Octavia Boulevard was a vision of activist neighbors and bicycle advocates who mobilized after the 1989 quake to campaign against Caltrans's efforts to rebuild the Central Freeway. In a reprise of the old freeway revolt of the 1960s, torrid campaigns rocked the city, and three consecutive elections saw nail-biters decide the fate of the Hayes Valley area. In the first vote, a 51–49 majority favored removing the freeway in favor of the Boulevard plan. Sunset and Richmond dwellers used to driving on the freeway daily feared total gridlock and returned to the ballot and prevailed by an equally narrow 51–49 margin. Redoubling their efforts in a last gasp to alter the landscape, neighbors and new ur-banists and cyclists coalesced once again and in the third election won by a small margin again. This time, Mayor Willie Brown ordered the demo-lition to begin within weeks in order to prevent any further efforts to change course. The ensuing property boom and gentrification of the neighborhood has surprised even the most ardent supporters of the surface boulevard plan (Henderson: 2013).

T12: BART

Powell Street Station

In the late 1950s, an extensive, decades-old grid of electric streetcars called the Key System covered most of Oakland and Berkeley and crossed the Bay Bridge into San Francisco's Transbay Terminal at 1st and Mission. Like many municipal railways in the 1930s and '40s, it had been acquired by a subsidiary of the National City Lines, a company created by General Motors, Standard Oil of California (later Chevron), Firestone Tire, and Phillips Petroleum. These four companies were later found guilty of conspiracy and fined a paltry $5,000 for having bought up railways around the country and replacing them with buses, destroying essential urban transit infrastructure in the process.

After a 1947 defense department study concluded that more transit would be needed regionally, business leaders began hatching a plan for a Bay Area Rapid Transit District. In 1958, the directors of the newly formed BART board were granted authority over transbay rail service, and when the East Bay's public transit agency AC Transit (which had taken over the Key System at the end of its days) and their consultants argued for maintaining tracks across the Bay Bridge, the BART directors blocked them. Their action led to the dismantling of the Key System's tracks, which heightened the political momentum to build the new rail system the BART directors backed.

BART began construction after original tax funding was approved at the ballot box in San Francisco, Alameda, and Contra Costa counties in 1962. Fearing that they might not get the 60 percent majority required because of rural and suburban opposition in Marin County, BART directors asked Marin County to withdraw from the original plan to extend BART across a new lower deck of the Golden Gate Bridge and into Marin county. Marin County supervisors complied with the request against their will, and later tried to be readmitted to BART but were denied (Healy: 2016).

BART opened its first line, the Richmond-Fremont north-south route in the East Bay, in 1972, and transbay service began in 1974. A conflict with the city of Berkeley over undergrounding the train was eventually won by Berkeley, and BART was forced to go underground from the Oakland border to nearly Albany. Combined with freeway construction in West Oakland and a massive new post office, the BART line contributed to the destruction of one of Black Oakland's most dynamic neighborhoods along West Oakland's 7th Street corridor. Downtown Oakland, San Francisco's Market Street and Mission District shopping districts were all permanently upended by the years-long trench-and-tunneling that built BART. In San Francisco's Mission District, neighbors mobilized against BART, recognizing the grandiose plans for the areas around its stations at 16th and 24th Streets would galvanize gentrification and drive out the existing working-class Latino community. Dovetailing with the mobilization of the Mission Coalition Organization in 1970, BART was forced to scale back its development plans, and Mission Street was not bulldozed as planned. A half century later, after Mission Street's formerly dynamic "miracle mile" has languished with dollar stores, derelict storefronts, and abandoned theaters for decades, a noticeable uptick in commercial rentals and new construction began to reshape the corridor in the 2010s (and the Mission Economic Development Agency has been busily buying up key corner properties along the street to help preserve at least some of its historic businesses and character).

The chief engineers responsible for BART's design worked in a consortium of several engineering firms called Parsons Brinckerhoff-Tudor-Bechtel, combining Parsons Brinckerhoff Hall & McDonald Engineering consultants (based in New York, they had been part of the earliest rail-planning efforts that began in 1953), Tudor Engineering, and San Francisco-based Bechtel Corporation, better known for its involvement in dam building and nuclear power plant construction. In fact, the BART system was poorly designed, from the 700-foot-long stations that prevented trains longer than ten cars from using the platforms, to the nonstandard gauge of the tracks ($5'6''$ wide instead of the standard $4'8.5''$ of most train systems). Maintenance and replacement equipment would always be prohibitively expensive. Strangely, the engineers chose to use steel rails and wheels, which in recent years has led to ear-shattering screeching as the trains make their turns deep in various tunnels. At the outset it was argued that the sensible rubber tires used in Paris, Mexico City, and other places were "too noisy!" BART has also suffered with inadequate sidetracks and turnaround facilities since its founding, leading to chronic systemwide delays and occasional blockages. After a half century of growth, the most crowded stations are bursting at the seams and desperate for an expansion that is logistically nearly impossible. Talk of building a second transbay tube and expanding lines in the core service areas have been met with skepticism due to the prohibitive cost, social and commercial disruption, and general dissatisfaction with the inflexibility of its design.

Puzzlingly, when plans in the late 1980s were nearing completion to connect the San Francisco Airport (SFO) to the Caltrain line (formerly operated by Southern Pacific, now publicly owned and maintained) running just west of the airport, and to extend Caltrain from its 4th and Townsend Street terminus to the Transbay Terminal at 1st and Mission Streets, the regional Metropolitan Transportation Commission suddenly pulled back. Instead of funding that plan, they became convinced to extend BART from its Daly City terminus to SFO, as part of a multibillion-dollar expansion of the airport that included adding a six-mile looping automatic Airtrain shuttle system. The Airtrain system reaches the car rental facilities, and BART got a station inside the airport, adjacent to the new International Terminal. The BART extension alone cost over $750 million, and the stations along the line between the airport and the original end of the line in Daly City have never had heavy usage. The alternative would have been to build the Airtrain to the same Caltrain station that BART also connects to at Millbrae, and then use the existing train to bring people into San Francisco. If the money had been spent then to extend Caltrain to the Transbay Terminal, the connection to BART and buses could have been accomplished at far less cost. As it happened, the BART extension was built, and now the Caltrain extension is being built additionally as part of the projected arrival of California High-Speed Rail into the heart of San Francisco. With the advantage of hindsight looking back several decades, we can see that terrible regional transportation decisions were made, apparently to benefit the locally connected corporations who most handsomely benefit from the design and construction of the BART system. We are now building for a far greater cost what we could have built in the first place without the enormous public expense to extend BART unnecessarily.

T13: SAN FRANCISCO AIRPORT

SFO

In 1915, San Franciscans were thrilled and then horrified by the aerial ac-
robatics of Lincoln Beachey as he did stunts over the bay as part of the
Panama-Pacific International Exposition—until plunging to his death
during a failed trick. Just west of the Exposition grounds was the city's first
airfield, a military post on Crissy Field in the Presidio. Commercial air
traffic was still a couple of decades away. For a brief time it was projected
that Treasure Island, built originally for the Golden Gate International
Exposition in 1939–40, would be converted to an airport after the World's
Fair. But when WWII interceded, Treasure Island became a naval base
with the Navy taking over the original terminal building and the hangars.

Plans were floated in the 1920s to build an airfield in India Basin over
the Islais Creek marshes. Eventually, the city of San Francisco purchased
the tidelands at the eastern edge of the Darius Ogden Mills estate (which
was eventually subdivided and became the town of Millbrae) in San Mateo
County, and there opened the airport as Mills Field in the late 1920s. On
June 9, 1931, the name was changed to San Francisco Airport and was soon
added to the purview of the City's Public Utilities Commission.

In the early 1930s, 350 acres of tidelands were "reclaimed," and by
1935, the airport had extended its runway C from 1,900 feet to 3,000
feet. The airport construction also created a basin for the amphibious
planes that were still a common part of early air travel. Pan American
chose the San Francisco Airport as its location to do the first regularly
scheduled transoceanic air service. The flight took off from the San
Francisco Airport, and 59 hours later, after four stops, it landed in Manila,
Philippines. The plane was so heavy that when it took off from the airport
it had to fly under the cables of the East Bay Bridge that had not been completed yet. The plane, China Clipper, became instantly famous and set off
a rage of new toys, beer, and food all with the name China Clipper. After
WWII, the rechristened San Francisco International Airport (SFO) began
its inexorable expansion, with a new terminal building, a new control tower,
and expanded runways all taking shape.

In the late 1990s, during the first dot-com tech boom, SFO became the
nation's ninth-busiest airport. SFO found itself confronted with chronic

delays, which were blamed on the old mid-century runways, no longer separated enough to accommodate a higher flow of airline traffic. Mayor Willie Brown, the consummate dealmaker, embarked on a campaign to build new runways into San Francisco Bay in order to allow expansion of the airport. But strong opposition by Supervisor Aaron Peskin and a panoply of local environmental groups, plus the Bay Conservation and Development Commission, ultimately derailed the plans. Air traffic has fallen considerably since those booming times, and SFO now ranks twenty-first in airport business. Oakland and San Jose airports have also taken up some of the pressure on SFO.

In the early 2000s, the city-owned facility completed its most recent expansion, adding a dedicated International Terminal, as well as building a six-mile automated shuttle train system, and running an extension of the BART train system directly to the airport (see T12 for more on this).

San Francisco International Airport is a bastion of union labor in the Bay Area. Nearly everyone working there belongs to one of over a dozen unions associated with the airline business, from machinists and pilots to flight attendants and custodial workers at the airport. Still, in 1981 the Professional Air Traffic Controllers Organization (PATCO) went on strike at the beginning of the Reagan administration, and threw up a picket line at SFO. They were all fired by the government, which sought to make an example of them to intimidate organized labor more generally. Their union was destroyed after a few months, in part due to a lack of solidarity from other airport unions.

After the 9/11 terror attacks in New York and Washington, D.C., a radically ramped-up security system was put in at SFO as at all airports nationwide. It was no longer enough to pass through the metal detectors that had existed for years. Now a whole theater of police state "security" had to be performed, from taking off shoes, hats, belts, and jackets, to removing everything from pockets, prohibiting all containers of liquid, and so on, all while standing in long, slow-moving lines. (Since 2017, the government has begun offering frequent travelers a way to get pre-checked and avoid some of the worst of the humiliating and pointless Transportation Security Administration rituals.) The absurd system of color-coded warnings implemented by the ominously named "Department of Homeland Security" quickly became a meaningless joke. Repeated breaches of the security system at most airports underscore the reality that the whole system is designed to teach-and-test docility and obedience to the average traveler and has very little to do with anything that might be called "public safety."

In January 2017, the incoming Trump administration promulgated draconian new rules to prevent immigration by Muslims, even banning green-card holders and people already holding valid visas and en route to U.S. airports. Thousands of people quickly besieged airports around the country, including SFO. For several days prior to a federal court judge reversing the ban (something that would happen twice more in the year), thousands of Bay Area residents marched, sang, chanted, and occupied the lobby of the International Terminal in a stirring rebuke to the xenophobia and racism that had taken over the government.

T14: Bicycling's Rebirth to Critical Mass

Duboce Bikeway

Bicycling had boomed in the 1890s, but was soon overtaken by the explosion in automobiles. While the bicycle remained a recreational and practical device for the decades that followed, it never had the cachet that it had

Critical Mass laboring up the steep Potrero Hill in August 1999. (Chris Carlsson)

enjoyed during its nineteenth-century boom. But by the 1970s, as ecological consciousness spread and the first oil embargo shocked Americans into a new way of thinking about cities and transportation, a new bicycling craze began. It was helped in part by the emergence of mountain biking in Marin County, which opened up a new way to enjoy the abundant open spaces of the Bay Area. In Berkeley for several years from 1969 into the early 1970s, there was an annual mass bike ride on Telegraph Avenue called "Smog-free Locomotion Day." In San Francisco, cycling advocates promoted bike lanes and successfully opened the City's first on Lake Street in the Richmond district. Organizing themselves as the San Francisco Bicycle Coalition, they pushed for more, but made little progress. Green signs indicating "bike routes" were installed on many streets, but nothing was done to alter the streetscape, which remained utterly dominated by the storage and movement of private cars.

The initial 1970s surge of cycling interest waned as the Reagan administration recommitted the United States to the oil and car industries, and the military that sustains and is sustained by them. Bike messengers in the 1980s became the most visible population of daily cyclists, along with a few hundred hardy commuters. In the late 1980s, after a crescendo of complaints about so-called scofflaw messengers dashing through downtown stoplights and weaving through traffic, the mayor suggested licensing and registration might be appropriate. Bike messengers organized a mass ride and encircled City Hall, demanding that no such action be taken, and gained the support of leading columnist Herb Caen. Other cyclists, about a dozen of whom were still members of the nearly moribund SF Bicycle Coalition, came together as "Bay Area Bike Action," and in 1990 staged actions in Golden Gate park clamoring for street closures on weekends (something taken for granted now) and insisting that the park not be a parking lot.

When the United States started threatening war against Iraq in 1991, mass demonstrations were held regularly in San Francisco, and surprisingly, many people began attending on bicycles. Small squads of cyclists would ride out as scouts for larger demonstrations, a pattern that was to repeat itself during other political movements in the years that followed. A spirit of politics and bicycling was in the air, and many people were discussing how to use bicycles more aggressively to advance a politics of pleasure, self-assertion, protest, and more. From this ferment among messengers, commuters, and other cyclists, arose Critical Mass.

Critical Mass, the monthly mass bike ride, started in San Francisco in September 1992 and within a decade had spread to over 400 cities around the world. More than 25 years later, the ride continues on the last Friday of every month in San Francisco and in hundreds of other cities worldwide. San Francisco's ride is a pale shadow of its heyday in the 1990s and first decade of the 2000s, but it rolls along nevertheless. Throughout major cities of South America and in Spain, Italy, and many European cities, the ride continues to draw thousands and challenge the dynamics of modern city life.

Beginning a year after the first Gulf War was used by George Bush Sr. to declare a post-Soviet Union "new world order" (widely recognized as an oil war to drive Iraq out of Kuwait and restore Kuwait's petroleum-dependent and Western bank-friendly royal family), Critical Mass opened a new mobile public space created by defiant bicyclists. Thanks to the political energy that Critical Mass unleashed, the City dedicated the block of Duboce between Church and Market to bicyclists and pedestrians in 1998, the first and only street of its kind in the City.

In 1998, artist Mona Caron painted her first mural on a remarkable 6,000-square-foot wall along the newly inaugurated Duboce Bikeway, covering the back of the Safeway store at Church and Market Streets. The mural traces the route that bicyclists had come to customarily use to go from the Mission District and Civic Center areas to the Haight and the western neighborhoods by way of the lowest, most gradual grade between the lower and higher elevations. This route was nicknamed by Joel Pomerantz in the late 1980s "the Wiggle," due to the quick turns cyclists typically take at each intersection along the route.

The Duboce Bikeway/Wiggle Mural depicts at its far eastern end a Critical Mass of bicyclists surging onto the foot of Market Street, but cleverly shows how the streets are *already* clogged with cars before the cyclists even arrive. But Caron, an early participant in the ride herself, set out to do much more with her epic mural. Multiple pedal-powered "airships" trail long yellow banners in the sky at the left of the mural, only to give way to one massive banner that becomes the bulk of the center of the art, representing—as she has declared—one vision of many possible San Franciscos. The mural itself is depicted along with the many people who contributed to it shown riding bikes, unicycles, walking, riding a MUNI car, and eventually making their way through the Wiggle's streets to the west side. The paths that go through the Panhandle and Golden Gate Park eventually terminate in a giant bicycle disappearing into the Pacific Ocean. Cleverly, the plants and critters that populate the western side of San Francisco appear in giant proportions, centered on a brown snake that breaks the pavement of the park and connects the rider to the sand dunes that once covered the entire west side of the peninsula and will likely encroach again in an unknown future. The snake's elaborate skin magically turns into the giant cycle's tire track to knit the whole 340 feet together as a commentary on the fin de siècle bicycling culture that was transforming San Francisco, and urban life across the world.

Critical Mass connected antinuclear and antiwar activists of the 1970s and 1980s with a new cohort of political people. It opened a monthly mobile space in which people were able to find each other, and a variety of initiatives began in the serendipitous encounters that took place there. As the contagious pleasure of the ride became known, dozens, hundreds, and eventually thousands of people began showing up to join in. In San Francisco, the first heady years of Critical Mass were unforgettable, with themes, costumes, music, and spontaneous eruptions of exploration all finding an easy embrace among riders. Annual Halloween rides became pageants of hilarious and pointed commentary, while month after month for years the City's streets were seized by thousands of leaderless riders, "corking" intersections, inviting passersby, bus riders, and motorists to join the ride the following month.

The sudden explosion of Critical Mass also gave impetus to the San Francisco Bicycle Coalition to redouble its efforts to change city streets. By 1994, a citywide Bike Plan was being concocted and debated in public hearings, but it would be many years before actual changes on the ground would begin to appear. Valencia Street was an early example where traffic was reduced from two lanes each way to one, and a bike lane was painted alongside parked cars. It felt like a breakthrough for a while, but eventually the bike lane was overtaken by double parked cars, especially in the latter 2010s when private car services suddenly and dramatically expanded, filling San Francisco streets with tens of thousands of new cars driven by people unfamiliar with the City, and Valencia's once cherished bike lanes became chronically blocked by amateur taxi drivers.

One reason Critical Mass was such a magnet for new participation was that nobody asked for your ID, your money, your soul, or your brain at Critical Mass. People would arrive and find a euphoric gathering sharing stories, drinks, and conversation. After 6 o'clock, bells began to ring and quickly cyclists would begin to circle until an excited mobile occupying army of noisy revelers rolled into the traffic-clogged streets. The streets were filled with people laughing and talking, hooting and whistling, tinkling bells and spinning gears. Critical Mass was a place to taste the imaginary (but suddenly and briefly real) power of collective spirit, to feel alive and aware in an uncorrupted sliver of autonomous, self-directed public space. Critical Mass provided encouragement and reinforcement for desertion from the rat wheel of car ownership and its attendant investments. But even more subversively, it did it by gaining active participation in an event of unmediated human creation, outside of economic logic, and offering an exhilarating taste of a life practically forgotten—free, convivial, cooperative, connected, collective.

Predictably, the police were not enthused about Critical Mass. In San Francisco, as in other cities, individual officers were deeply offended by what they saw as a violation of the American Way of Life, and felt it their duty to punish the revelers, even if the only illegal activity was the occasional running of a red light while in a mass of dozens of cyclists. A cat-and-mouse logic played out with occasional tickets and arrests by officers, until summer 1997, when Mayor Willie Brown decided to crack down on Critical Mass. He unleashed the police after unsuccessful efforts to lure "leaders" into negotiating a controlled experience, and after the police riot of July 1997, over 100 people were arrested. No one was ever charged or convicted of any crimes, though in local media memory the *San Francisco Chronicle*'s false headline of "250 arrests" is still invoked as evidence of the "violence" that has "plagued" the ride. In fact, the following month more riders showed up than the several thousand who had been attacked in July. But instead of an anarchic scattering, the group "rode to rule," meaning everyone obeyed ALL the laws, which had the effect of jamming traffic much worse than any prior ride. From then on, the police backed off and the ride went on for years more. Efforts to propose specific routes with specific themes disappeared, and the culture of Critical Mass began to erode. The much-touted leaderless quality of the ride led many people to prefer an open-ended meandering ride without any particular direction or destination, unlike earlier years. As a result, during the 2000s, the ride became very repetitive, going again and again to the Broadway Tunnel, the Giants stadium, the Mission, the Wiggle. Longtime riders abandoned the ride out of boredom or despair at the macho youth who had come to dominate the front of the ride, the long-disdained "testosterone brigade" who would posture and taunt motorists, flaunting an empty machismo. The month-after-month conversations and organizing that kept that in check during the early years were harder to sustain, and Critical Mass became a predictable monthly ritual in San Francisco.

Elsewhere, Critical Mass, or Massa Crítica, or Críticona, or Ciemmona—the many other cultures that embraced and extended and reinvented the mass bicycle ride in the world's great cities—continued to innovate and challenge the car-centric policies of cities from Brazil to Italy to India to South Korea (Carlsson, Elliott, Camarena: 2012).

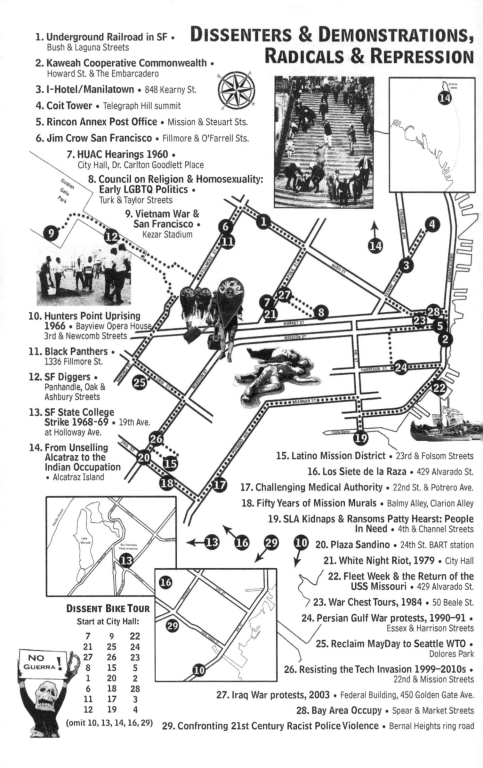

DISSENTERS & DEMONSTRATIONS, RADICALS & REPRESSION

1. **Underground Railroad in SF** • Bush & Laguna Streets

2. **Kaweah Cooperative Commonwealth** • Howard St. & The Embarcadero

3. **I-Hotel/Manilatown** • 848 Kearny St.

4. **Coit Tower** • Telegraph Hill summit

5. **Rincon Annex Post Office** • Mission & Steuart Sts.

6. **Jim Crow San Francisco** • Fillmore & O'Farrell Sts.

7. **HUAC Hearings 1960** • City Hall, Dr. Carlton Goodlett Place

8. **Council on Religion & Homosexuality: Early LGBTQ Politics** • Turk & Taylor Streets

9. **Vietnam War & San Francisco** • Kezar Stadium

10. **Hunters Point Uprising 1966** • Bayview Opera House 3rd & Newcomb Streets

11. **Black Panthers** • 1336 Fillmore St.

12. **SF Diggers** • Panhandle, Oak & Ashbury Streets

13. **SF State College Strike 1968-69** • 19th Ave. at Holloway Ave.

14. **From Unselling Alcatraz to the Indian Occupation** • Alcatraz Island

15. **Latino Mission District** • 23rd & Folsom Streets

16. **Los Siete de la Raza** • 429 Alvarado St.

17. **Challenging Medical Authority** • 22nd St. & Potrero Ave.

18. **Fifty Years of Mission Murals** • Balmy Alley, Clarion Alley

19. **SLA Kidnaps & Ransoms Patty Hearst: People In Need** • 4th & Channel Streets

20. **Plaza Sandino** • 24th St. BART station

21. **White Night Riot, 1979** • City Hall

22. **Fleet Week & the Return of the USS Missouri** • 429 Alvarado St.

23. **War Chest Tours, 1984** • 50 Beale St.

24. **Persian Gulf War protests, 1990–91** • Essex & Harrison Streets

25. **Reclaim MayDay to Seattle WTO** • Dolores Park

26. **Resisting the Tech Invasion 1999–2010s** • 22nd & Mission Streets

27. **Iraq War protests, 2003** • Federal Building, 450 Golden Gate Ave.

28. **Bay Area Occupy** • Spear & Market Streets

29. **Confronting 21st Century Racist Police Violence** • Bernal Heights ring road

DISSENT BIKE TOUR

Start at City Hall:

7	9	22
21	25	24
27	26	23
8	15	5
1	20	2
6	18	28
11	17	3
12	19	4

(omit 10, 13, 14, 16, 29)

NO GUERRA!

V

DISSENTERS AND DEMONSTRATIONS, RADICALS AND REPRESSION

Generations of rebels, outcasts, contrarians, and misfits have come to San Francisco to change the world. San Francisco has welcomed them with good food and strong drink to a port city at the edge of the continent that seemed to have space for everyone and everything. Waves of creative radicals have washed over the City repeatedly, leaving their marks on music, poetry, literature, dance, photography, and painting. Others have reshaped sexuality, politics, media, medicine, transportation, and helped spawn the Internet. San Francisco is the capital of the Left Coast of the United States, the home to the Beats, the Flower Children, and rock 'n' roll. It's also where citizens have revolted against every war since 1898; where residents stopped freeways, saved the bay, and fought the nuclear industry to a standstill; where in less than a decade civil rights protesters ended discrimination in employment and housing and established the first university-level Ethnic Studies curriculum in the country. The explosion of gay liberation that made San Francisco its "mecca" starting in the early 1960s, and the longer thread of sexual and gender radicalism, has also been prominently associated with a particular—even peculiar—urban culture that has percolated and occasionally bubbled to the surface in the City by the bay over its entire history. The threads that connect dissent and protest in San Francisco can be traced back to the nineteenth century, even if they seem to erupt anew each time.

Sitting at the edge of the continent has infused San Francisco with a vaguely "end of the world" sentiment from its beginnings. Wealthy families dispatched their wayward homosexual offspring to live as "remittance men" in San Francisco in its first decades, and the lack of traditional institutions and the entrenched moral and political norms that had developed in the East provided space here for cultural dissidents to create and inhabit spaces where experiments were possible—and even welcome. This is not to argue that early San Franciscans were not fully immersed in the racist and sexist assumptions that prevailed in nineteenth-century North America; only that the dominant culture was full of fissures and holes that soon gave San Francisco a reputation as a place where one could go and escape the strictures of bourgeois respectability with less of the severe consequences that accompanied such transgressions in the more established cities of the East, and beyond that in Europe.

Dissent, of course, is not limited to sexuality (even if today's ever more boundary-less queer politics has even confronted the centuries-long certainties over binary gender). San Francisco's lefty reputation also has deep roots in the endless class war that erupted into gun battles and riots on many occasions over many decades, leading to the epic General Strike of 1934 before subsiding into the orchestrated labor peace of the post-WWII "golden era." After the City was deindustrialized by the 1970s, social conflict has largely focused on housing, racial discrimination, and poverty rather than the terms of work (which in any case has been utterly transformed by the digital, medical, and tourism economies that have taken over since the beginning of the twenty-first century).

This chapter traces threads of dissent primarily through literary and journalistic expressions until the past half century or so. Starting in the 1960s, a rich history of activism and dissent is easier to plumb. Combined with my own lived experiences from my 1978 arrival in San Francisco to the present, the accounts grow more detailed with the advantages of talking to living people full of vital memories.

San Francisco was home to a freewheeling press from its founding in 1849 until at least WWII. After a decade of rampant slaughter during public campaigns of Indian extermination, the *Alta California* sardonically editorialized on February 29, 1860, under the title "Our Indian Massacre Policy": "We . . . propose to the Legislature to create the office of Indian Butcher, with a princely salary, and confer it upon the man who has killed [the] most Indians in a given time, provided it be satisfactorily shown that the Indians were unarmed at the time, and the greater portion of them squaws and papooses." J. Ross Browne, who once remarked about Mark Twain that "he made plenty of money on his books, some of it on mine," was the son of an Irish writer jailed for seditious libel and inciting revolt against England. He was able to decipher the treatment of California's original inhabitants: "[T]heir history in California is a melancholy record of neglect and cruelty," and he urged the government to admit it encouraged genocide. Another writer to take a Swiftian tone, he wrote:

> Unacquainted with our enlightened institutions, they could not understand why they should be murdered, robbed, hunted down in this way, without any other pretense or provocation than the color of their skin and the habits of life to which they have been accustomed . . . the idea, strange as it may appear, never occurred to them that they were suffering for the great cause of civilization, which, in the natural course of things, must exterminate Indians. (Ferlinghetti and Peters: 1980)

California entered the union as a "free state" under the 1850 Compromise, which formally banned slavery but accepted the requirement to enforce the Fugitive Slave Act. Though slaves were captured and returned to their "owners" by local courts in the first years of statehood, an active movement of abolitionists convinced growing numbers of African Americans in California to escape. San Francisco had its own role in the Underground Railroad, supported by the legendary Mary Ellen Pleasant (D1).

In its first year, the state legislature passed laws allowing for the legal custodianship and indenture of Indians in California, which was tantamount to slavery—according to recent scholarship, fully one-fourth of Northern Californians in the 1850s had an indigenous slave child in their homes! It wasn't until these laws were repealed on April 27, 1863, almost five months after Lincoln's Emancipation Proclamation freed slaves in the Confederacy, that Indian slavery in California became illegal (Madley: 2016).

White supremacist beliefs sustained systematic racism against blacks, Chinese, Mexicans, Chileans, and Indians, while at the same time a commitment to "free labor" drove most San Franciscans into the abolitionist camp. The Civil War split San Francisco between its Confederate sympathizers who originally hailed from the South and the majority of working men who rallied to the Union cause. Thomas Starr King, a charismatic Unitarian minister, publicly exhorted San Franciscans to back the North, and the City became a major source of funds for the war effort. By the end of the war, the City remained divided between its new Republican majority and the many pro-slavery Democrats who had long opposed Lincoln and wanted to settle the war short of total victory for the North. When Lincoln was assassinated and a number of Democratic "Copperhead" newspapers gloated over his demise, a mob rioted and destroyed the presses of each one of them. (As the story goes, the ambitious de Young brothers followed behind the mob's destruction to scoop up as much equipment as they could from the streets, which allowed them to put together their own press and launch the *Daily Dramatic Chronicle* in 1865, still surviving to this day as San Francisco's last standing daily newspaper!)

In the post-Civil War political climate, a new configuration of power took shape. The rising working class became a force, while women's efforts to gain the right to vote in the mid-1870s failed. A forgotten radical writer, Prentice Mulford, was skeptical of material "progress," admired laziness, and defended women's rights. Finding his ideas less than popular, he moved onto an old whaler and spent his days living on the bay. *The Overland Monthly* was founded in 1868 and carried on into the twentieth century under a variety of different editorial voices and purposes (Mexal: 2013). At its inception it was edited by Bret Harte, who published the new writers of the West in its pages. Henry George's *Progress and Poverty* predicted economic disaster rooted in the private ownership of land that he argued should be heavily taxed to redistribute wealth, end speculation, and provide an abundant source of public funds. More radical still was Victoria Woodhull, a writer who exposed Henry Ward Beecher for his sexual hypocrisy, and later with her sister, was the first American publisher of Karl Marx's *Communist Manifesto*.

As the railroads expanded their reach geographically, they also consolidated their control over the federal government, leading to populist movements against monopolies that by the end of the nineteenth century took the form of a rising progressive movement committed to public ownership of water, power, and transportation. In San Francisco, the Spring Valley Water Company monopolized local water and joined the Southern Pacific Railroad Company as objects of scorn and resentment. A beautifully printed journal full of satirical lithographs, *The Wasp*, took on politicians, monopolists, and the rich in scathing cartoons and essays, edited for six years in the 1880s by the incomparable Ambrose Bierce. With bitter cynicism at his core, he easily punctured the abundant hypocrisy and fraud of the era. His *Devil's Dictionary* has remained in print for over a century, featuring scathing denunciations cloaked as definitions:

FAITH, n. Belief without evidence in what is told by one who speaks without knowledge, of things without parallel.

DISTANCE, n. The only thing that the rich are willing for the poor to call theirs, and keep.

EGOTIST, n. A person of low taste, more interested in himself than in me.

DIPLOMACY, n. The patriotic act of lying for one's country.

CORPORATION, n. An ingenious device for obtaining individual profit without individual responsibility.

DEBT, n. An ingenious substitute for the chain and whip of the slave-driver.

RELIGION, n. A daughter of Hope and Fear, explaining to Ignorance the nature of the Unknowable . . .

European utopians poured into California in the last quarter of the nineteenth century, determined to find new ways to live freely beyond the constraints of established society. Followers of Etienne Cabet, a French socialist, founded Icaria Speranza in Cloverdale, though it didn't last a decade. Another utopian community was launched among the giant Sequoias of the southern Sierra Nevada mountains by a homegrown San Francisco radical, Burnette Haskell, and his comrades (D2).

By the 1890s, American businessmen and politicians were hatching more ambitious plans. When Frederick Turner's famous essay declared the closing of the Western frontier, U.S. elites turned their attention across the Pacific Ocean. Already Americans were well established as missionaries and sugar barons in the Hawaiian Islands, then an independent monarchy. Hawaii lost its independence when those Americans seized power in the mid-1890s, leading to formal annexation in 1898, the same year the United States declared war on Spain. When the USS *Maine*'s boiler exploded in the harbor of the Spanish colony of Cuba, the United States declared war and quickly seized Cuba, Puerto Rico, and steamed into Manila harbor and took over the Philippines in a sordid double-cross of the Independence movement there (D3).

One of San Francisco's most famous early writers, Mark Twain, became an outspoken critic of U.S. policy as a leader of the Anti-Imperialist League. Speaking publicly across the country and writing incessantly, Twain eloquently denounced the U.S. war on Philippine independence and the fraudulent seizure of Cuba and Puerto Rico. When General Frederick

Funston faked an injury to capture Filipino leader Emiliano Aguinaldo, Twain loudly denounced his cowardly tactics (Twain: 1992).

In 1899, radical poet Edwin Markham published in the *San Francisco Examiner* a poem protesting the brutal treatment of farm labor, "The Man with the Hoe." It took the world by storm and was translated into 40 languages, and vaulted Markham into a long career as a much-loved public speaker. In 1922, over 100,000 people attended his reading at the opening of the Lincoln Memorial in Washington, D.C., also broadcast on the radio nationwide in one of the first such mass-media events.

John Muir lived in rural Contra Costa County to the east of San Francisco, but became one of the City's most famous writers and dissidents. He was one of the founders of the Sierra Club in 1892, and his reverence for untrammeled nature, especially the wild and untamed Sierra Nevada mountains, was legendary. He led a long, ultimately unsuccessful, campaign to save Yosemite's Hetch Hetchy Valley from being dammed by the city of San Francisco to create a permanent supply of publicly owned drinking water and electricity. He lost that battle, but the conservation movement he helped pioneer continued to affect the shape of the Bay Area, California, the nation, and the world for the rest of time.

Lincoln Steffens, born in San Francisco in 1866, was perhaps one of the best-known journalists of his era, becoming famous in 1904 for his *Shame of the Cities* and his relentless muckraking that brought to light scandals and corruption. His writing attacked trusts and government collusion with big business and helped fuel a climate of "progressivism" that led to antitrust legislation, protective labor laws against child and women's work, and more. He returned to San Francisco in 1907 to cover the unraveling corruption of the Union Labor Party municipal government, but knew the real power was in the system rather than the individuals being charged. He wrote, "I labored humorously, and I think pleasantly, for the exposure in San Francisco of the universal state of business corruption of politics to show what was hurting us, and not who." He settled in Carmel in the late 1920s and died in 1936 as an avid supporter of the Soviet Union (Ferlinghetti and Peters: 1980).

In 1911, Italian radicals in North Beach began soapboxing against patriotism and government not far from the St. Peter and Paul Catholic Church on Washington Square. In an unsung free speech fight during the pre-WWI era, Wobblies and others who had fought with the Mexican Liberal Party during an ill-fated invasion of Baja California returned to

San Francisco where they "spoke disparagingly about the American flag, condemned law and order, denounced all forms of government, and ended with a tirade against the Pope." When police arrested the speakers and marched them to a fire station on Broadway, thousands of protesters converged on the scene. Throwing rocks and bricks and even a knife at the police in front of the firehouse, the rioters were eventually subdued by police action. Hilariously, North Beach merchants did not want police repression because the free speech street meetings were bringing them so much business! (Zimmer: 2015).

When World War I broke out in Europe in 1914, San Francisco was busily building fairgrounds on the north shore of the City for the 1915 Panama-Pacific International Exposition (PPIE). Upwards of 30,000 unemployed men had poured into the City in 1913 seeking work on the big project, and their demonstrations had brought business leaders and organized labor together in a labor truce for the duration of the fair. In spite of the carnage in Europe, most countries sent delegations and exhibits to the PPIE, and it was a huge success, serving as a festival dedicated to promoting the latest technological marvels of the era (including Model T automobiles, Victrola record players, and a profusion of newly available packaged foods).

After the close of the PPIE at the end of 1915, San Francisco's buried class tensions quickly reemerged. When business leaders staged a big Preparedness Day march on July 22 to promote entry into WWI, a terrorist bomb exploded in the middle of it, killing ten and injuring several dozen. At this time, the City was home to a substantial population of Irish, Germans, and Italians. Anarchists and members of the Industrial Workers of the World (the IWW) were prominent among the antiwar agitators in San Francisco, most notably the famous Emma Goldman and Alexander Berkman, who were then living at 569 Dolores Street across from Dolores Park and publishing their regular newspaper *The Blast!* (L9).

There are many possible candidates for the real bombers (not the labor leaders who were framed for the crime). Germans in the Bay Area were angry that the United States was leaning toward (and eventually joined) the English and French in WWI. Mexicans were angry about the role of the United States in manipulating events during the ongoing Mexican Revolution—General John "Blackjack" Pershing led an expeditionary force into northern Mexico to "punish" Pancho Villa and his troops, but couldn't find them. Anarchists were famous for their use of dynamite against their class enemies. Italian anarchists were promoting an upcoming speech by birth control advocate Margaret Sanger and distributing thousands of pro–birth control flyers published in Italian to Catholic Italians in North Beach (Berkman: 2005).

British intelligence was quite active in San Francisco during the war, too, trying to combat the Irish nationalists in the Mission District who helped finance the failed Easter Rising in 1916 for Irish independence. Across town, activists for the independence of India founded the Ghadar party, and to the British and their U.S. allies, this smacked of a conspiracy to support the Germans in WWI. Before long, headlines were screaming about a Hindu-German conspiracy, leading to arrests and a very public trial (Ramnath: 2011). Once the United States entered WWI, a new federal Sedition Act was used to shut down a wide range of anarchist, socialist, and other periodicals in blatant violation of the First Amendment. After WWI, a wave of repression culminated in the infamous nationwide Palmer Raids in 1919–20 that led to the summary deportation of over 20,000 "undesirables"—foreign radicals and labor agitators. Organized labor was crushed, and the emerging consumer culture became the pulsing heart of the Roaring Twenties.

After a lengthy hike down the mountains from his starting point in Washington state in the late 1920s, a young autodidact named Kenneth Rexroth arrived in San Francisco and decided to stay. Having grown up in Chicago's bohemian underground, by the mid-1930s Rexroth was deeply involved in the political upheavals along the waterfront and among muralists and other artists. He also hosted a Libertarian Circle at his home at Scott and Page Streets where many of the poets who comprised the San Francisco Renaissance met with freethinkers and other cultural outlaws (Rexroth: 1991). Rexroth joined with muralist Bernard Zakheim to organize a meeting among painters, many of whom lived in the Montgomery Block. Desperate for work in the depths of the Depression, they sent a telegram to a contact in Washington, D.C., seeking support. Surprisingly, thanks to a parallel effort already under way at the federal level, their message was well received, and they soon were at work on the Coit Tower murals, sponsored by the New Deal Public Works of Art Project (PWAP). Painting during the tumultuous waterfront strike of 1934, the artists formed their own San Francisco Artists' and Writers' Union, and painted images that echoed the class conflicts erupting along the waterfront and around California during the Depression (D4).

Part of the milieu that gave rise to the rich Libertarian Circle at Rexroth's place had its roots in the Italian anarchist insurrectionists that had rallied around the famous Boston trial of Sacco and Vanzetti in the 1920s. In 1927, the Emanzipazione Group convened a new International group consisting of Spanish, Russian, Yiddish, French, Chinese, and Italian anarchists who met regularly at 2787 Folsom at 24th in the Mission District. Hosting regular spaghetti dinners and performances of Russian balalaika orchestras, piano recitals, and songs in German and English, the club became a vital source of support for radical projects in the 1930s. In 1932, Marcus Graham founded a new journal in downtown Oakland called *Man!* that was largely supported by the International Group of San Francisco. In the pages of *Man!*, editor Graham wrote incendiary tracts denouncing any type of organized labor, declaring "Anarchists don't support the so-called sane, practical movements. . . . For the anarchist is the prophetic fiery denouncer of everything unjust and unfree, holding forth the Day of Liberation." Graham even advocated a romantic opposition to technology long before it became fashionable in the late twentieth century, echoing William Morris's 1893 denunciation of useless toil, discrediting the idea that machinery would promote happiness by alleviating toil. Working for oneself to Graham was inherently joyful and rewarding, a view shared with Morris and many other nineteenth-century romantic radicals (not to mention many at the turn of the twenty-first century!). "Every new device becomes in turn a power to ensnare, mislead, delude and deaden man's need or possibility of employing his own thinking faculties," he prophesied (Graham: 1933).

When WWII began, Kenneth Rexroth was among the principled few who opposed Japanese internment and supported the conscientious objectors who refused to go to war and ended up in CO camps in eastern Oregon. Rexroth was a Bay Area distributor of anarchist antiwar journals such as *Why?* and *Retort* from New York during the 1940s, which helped cement relations among a dedicated core of radicals. After the war, some of these same folks founded Pacifica and KPFA radio in Berkeley, which gave Rexroth a regular platform for his remarkable array of interests, from Eastern philosophy to anarchism to local music and poetry.

With Berkeley's KPFA being an outlet for all sorts of unpopular and controversial views, staid 1950s San Francisco also harbored a simmering undercurrent of dissent. The last Depression-era murals were painted at the Rincon Annex Post Office in 1947–48; and by the early 1950s, Richard Nixon and other Republicans in Congress were demanding their destruction as anti-American propaganda (D5). Local communists were being hunted by repeated visits of the House Un-American Activities Committee (HUAC), while Longshore Union leader Harry Bridges was on trial multiple times for sedition and to deport him back to his native Australia, all efforts that finally failed. In 1957, the IRS forced the closure of the California Labor School. The Labor School, named for Tom Mooney at its 1942 founding, had provided a thriving educational space for GIs returning from WWII and local workers. They could encounter radical ideas, learn modern painting and theater, study literature and philosophy, subjects that were often denied working-class students elsewhere (L18). But after enduring several HUAC inquisitions during the 1950s, in May 1960, San Franciscans had had enough. Students from area universities besieged City Hall where HUAC was meeting, and though they were driven out the first day, the cumulative effect of three days of mass protest was to end HUAC's public hearings for good (D7).

In the early 1960s, the Congress on Racial Equality, the NAACP, and the Ad-Hoc Committee to End Discrimination were organizing mass demonstrations against employment discrimination on Auto Row along Van Ness and at the Palace Hotel on Market and New Montgomery. Juxtaposed to the Freedom Summer efforts down South, liberal San Francisco was not happy to find itself confronted with its own deeply segregated and white supremacist daily life. When the state legislature passed the Rumford Fair Housing Act in 1963, a "whitelash" led to a statewide referendum to repeal it in November 1964 that passed 2–1 and won a majority of voters in every major city, including San Francisco. But the repeal was canceled a year later by the state Supreme Court, and slowly but surely the unacknowledged Jim Crow segregation in San Francisco gave way to a fairer legal environment (if not a fairer economic one!) (see D6).

In 1957, San Francisco customs officials seized a shipment of City Lights Books' new poetry book *Howl* by Allen Ginsberg, leading to an epic censorship battle that was won by the plucky North Beach publisher, helping ensconce it in the pantheon of vital counter-institutions that have renewed dissent here again and again. (A decade after *Howl*, another poetry book, *The Love Book* by Lenore Kandel, became the poster child for censorship during the Summer of Love in 1967, this time leading to a verdict of guilty against the writer and bookstore sellers of the small "obscene" chapbook. But thanks to the publicity of the arrest and trial, *The Love Book* had sold over 20,000 copies, and Kandel, with tongue firmly in cheek, graciously donated 1 percent of her unexpected earnings to the San Francisco Police Department Retirement Fund.) The *Howl* trial also began a process of unraveling the unquestioned moral power that the San Francisco police had long held on behalf of the Catholic Archdiocese. The ribald stand-up comedy of Lenny Bruce, Mort Sahl, The Committee, and others in North Beach during the late 1950s and early 1960s, risqué art and film pouring out of the Art Institute and appearing at local galleries, all helped open the culture, reinforcing a frankness about sex and race that soon also led to topless dancing, and circuitously, to the 1970s pornography industry. In the Tenderloin, liberal religious leaders joined with community activists to form the Council on Religion and Homosexuality (CRH). When they held a New Year's Eve Ball at the end of 1964 at California Hall on Polk Street, police photographed, filmed, and arrested dozens of patrons in full drag. The police lost the battle for public opinion, however, when the CRH denounced their attack on a private event at a subsequent press conference. A community of self-organized queers and transsexuals soon emerged in the Tenderloin; in August 1966, a mini-riot at Compton's Cafeteria at Turk and Taylor confronted police harassment (D8).

San Francisco had its antiwar dissenters going back to the nineteenth century, but nothing like what burst upon the city from about 1966 to 1974 during the Vietnam War. Countless groups mobilized, an underground press emerged, mass marches and rallies were held repeatedly, a mutiny of imprisoned soldiers took place at the Presidio, and the broad countercultural revolt infused the breakdown of military discipline and ended popular support for the Vietnam War (D9).

The initial desegregation successes gained by the civil rights sit-ins and demonstrations in the early 1960s soon stagnated into a familiar pattern of structural racism. When the police stopped a suspected stolen car and Matthew "Peanut" Johnson ran away from the scene, an officer shot and killed him. An uprising in Hunters Point followed, and for over a week, daily confrontations between police and angry youth and neighborhood residents, soon joined by National Guard patrolling with machine guns on jeeps to enforce the martial law declared by Governor Pat Brown, brought daily life in black San Francisco to a halt (D10). Organizing efforts on both sides of the bay took the name "the Panthers," but it was the Black Panther Party for Self-Defense that began in Oakland that ultimately dominated the next wave of self-organization in the African American community, not just in San Francisco but across the country (D11). After Black Panther leader Huey P. Newton had been arrested for allegedly killing a police officer, mass rallies to "Free Huey" were held in Oakland and at San Francisco Federal Building on Golden Gate Avenue. At a May 1, 1969 rally there, Latino supporters heard police radio reports of an officer down in the Mission—a saga that became a years-long effort to defend seven young men falsely accused of the crime, Los Siete de la Raza (D16).

Parallel to these cultural shifts were newly emergent ecological movements opposing nuclear power, freeways, and further filling and development of the San Francisco Bay (see chapter 2). In 1967, the San Francisco Diggers challenged the burgeoning youth movement to transform life completely by doing everything for free (D12). Plastering the city with posters and handbills, engaging in theatrical interventions such as the 1966 "Death of Money" and the late 1967 "Death of Hippy" marches on Haight Street, the Diggers also pioneered the distribution of free food in the Panhandle, which years later inspired the group Food Not Bombs (1980s–2010s).

The Black Panther Minister of Education George Mason Murray was suspended from his job as an English teacher at San Francisco State College in fall 1968. By November, students at the university, led by the Black Student Union and joined by the Third World Liberation Front, were on strike. The San Francisco State strike, eventually joined by the faculty as well, lasted until March 1969, the longest university strike in U.S. history. The settlement created the first School of Ethnic Studies, and the experience changed San Francisco politics in countless ways. Hundreds of students who became radicalized through the strike and the extreme violence administered by the new Tactical Squad of the SF Police went on to become community organizers, housing activists, and more, in the following years (D13).

Alcatraz is world-famous for the harsh prison that once held the "worst prisoners." After its decommissioning in the early 1960s, though, it became a symbolic example of a broken relationship between federal government and Indian peoples. San Francisco, thinking it had jurisdiction, sold the island to some Texas oilmen before being forced to backtrack on that deal after a popular revolt. In 1969, following an earlier attempt in 1964, a group of Native American activists managed to get to Alcatraz and begin a year and a half occupation that galvanized popular support, and rekindled a vibrant movement of dignity and self-assertion among Indian tribes across the United States (D14).

In 1967, Mission District residents banded together with longtime merchants to block the Redevelopment Agency from unleashing its bull-dozing "improvement" plans. A year later, many of the same groups and individuals came together to form the Mission Coalition Organization (MCO), which eventually encompassed over 100 groups and embodied what one analyst called the largest community-based urban movement in history. For the five years of its existence, the MCO mounted major campaigns to control jobs, housing, and neighborhood development in the Mission (D15). During the height of community involvement in planning and economic development, a grassroots mural movement appeared on the walls of the neighborhood. Clusters in Balmy Alley and Mission Playground on 24th Street became widely recognized, but the remarkable efforts to forge a new creative public art, rooted in the famous muralists of mid-twentieth-century Mexico, brought women to the fore, and helped the Mission to define its own *latinidad*.

At SF General Hospital, traditional medicine was both racist and sexist. The blossoming feminist movement of the late 1960s began to challenge the control that patriarchal medical practices held over well-being, especially for women. But their years-long efforts to gain access to new medical practices, new physiological knowledge, and open up access to medical employment permanently altered the field. Their efforts dovetailed with a community clinic, El Centro de Salud, opened by the Los Siete Defense Committee when a strike closed down General Hospital. The free bilingual services offered at the clinic pushed the public hospital to begin offering services in multiple languages soon after. When the AIDS crisis hit in the early 1980s, a fertile foundation had been set for what became of necessity an enormous grassroots political movement to wrest control over research and development in medical care and pharmaceuticals from the government and corporations who refused to adequately fund or research remedies. Again, a grassroots science emerged to counter the automatically accepted authority of professionals and experts (D18).

Political violence was not unusual in the early 1970s. When the Symbionese Liberation Army (SLA) announced itself after assassinating the Oakland Superintendent of Public Schools, many thought they might be a fake group, funded by the police. Such doubts dogged the group, but most SLA members were eventually consumed by flames in a horrific live-TV siege by the Los Angeles police. Prior to that, their most famous act was kidnapping *San Francisco Examiner* publisher William Randolph Hearst's granddaughter, Patty Hearst, from her dorm room near UC Berkeley. The SLA ransom demand that free food be given to poor people led to the "People in Need" program that later changed local politics (D19).

The Mission District had become home to thousands of Nicaraguans fleeing the Somoza dictatorship, especially after the 1972 earthquake that devastated the capital Managua. Activists determined to overthrow the dictatorship lived and worked in the neighborhood and were in close contact with the revolutionaries fighting in Nicaragua. Many of the main leaders of what became the Sandinista government spent time in San Francisco in the 1970s, and the weekly rallies that filled the 24th Street BART plaza soon gave it the name Plaza Sandino (D20).

After the horrifying mass murder/suicide of the People's Temple congregation in Guyana (nearly all of them originally from San Francisco) and the double murder of Mayor Moscone and Supervisor Harvey Milk in November 1978, San Francisco was a dark place. When Dan White was given a "voluntary manslaughter" verdict by an all-white jury convinced by his attorney's improbable "Twinkie" defense, the so-called "White Night Riot" erupted at City Hall on May 21, 1979 (D21).

The Democratic National Convention was held in San Francisco in 1984, a time when Dianne Feinstein was mayor and determined to revive the moribund waterfront by luring back the USS *Missouri* to be homeported in the City. She relaunched "Fleet Week" as part of her PR campaign to renew support for the military, but activists used rowboats, yachts, and all manner of waterborne craft to launch the "Peace Navy" and blockade her efforts. During the convention, activists renewed tactics invented during anti-Vietnam War protests to carry out "Warchest Tours" of the merchants of death in the City's Financial District (D22, D23). The antiwar and antinuclear movements, combined with the ongoing support for liberation movements in Central and South America, as well as the anti-apartheid movement in South Africa, made for a thriving anti-militarism culture that dominated San Francisco's politically active communities. When George H. W. Bush declared a "new world order" after the fall of the Soviet bloc, and then launched the Persian Gulf War to prove that a "peace dividend" would be impossible, hundreds of thousands of San Franciscans marched against his agenda (D24). Early video activists documented the surprising depth and breadth of the opposition in the Gulf War Video Project, a precursor to the self-documenting work now so common on YouTube.

The neoliberal agenda was consolidated in the 1990s when Bill Clinton triangulated his way through the decade as a conservative Democratic president facing an increasingly ultraright Republican congress. Harsh sanctions on Iraq, bombings in the Balkans and Somalia, and the marketized disruptions engendered by NAFTA provided the geopolitical context for the sudden emergence of the World Wide Web and a tech boom based on digital media and games. In San Francisco, hundreds of activists regrouped in a creative effort to "Reclaim May Day," with major processions in 1998 and 1999 culminating in festivals at Dolores Park. Meanwhile, efforts to promote NAFTA-style pro-corporate "reforms" were focused on the World Trade Organization, which was due to meet in Seattle in 1999. Some of the local Reclaim May Day organizers spent most of 1999 traveling up and down the West Coast to encourage people to come to Seattle to protest the WTO. Surprisingly, the "teamsters and the turtles" successfully blockaded the opening day in Seattle, and caused enough havoc in the City's streets that negotiators from smaller countries refused to be steamrollered by the United States and its allies. The WTO failed in Seattle, and never really recovered (D25). The tech boom continued apace, and as it grew into a bulging bubble focused in San Francisco and Silicon Valley, the City's housing and real estate markets came under intense pressure, radically raising rents and prices. An eviction crisis hit several of the neighborhoods that had long been home to culture producers, ethnic enclaves, and the soul of San Francisco. Artists and activists mobilized and for two years confronted project after project, developer after developer (D26).

In the twenty-first century, building on the many prior antiwar efforts, more than 20,000 San Franciscans seized intersections and key streets on the first day of the 2003 Iraq War and shut down the City (D27). The logic and experience of repurposing public space that many thousands learned in Critical Mass (T14) and the antiwar and antinuclear movements came to a new head in the Occupy movement that was part of a global wave of such movements in 2011, stretching from Tunisia and Egypt to Spain to the United States (D28). But the encampments were soon dismantled, succumbing to their own internal contradictions as much as the harsh repression local police forces meted out to them. The militarization of local policing visible in the repression of Occupy camps has been applied widely and more randomly to young men of color across the country, and also prominently in San Francisco. A number of unjustifiable police murders have devastated families of longtime residents and immigrants in the past 15 years, and a robust community-based movement repudiating police violence has made itself felt here too (D29).

San Francisco keeps surprising us. In spite of the overwhelming gentrification of the City, countless longtime residents still live here. From the once-ubiquitous sidewalk "free box" to the repeated waves of literary, musical, and artistic dissent, San Francisco continues to attract and launch voices contrary to both the prevailing wisdom and politics. Amid the ubiquitous app developers and data warehousers who are the current apple of investors' eyes, dissident programmers, writers, historians, and sociologists are using digital tools to produce free and open archives, maps, and databases that undergird current and future efforts to rethink how we live. From the Anti-Eviction Mapping Project to the Coalition on Homelessness, from Shaping San Francisco to the Internet Archive to a half-dozen vital neighborhood newspapers, the Tenants Union to Our Mission No Eviction, dissent finds its contemporary voice in San Francisco, carrying on a tradition that stretches back to its earliest days. Hidden histories of dissent lie in surprising corners of the City. Read on!

D1: Underground Railroad in San Francisco (1850s)

Bush and Laguna Streets

A year after the 1857 Supreme Court *Dred Scott* case (which disallowed rights for any African-descended people in the United States), Archy Lee, a slave when he lived with his owner in Mississippi, became a cause celebre for the free black population of California. After being employed for wages during several months in Sacramento to raise money for his owner, Lee, who was in daily conversation with free blacks, realized that in California he could not be kept as a slave. Abolitionist lawyers eventually won his freedom by arguing that Archy Lee wasn't a fugitive slave since he hadn't run away during his time in Mississippi, nor en route to California. Since California was a free state, there was no law regarding *becoming* a fugitive slave in the state, and slavery itself was not legally permissible in California.

During the lengthy dispute, the waterfront was patrolled by small crowds of San Francisco's free black population in search of Lee and/or his owner in order to ensure Lee's escape. Eventually, a deputy sheriff and two officers grabbed Archy Lee from an approaching rowboat and brought him to San Francisco, where he was later released directly from the courtroom. He purportedly went to the home of Mary Ellen Pleasant. Later in 1858, nearly 1,000 members of San Francisco's black community, sensing the rising tide of racial enmity from *Dred Scott* and more, emigrated permanently to Victoria, British Columbia, in Canada.

The Underground Railroad had an important, if not widely recognized, conductor in San Francisco in the person of Mary Ellen Pleasant, a biracial woman born on Nantucket Island off Massachusetts and a longtime abolitionist. It was she who met arriving fugitives of African descent at the docks of San Francisco and found them abodes and employment as maids and butlers in the richest homes of early San Francisco. In return, they became her eyes and ears on the machinations of wealth in town. Pleasant herself was a successful entrepreneur and investor behind the scenes. In 1858, she traveled to Chatham, Ontario, Canada, to attend an abolitionist gathering with Frederick Douglass and John Brown. Apparently Pleasant was the source of $30,000 in cash given to Brown to help finance his upcoming (and ultimately unsuccessful) raid on Harper's Ferry (then the U.S. Army's state-of-the-art arsenal). She later returned to San Francisco, where she sued a local streetcar company to desegregate it and won. A memorial to her is in the sidewalk at Bush and Laguna Streets under the massive eucalyptus trees planted in front of what was her mansion at this corner (Hudson: 2003).

D2: Kaweah Cooperative Colony (1890)

Howard Street and the Embarcadero

Burnette Haskell, a homegrown California radical born in the foothills in 1857, edited a labor newspaper called *Truth* in the 1880s whose motto was "Truth is five cents a copy and dynamite is forty cents a pound." But after helping establish the Coast Seamen's Union (later the Sailors Union of the Pacific—see L3), Haskell's impatience for radical change led to his departure.

Haskell decided to join with a group of radical friends and go to the mountains and start a commune. In 1889, he and his comrades laid claim to lands above the Kaweah River, in the southern Sierras east of Fresno and Visalia. They filed federal land claims as they painstakingly built a road from the river up into the groves of ancient Sequoia trees that they planned to harvest and turn into railroad ties. Two years later, their land claims had never been granted, they were hungry and tired, and morale was low. The co-op was in trouble—free love didn't suit everyone, and the failure to get land claims certified left them short of collateral and running out of money.

Between September 25 and October 1, 1890, two bills were passed in Washington, D.C. The first created Sequoia National Park, and the second just days later created the federal Yosemite National Park but also mysteriously tripled the size of the previously created Sequoia Park. A Southern Pacific Railroad Company attorney got additional language inserted into the Yosemite National Park bill. After the senators voted, they realized they had created not just Yosemite, but also vastly expanded Sequoia, the latter encompassing precisely the lands claimed by the Kaweah Cooperative Colony. The railroad had pulled a fast one in order to prevent these "reds" and radicals from entering the railroad tie business in competition with the large corporation. By this strange twist of fate, the remarkable, thousand-year-old giant sequoia trees were saved, preserving dozens of specimens that could not be replaced, including what we now call the General Sherman tree. For the Kaweah Cooperativists it was the "Karl Marx" tree! Sequoia National Park, with its amazing ancient trees, has long been the southern Sierras' biggest tourist attraction (O'Connell: 1999).

D3: I-Hotel/Manilatown (1898–1977)

848 Kearny Street

In 1898, a U.S. Navy fleet under Admiral Dewey steamed into Manila Harbor in the Philippines. Filipino revolutionary nationalists had been fighting against the Spanish colonial regime for years and were on the cusp of achieving independence. Their troops surrounded Manila after they had

Sheriff Richard Hongisto outside the I-Hotel, August 4, 1977, after overseeing the brutal eviction of I-Hotel tenants. (Calvin Roberts, Granmas Camera)

defeated Spanish garrisons in most other parts of the archipelago. Looking to the United States for inspiration, the rebels were intent on establishing a federal government patterned after the United States, and expected the arriving American fleet to support their efforts.

Instead, a mock battle was staged between U.S. and Spanish troops, followed by a backdoor sale of the Philippines for $20 million. When the

U.S. Senate was going to vote on a formal annexation declaration, it seemed the anti-imperialist agitators in the United States, prominent among them Mark Twain, would prevail and defeat the annexation. But two days before the vote was to take place, in the middle of the night, U.S. troops crossed a neutral bridge between their forces and the Filipino insurgents, sparking a gun battle. Cables were quickly sent to Washington claiming that the United States had been attacked without provocation, and with the *causus belli* in hand, enough senators were swayed to change their vote. It took more than a decade of war, but after employing waterboarding and strategic hamlets and a whole panoply of barbaric tactics to defeat the Filipino independence fighters, the United States had full possession of the Philippines (Ignacio et al: 2004).

The United States called it the Philippine Insurrection, but to Filipinos, the Philippine-American War was another war of independence against another imperialist nation. It lasted from 1899 to 1902, when General Aguinaldo was captured by Col. Frederick Funston, but sporadic fighting continued in the countryside until 1904. American historians acknowledge that the war cost Filipinos over 200,000 lives, most of whom were innocent civilians. Filipino historians, however, claim a much higher number. Citing figures given in the *New York Times* that over 300,000 civilians alone were killed in U.S. military campaigns in Samar Island in the Visayas, Filipino historians claim that the casualties were closer to 1 million (Ignacio et al: 2004). It was in the Philippines that "concentration camps" and "free fire zones" would be practiced by the U.S. military, which led to outbreaks of starvation and diseases, killing thousands of civilians.

After annexing the country, the United States brought thousands of Filipino men to work in the fields of California. It had been more than 20 years since Chinese immigration was banned in 1882. In 1903, Japan defeated Russia in a war that sparked a wave of hysteria and fear on the West Coast of the United States, reinforcing a strongly xenophobic mistrust and fear of Japanese farmers who were thriving on leased properties in many parts of rural California. Facing a severe shortage of agricultural labor, California growers turned to Filipino farm labor, since men from the Philippines were now in U.S. territory and could easily immigrate (though they were not allowed to become citizens, nor could they bring their wives or children until long after WWII). Thus began a decades-long migration of Filipino men into California, most of whom worked seasonally in the fields and stayed in transient hotels in San Francisco during the winters. Many of these hotels stretched along ten blocks of Kearny Street in the 1920s and 1930s, from Market Street to Jackson Street, and at the corner of Kearny and Jackson Streets stood the International Hotel (I-Hotel).

Early twentieth-century Filipino immigrants who remained in San Francisco formed a bachelor community in a three-block radius around Kearny Street and Jackson Street, next to Chinatown. These San Franciscan Filipinos worked in restaurants as cooks and waiters and in hotels as bell-hops and "elevator boys." Others worked in the domestic service sector as house servants, cleaners, and chauffeurs. Some even started their own businesses that catered to a primarily Filipino clientele. Filipinos owned and operated pool halls, lunch counters, restaurants, coffee shops, clothing and grocery stores, and gambling establishments. They had names like the Manila Cafe, the New Luneta Cafe, the Bataan Lunch, and the Sampagita Restaurant.

By the mid-1960s, downtown was rapidly expanding in all directions. Much of Kearny Street had become the wealthy border between the Financial District and the tony Union Square shopping district. But at the far northern edge of the old Manilatown stood the I-Hotel, a bastion of low-cost housing for elderly *manong*, the men who had been working as migrant labor in California for decades. In 1968, Democratic Party bigwig and wealthy real estate investor Walter Shorenstein used his Milton Meyer & Co. property firm to buy the site with the intention of tearing it down and building a parking lot. He started eviction proceedings, but did not expect the organized and community-inspiring resistance he would face. When a mysterious fire killed three tenants days before the planned eviction, the political pressure forced Shorenstein to agree to a three-year lease for the remaining tenants. He would later sell the property to a Hong Kong-based company that intended to complete the eviction.

Dozens of students, largely Asian American, converged on the I-Hotel to support the elderly men confronted with eviction. Many of these young radicals had cut their teeth in the violent strikes at UC Berkeley and San Francisco State prior to joining the I-Hotel fight. Those of Japanese descent were driven by family memories of humiliating incarceration during WWII. Moreover, the Vietnam War was raging and antiwar demonstrations rocked San Francisco and Oakland regularly, drawing ever more people who made the connections between the war abroad and the war at home. The I-Hotel also housed elderly Chinese men, a pool hall, small restaurants, and during the years-long eviction process, a small cooperative garment factory. Cultural organizations such as the Kearny Street Workshop arts group, the Asian Community Center, the Chinese Progressive Association, and others called the I-Hotel home. Also published at the I-Hotel was the leftist *Kalayan* newspaper, precursor to *Katipunan ng mga Demoratikong Pilipino* (KDP), the largest Filipino socialist organization in America. With its left-wing residents and community, people began to call the brick hotel the Red Block.

After nine years of threats and resistance, the I-Hotel eviction was violently carried out starting at 4 a.m. on August 4, 1977. In spite of a mobilized community of approximately 3,000 supporters blockading the building with their bodies, riot police, cavalry, and firemen were able to gain access to the building and evict the remaining elderly, destroying the plumbing and fixtures in the process. Famously, Sheriff Richard Hongisto, who had spent five days in jail for refusing to carry out the eviction order, led the charge. Extension ladders reached the upper floors, and police poured through the less-defended windows (Habal: 2007).

National headlines proclaimed the final eviction of the I-Hotel tenants. The City had spent over $3 million and suffered a spate of negative publicity. The ferocity of the eviction attack stunned the City and galvanized activists into the following years' efforts to establish rent control in San Francisco, an effort that came to fruition two years later in 1979 (Shaw: 1998).

After the building was cleared, it was demolished, and the lot sat empty for more than 20 years. Finally, a deal was struck with the Thai investor who had purchased the property prior to the final eviction. The Catholic Church took over and eventually built the high-rise senior housing that is there now, and provided space for the Manilatown Heritage Foundation on the ground floor. The *manong* who had been evicted were relocated in various other buildings, their relationships and community shattered, but none lived long enough to see the replacement housing that rose on the site of the storied I-Hotel.

D4: COIT TOWER (1934)

Telegraph Hill summit

Coit Tower sits atop Telegraph Hill. Built with a bequest from Lillie Hitchcock Coit, a storied character of antebellum San Francisco where she was famous for her enthusiastic participation in volunteer firefighting (later, during the Civil War, she actively supported the South alongside many of her wealthy San Franciscan contemporaries). The Romanesque column was not designed to resemble a fire hose as some have asserted, but was designed as a classic fluted column. The tower is now dwarfed by the nearby high-rises of the Financial District, but when it was built in the early 1930s it was a prominent monument.

City officials, working closely with New Deal officials in Washington, chose the tower's lobby as a site for a significant public mural project, employing a dozen artists who had been organizing and clamoring for publicly funded art. Many of them had worked with, or been inspired by, Diego Rivera and his wife Frida Kahlo, during their time in San Francisco in the late 1920s and early 1930s. When Rivera's just-completed mural in the Rockefeller Center in New York was destroyed in early 1934 because it included a prominent portrait of Lenin, the Coit Tower muralists rallied to his defense. Ralph Stackpole used a sketch of Rivera's mural in New York as an inspiration for his contribution to the Coit Tower murals. Elements throughout several of the Coit Tower frescoes were considered politically controversial, from Bernard Zakheim's library scene with a patron pulling Marx's *Capital* from the shelf, to Victor Arnautoff's *City Life* that portrayed an overturned car and a street mugging along with a newsstand selling left-wing magazines. Other muralists focused on themes promoting work and production, though in one case including an obvious allusion to the just-defeated 1933 Central Valley cotton strike. All of these murals can be seen today. Only Clifford Wight's banner juxtaposing three ideas—rugged individualism (with a seal proclaiming "in God We Trust"), the New Deal (showing the National Recovery Act logo), and communism (showing a hammer and sickle)—was deemed too much and whitewashed before the public opening (Zakheim: 1983).

While the artists worked in Coit Tower, the massive, epoch-shaping waterfront strike erupted, shutting down the West Coast as of early May 1934. By the time the public opening rolled around on July 7, the City was paralyzed by a spontaneous general strike in support of the waterfront workers who had been attacked and shot by police and national guard. (After two were killed on "Bloody Thursday" July 5, 1934, the City ground to a halt. See L10.) The murals had been designed and painted in a city at the depth of the Depression and undergoing an unprecedented revolt in its port, and the men in charge of New Deal public art decided the works were too controversial to open in the midst of the ongoing social upheaval. The artists protested, but to no avail. Finally, the Coit Tower murals were opened to the public in October 1934, and the activated working class, by whom and for whom the paintings were made, enthusiastically flocked to see them.

Decades later—the murals and the working-class movement they were rooted in largely forgotten—the art had fallen into disrepair, with water leaking onto some parts and graffiti scarring other areas. A public campaign was launched to save and restore the murals, and to prevent the privatization of Coit Tower, seen as the logical solution to its maintenance problems through the eyes of the Recreation & Park Department managers. A successful ballot proposition in 2012 put permanent limits on the private rental of Coit Tower and ensured that revenues from the existing gift shop and elevator would be dedicated to mural and tower restoration and maintenance.

D5: RINCON ANNEX POST OFFICE (1947)

Mission and Steuart Streets

A remarkable series of 30 murals depicting the history of California grace the Art Deco lobby of the former Rincon Annex Post Office, painted in the mid-1940s by Anton Refregier. Anti-communist San Franciscans besieged the Russian-born artist during the painting of these panels, and once they were finally completed, the Republican-majority Congress that came to power with the 1952 presidential election of Dwight Eisenhower held public hearings with the intention of condemning and then destroying the art. Not only do the nearly 30 distinct murals tell many important tales of San Francisco history, but their creation and lasting presence are themselves loaded with historical significance and controversy.

Republican representative Hubert Scudder of Sebastopol, California, opened a House Committee debate by claiming that the artist was tantamount to a Soviet agent. Scudder claimed that Refregier's detailed history of California was nothing but propaganda designed to slander the state's pioneers and convert patrons at San Francisco's main post office to communism. Refregier had arrived in San Francisco with the goal of painting historic murals not as romantic decorations but as part of the social movements that were unfolding all around him in the 1930s and early 1940s.

Before he had finished painting, his work was already being protested. The Catholic Church objected that a friar preaching to Indians at Mission Dolores was too fat, so in response Refregier slimmed him. In 1947, the Public Buildings Administration ordered Refregier to take President Roosevelt out of his panel *The Four Freedoms*. He asked San Franciscans to back him, but the momentum was with the opponents of his work. He eventually complied. During the height of early 1950s Cold War hysteria, Michigan representative George Dondero, for one, launched a campaign against all that was "modern" in art, a term which he defined as "communistic because it is distorted and ugly, because it does not glorify our beautiful country, our cheerful and smiling people." Dozens of protests put into the Congressional Record during that 1953 hearing were nearly unanimous in their claim that "said murals do not truly depict the romance and glory of early California history, but on the contrary cast a most derogatory and improper reflection upon the character of the pioneers, and the other murals are definitely subversive and designed to spread communistic propaganda and tend to promote racial hatred and class warfare" (Brechin: 2015).

Somehow the efforts to destroy the murals fell short, and life went on at the post office under the glare of the so-called subversive murals. After several decades, the post office decided to vacate its bulk mail facilities at Rincon Annex in the late 1980s and close its post office. Emmy Lou Packard led a successful public campaign to save and restore the historically important murals. Today they are in great condition. Fully restored inside and out, but now a foyer to the sprawling high-rises accessible through a walkway in its southern wall, the lobby is open 24 hours a day and is one of San Francisco's better-kept historical sites. Within its walls are also a dozen glass cases full of artifacts dug up from the mudflats and sand dunes that were once the shallow bottom of Yerba Buena Cove, and later were covered by piers, ships, and warehouses.

D6: JIM CROW SAN FRANCISCO (1950–65)

Fillmore and O'Farrell Streets

San Francisco never had a very large African American population. Blacks numbered only about 2,500 as late as 1940. After heavy recruitment campaigns in the South on behalf of Kaiser Industries and others, tens of

Anti-discrimination protesters occupy lobby of Cadillac dealership on Van Ness Avenue in San Francisco, 1964. (San Francisco History Room, San Francisco Public Library)

thousands migrated to California, seeking employment in the war industries that ringed the bay. When President Roosevelt authorized the mass incarceration of thousands of Japanese American residents on the West Coast in 1942, the Fillmore District's Japantown was suddenly depopulated. Combined with a pre-war black community in the southern part of the district and the dire housing shortage region-wide, over 40,000 new African American arrivals poured into San Francisco and settled in the emptied apartments left by the Japanese as well as crowding into the existing neighborhoods that allowed nonwhite residents.

In 1937, the federal government, expanding its New Deal approach to public spending, began supporting public housing, but under the control of local agencies. In San Francisco, several projects were initiated during this time, including Holly Courts on Bernal Heights, Sunnydale in Visitacion Valley, and the Potrero Terrace development on the southeast slopes of Potrero Hill. When WWII hit, the government began rushing to finish these projects to house wartime workers. The neighborhood pattern clause of a 1942 Housing Authority resolution barred the "co-mingling of races"; early marketing brochures for Sunnydale and Valencia Gardens, for example, featured white children playing in the shared inner courtyards.

The stated goal of the Housing Authority was to preserve the racial composition of the neighborhoods in which projects were placed. This meant that blacks could only move into projects in sufficiently black neighborhoods. Westside Courts at Post and Broderick Streets on the western side of the Fillmore was the only project at this time that had what was called a Negro Experiment, allowing the inclusion of blacks.

The anxiety of white postwar San Francisco was palpable in 1947, when at a press conference Mayor Roger Lapham asked journalist Tom Fleming, "Mr. Fleming, how long do you think these colored people are going to be here?" Fleming, a California native who grew up in the Central Valley and was a reporter for the *Sun-Reporter*, replied, "Mister Mayor, you know how permanent the Golden Gate is out there? The Black population is just as permanent as the Golden Gate!" (Carlsson: 1996).

It wasn't until the early 1950s, when the NAACP won a case before the California Supreme Court that overturned the neighborhood pattern rules, that public housing was legally desegregated. But that only applied to public housing. In fact, San Francisco housing was still legally racially segregated well into the 1960s thanks to racial covenants on property deeds and widespread white racism.

When the baseball Giants moved to San Francisco from New York in 1958, all-star centerfielder Willie Mays tried to buy a house in the upscale Miraloma neighborhood but was refused because of a racial covenant on the property. Rocked by the ensuing uproar, then mayor George Christopher invited Willie to stay at his house until the owner relented and agreed to sell the house to Mays. But redlining by insurance companies and banks persisted and de facto segregation continued.

San Francisco's black community, led by the NAACP and the Congress on Racial Equality (CORE), connected life in the City to the civil rights movement unfolding in the South. When sit-ins began at lunch counters in 1960 to demand desegregation, San Franciscans picketed at Kress and Woolworth's in solidarity. By 1963, a sustained campaign to abolish racial employment discrimination was under way in San Francisco. The Palace Hotel (which had employed African Americans until 1882 when white unions demanded that black workers be fired) came under steady pressure with mass sit-ins in the lobby and picket lines blocking their doors on New Montgomery. Safeway and Lucky's grocery chains were picketed with demands to desegregate hiring, and according to CORE activist Darrell Rogers, Safeway ultimately agreed to hire a number of Latinos and Asians but continued to refuse black employees until many years later (Carlsson: 2016). Lucky's decided to leave San Francisco rather than succumb to the pressure to desegregate their hiring practices. Mel's Drive-in diners were picketed, and the culminating struggle took place at the Cadillac dealership on Van Ness in the middle of Auto Row. Dozens of protesters, black and white students from local universities along with the active members of CORE and the NAACP, besieged the Cadillac showroom until the owners relented and agreed to hire black salesmen.

By 1965, the San Francisco Redevelopment Agency's plans to bull-doze the Fillmore District to remove what they called blight were partly accomplished. The main corridor along Geary Boulevard, project area A-1, had been leveled and the new Japantown development was begin-ning, but the empty stretch from Gough Street to Masonic Avenue served as what was then referred to as a "Mason-Dixon Line" between the poor black southern part of the neighborhood (itself slated for clearance in the A-2 plan) and the wealthier white neighborhood in the northern part of the Fillmore reaching up to the very rich Pacific Heights. Neighborhood organizing accompanied the emergence of new black political efforts and put pressure on the Redevelopment Agency to alter their plans. Church leaders, black activists, students, and longtime residents banded together to resist the bulldozers with limited success. In this context, shaped in part by the ongoing Freeway Revolt that put a halt to plans to run a freeway up the Fell/Oak corridor and through the Panhandle and Golden Gate Park (T11), black residents moved steadily southward, filling the Lower Haight (which was then seen as part of the Fillmore), and west into the Haight Ashbury. By the 1970s, the black population was nearing 100,000 in San Francisco, a high point that would recede rapidly in the coming decades as gentrification began at the end of the 1970s. By the 1990s, formal housing discrimination was a thing of the past, but the concentration of African American residents had been largely dispersed by a more invisible eco-nomic cleansing involving deindustrialization and inexorable property inflation. In 2000, the African American population of San Francisco had fallen below 50,000, and has continued its downward trend ever since, falling to approximately 35,000 by 2018.

D7: House Un-American Activities Committee (1960)

City Hall, 1 Dr. Carlton B. Goodlett Place

When the House Un-American Activities Committee (HUAC) planned new hearings in May 1960 to investigate communist infiltration in the Bay Area, they didn't expect serious opposition. The same committee had held hearings in previous years. Beyond a few unrepentant members of the Communist Party, the committee's attention was widely feared. In 1960, the climate changed for good when hundreds of students from local universities converged on the hearing to witness the famous witch hunters. The HUAC was careful to allocate the public seats to reliable supporters of their efforts, leaving the students out in the hall unable to enter the hearing. They chanted and sang and demanded entry, leading police to declare their gathering unlawful. Perhaps inspired by civil rights protests in the South, students resorted to passive resistance in the face of police repression. The police then unleashed fire hoses and washed students down the marble steps inside the rotunda before arresting 64 and sending a half dozen to the hospital (no one was convicted, and most of the charges were dropped before trial).

In spite of the fear and trauma, everyone returned the next day, jamming Civic Center Plaza. Big, burly longshoremen showed up to defend the students from horse-mounted police, and with thousands of protesters in the streets, the HUAC canceled the rest of its hearing, and never held another public hearing again! In retrospect, the HUAC protest can be seen as the end of a paralyzing and paranoid repressive period in U.S. history, but also the beginning of the student movement that within a few years would be a powerful force in opposing the Vietnam War and in unleashing the wide-ranging cultural revolution we call "the '60s" (Jenkins and Hallinan: 1994).

D8: Council on Religion and Homosexuality/ Early LGBTQ Politics

On New Year's Eve in 1964, one of the San Francisco gay community's most important historical events took place at California Hall on Polk and Turk Streets. That night, the recently formed Council on Religion and

Homosexuality was scheduled to host a private New Year's Eve Ball. Attendees, overwhelmingly gay, planned to come in drag, given the rare opportunity to share a major holiday in public but at an officially private event. Knowing the long history of police harassment, the religious leaders spoke to police ahead of time and were assured that their event could go ahead without police intervention. But instead, the police created a gauntlet of spotlights and cameras, which discouraged many who showed up from attending, as this was a time when being openly gay or associated with homosexuality could still lead to being fired from your job or evicted from your apartment. The police not only filmed and photographed attendees, but they repeatedly entered the hall in search of fire code violations, and even arrested a few partygoers. Outraged by the duplicitous behavior of the police, religious leaders held a press conference the day after, denouncing police harassment. While homophobia was still very much the norm in society, popular opinion swung against the police repression of this event. The New Year's Eve Ball was officially a private party, and the police had overstepped a new sense of what the limits were. By 1964, one's sexuality was becoming a private concern, and in private one could dress as one liked. Ultimately the ball and its harassment led to a new sense of what was possible in public and private space. After the public backlash to the widespread press coverage, the police stopped imposing their personal idea of morality. Instead of arresting people for what they saw as *wrong*, they purportedly focused on arresting queer people who had *broken the law*, another small but important step on the long road to LGBTQ civil rights.

A Tenderloin resident, Mark Forrester, was a poor, politically active gay man, and in 1965 he helped draft "The Brief of Injustices," a ten-point document documenting the discrimination against homosexuals. This manifesto helped build and make public the hypothesis that the homosexual minority was similar to ethno-racial minorities. This document made public a sensibility that had been growing since the 1951 founding of the Mattachine Society and the 1954 founding of the Daughters of Bilitis, encouraging minorities with different sexualities and gender sensibilities to discover themselves as public actors.

The local San Francisco Equal Opportunity Council was responsible for allocating the monies flowing to San Francisco from President Lyndon Johnson's 1964 War on Poverty. Originally, millions targeted five neighborhoods, chosen based on ethnicity and historic discrimination and impoverishment: Chinatown, the Mission District, the Fillmore/ Western Addition, Potrero Hill, and Bayview/Hunters Point. A sixth, the Tenderloin, was only added after two years of organizing and agitation by neighborhood residents and organizers from area churches and social service agencies. The campaign to include the Tenderloin brought federal relief to the "Central City Target Area" (including blocks south of Market Street in addition to the borders of the contemporary Tenderloin district). The effort was pathbreaking for the entire country in redefining who was understood as disadvantaged, and thus eligible for federal anti-poverty support. The new Central City Target Area was largely inhabited in the mid-1960s by poor white residents, many of whom were homosexuals, sex workers, impoverished elderly, abusers of drugs and alcohol, and young runaways and outcasts. The social stigma attached to each of these categories (which largely derived from a sense that individual moral turpitude or personal failure was responsible) had made this poor population harder to include in the initial public anti-poverty support.

But, as historian Martin Meeker has shown, a "coalition of liberal ministers, gay activists, and Central City residents worked together to produce a new poverty knowledge focused less on racial discrimination and cross-generational poverty, but much more on social isolation and its causes" (Meeker: 2012). The Central City Target Area was the first time homosexuals, and others at the margins of mainstream acceptability, received benefits from the welfare state based on their different way of being. Moreover, with this new sense of entitlement came a growing awareness of a shared identity, and with it a growing commitment to dignity and basic civil rights—the foundation of today's widely accepted LGBTQ movement. The 1960s Tenderloin activists didn't try to minimize the role of race in defining poverty, but argued that social marginalization and individual isolation were also key factors, thus augmenting the mix of economic and ethno-racial factors already in play.

Transsexuality came of age in the Tenderloin in the mid-1960s too, arising from the confluence of gay organizing, anti-poverty claims on behalf of the isolated and socially marginalized so-called deviant characters in the Tenderloin, and the emergence of a medical approach to changing gender. New ideas about gender started with the famous Christine Jorgensen sex-change operation in 1952, but by the mid-1960s were entering more widespread acceptance due to the work of Dr. Harry Benjamin and other clinically trained professionals. Benjamin's 1966 publication of *The Transsexual Phenomenon* was the first book-length treatment of transsexuality and helped create a new orthodoxy in medical and psychotherapeutic circles. Dr. Benjamin ran his summer practice from an office off Union Square, just blocks from the thriving gay drag (aka queen) scene on Turk Street that included El Rosa, Sound of Music, Chukkers, the Camelot, and the Hilliard, along with other establishments in the surrounding streets.

In August 1966, the infamous mini-riot at Compton's Cafeteria on Taylor and Turk Streets took place. Police rolled in to carry out what had become routine roustings and mass arrests of queens and gays, but for the first time the patrons of Compton's fought back, smashing windows and fighting the police with shoes and handbags in the streets (Stryker and Silverman: 2005). Early historians of San Francisco's gay community recognized that the Tenderloin's legacy of transgender militancy contributed significantly to early gay liberation efforts in San Francisco, leading to the establishment later of the Gay Liberation Front, which evolved into the Gay Activist Alliance, ultimately founding the Helping Hands Center on Turk Street to provide support and services for transsexuals as part of its overall mission.

The presence of "deviant" sexuality and gender in San Francisco, specifically in the Tenderloin, clearly laid the foundation for the burgeoning sexual politics that erupted in the decades that followed. New ways of being and new identities forged in the oppressive mid-twentieth century found political voice and agency that transformed social norms not just in San Francisco but nationally and across the world.

D9: Vietnam War and San Francisco (1965–75)

968 Valencia Street, Kezar Stadium

San Francisco's port had its last stretch of intense usage during the first half of the 1960s when war matériel was being shipped by the ton to Vietnam. The local economy enjoyed a boom during the buildup to the Vietnam War, as it has for every major war in the Pacific during the twentieth century. By 1965, when Lyndon Johnson's draft was radically expanded to accommodate a half million troops in Vietnam, antiwar activists were already appearing around the City and the Bay Area. But the really big mobilizations against the Vietnam War didn't come until the Spring Mobilization

Anti-Vietnam War marchers on Market at New Montgomery Street, 1969. (H. K. Yuen)

in 1967, when 100,000 marched from downtown to Kezar Stadium at the edge of Golden Gate Park; thousands more besieged the Oakland Induction Center in October 1967 in a weeklong, multi-tactic effort to "Stop the Draft."

In the fall of 1968, military police at the Presidio jail shot and killed "Rusty" Bunch, a depressed young man who tried to run away in plain view. Angry at the blatant murder of their brother, 27 men, all conscientious objectors (COs), went on strike in the Presidio jail. When they sat down on October 14, 1968, they had seven main demands: elimination of shotgun details, complete psychological evaluations of all prisoners and guards, removal of racist guards, rotation of guards to prevent the buildup of antagonism, better sanitary facilities, decent food in sufficient quantities, and a chance to tell the press the prisoners' version of Bunch's slaying. They were put on military trial, accused of mutiny, and nearly all were convicted and spent at least a year in jail before an appeal reduced their sentences. Two escaped to Canada (Barnes: 1972).

By November 1969, the New Mobilization to End the War in Vietnam drew a half million in Washington and half that in San Francisco for another long march to Golden Gate Park that ended in the Polo Field. The underground press was full of antiwar articles. Hundreds of antiwar GI newspapers were founded around the world; at a Mission District storefront (at 968 Valencia) you could leave mail for *Up Against the Bulkhead*, a regular newspaper for antiwar sailors.

On May 5, 1971, thousands of protesters were determined to shut down the Financial District and to simultaneously expose the war-profiteering of numerous corporations with headquarters downtown. Office workers on their lunch breaks were herded and gassed just like the protesters who clogged the streets. Police on small motorcycles and on horseback repeatedly rode into groups of protesters and beat them with batons. Numerous serious injuries were inflicted, but demonstrators found some unexpected support when a corporate lawyer offered his services—he was horrified at the unprovoked violence the police meted out. Shell Oil, Chevron, Bank of America, Wells Fargo, Dow Chemical, Bechtel, Zellerbach Paper, and others were all besieged by protesters more than willing to point out the specific role each company was playing in supporting the war in Vietnam.

In 1974, a long campaign by sailors and their wives out of the Alameda Naval Air Station attempted to prevent the USS *Coral Sea* from sailing back to Vietnam. A number of sailors marched in antiwar demonstrations on Market Street under the banner SOS (Save our Ship, or Stop our Ship). This was the same year Nixon resigned the presidency, and the U.S. military was near collapse. Widespread mutiny and refusal to fight by the troops in Vietnam fed a generally seditious attitude among troops around the world. The United States was bringing soldiers home as fast as it could. When it was obvious that a draft-based military was not reliable anymore, the government switched to a so-called Volunteer Army (read: economically conscripted).

For many decades, starting with Reagan's 1983 invasion of the tiny Caribbean island of Grenada and later the attack on Panama City, leading crucially to President George H. W. Bush's 1991 invasion of Kuwait and Iraq, the U.S. government has been trying to overcome the "Vietnam Syndrome." This refers to a population who, either out of principle or exhaustion, oppose wars of empire and conquest (and maybe wars in general!) and will resist. Finally, after 9/11 and the invasions of Afghanistan and Iraq in the twenty-first century, Americans have learned to live with perpetual war. The Vietnam Syndrome has been outflanked by war from afar conducted with airpower and unmanned drones and few boots on the ground. The tight control of press coverage with the complicity of major media companies has also prevented the mayhem and violence of war from being seen directly as it was during crucial years of the Vietnam War.

D10. Hunters Point Uprising (1966)

3rd and Newcomb Streets/Bayview Opera House

On September 27, 1966, a white police officer shot and killed a 17-year-old African American teen, Matthew Johnson Jr., as he fled the scene of a stolen car. For two hours after the shooting, a large, angry crowd milled about the site along Navy Road. The police, meanwhile, were hurrying the African Americans on the City's Human Rights Commission over to the scene. Nathaniel Burbridge of the NAACP and Tom Fleming, editor at the *Sun-Reporter* newspaper in the Fillmore arrived at the Bayview Opera House public meeting in the early evening where the crowd pressed their demands that the cop be charged with murder, a concept that was incomprehensible to the assembled authorities. By the time Mayor Shelley arrived, the restive crowd was quick to jeer him and even throw tomatoes at him. When the mayor promised them that the officer had been suspended, it was

*Police open fire on Community Center at Newcomb and 3rd Streets, September 28, 1966.
(Author's collection)*

too late. The lone black supervisor, Terry Francois, known as an NAACP
and civil rights defense lawyer, was jeered and pelted with rocks when he
appeared (Carlsson: 1996).

That night saw sporadic looting, rock throwing, and petty arson.
Community leaders tried to calm the situation the next day, but Police
Chief Tom Cahill issued an ultimatum: calm by noon Wednesday or massive force would be introduced. Neighborhood leaders were unable to
calm the situation, and the streets continued to be a battleground.

Around six in the evening, a few hours after Governor Pat Brown
authorized the use of the National Guard and Highway Patrol, the police
responded to alleged gunfire by opening up on the Bayview Community
Center and surrounding buildings. After riddling it with hundreds of
bullets, the police found no gunmen or weapons but only several preteen
kids huddling in the corner. The long-suppressed anger over the abysmal
status imposed on African Americans was uncontainable, but the violence was largely limited to property damage.

Nevertheless, martial law was imposed on the Bayview and Fillmore
Districts for three days, Sept. 29–Oct. 1, with young, armed National
Guard troops patrolling the streets in jeeps with machine guns mounted on

the back. The rebellion continued with decreasing violence, and then finally petered out. The property damage (several hundred thousand dollars) compared with riots in comparably sized cities was minimal, as were the casualties (ten civilians reported as victims of gunshot wounds, no casualties among the police or National Guard). Like most urban uprisings it consisted primarily of running around, breaking windows, and ransacking unpopular establishments (Hippler: 1974).

The police had, until the early 1960s, dealt with black youth from Hunters Point by isolating them there. At the outbreak of the uprising, in spite of happening citywide, the same tactic was used. African Americans, no matter who they were or what their reason for being in the area of 3rd Street, were either arrested or herded back up the hill. The police rank and file assumed a war footing, heavily framed by their essentially racist outlook. While the brass made various mediation attempts, the cops on the street saw an undifferentiated mass of hostile enemies and behaved accordingly.

The best indication of the unreasonable magnitude of white fears at the time is the fact that, aside from long-range brick throwing, less than a half dozen assaults by blacks against whites were recorded in the course of five days. Also, the action took part in all parts of the City with sizeable black populations (the Mission District, the Potrero Hill area, the huge Fillmore District—which today includes the Lower Haight and North of the Panhandle areas) and yet resulted in so few injuries indicates the targeted nature of the protests, which mostly were directed at police and unfriendly businesses.

Immediately after the five-day upheaval, many Hunters Point residents hoped that it would lead to greater solidarity among community groups. Actually, the opposite occurred: greater community disintegration resulted. This was reinforced when the insurance industry refused to underwrite the losses incurred by business owners in the Bayview Hunters Point area. The general belief that "nobody cares" and "it's too late to do anything" became widespread. Automatic weapons, portable artillery, and federal troops—that is, military occupation—offered a vivid demonstration of how far San Francisco would go in the attempt to contain black rage. Very few community organizations continued functioning in Hunters Point immediately afterward, though they began to reemerge in the following years. Meanwhile, the Hunters Point Uprising itself almost disappeared down the memory hole.

D11: Black Panthers (1966–70)

1336 Fillmore Street (former offices)

The Black Panther Party for Self-Defense was founded in Oakland by Huey Newton and Bobby Seale in October 1966. Other groups using the Panther name were emerging at the same time, including a black group in San Francisco who just went by the moniker the San Francisco Panthers. But within a year and a half, the Oakland-based Black Panther Party had absorbed most other groups into their own structure. One of their most famous early actions was to invade the State Capitol in Sacramento during a legislative session fully armed (it was officially legal in California to carry loaded rifles as long as you didn't point them at anyone) (Rhodes: 2007). They followed this bold action with a public commitment to armed self-defense of the black community in Oakland and wherever the party was organized. This led to rapid growth in membership as thousands wanted to stand up to years of police violence and intimidation. As the Black Panthers went from a local group in the East Bay to a nationally prominent organization that attracted tens of thousands of young African Americans, the federal government led by the FBI's J. Edgar Hoover was determined to destroy them. Dirty tricks, false accusations, shootings, even direct police murders, all led to the Black Panthers losing many of their most charismatic members to murder and incarceration over the following years. Some Black Panthers are still in jail as you read this.

The San Francisco Diggers delivered bags of food to the Panthers in early 1967 (Minault: 2017), and later that year the Black Panthers launched their most famous initiative, the Free Children's Breakfast Program. The Breakfast Program became one of the best examples of how the Black Panthers were able to provide real resources to their community and members, and it was largely thanks to the unsung women of the Black Panther Party that the program was kept alive for several years. Hundreds of hungry children were being fed breakfast every morning. Worried that the Free Breakfast program was winning them converts and allies, the federal government began funding breakfast-at-school programs in many parts of the country.

Huey Newton was convicted of shooting a police officer under dubious circumstances in 1968, and that led to a national movement to Free Huey. (His conviction was overturned on appeal in 1969.) Also in 1968,

Black Panther Minister of Education George Murray was fired from his job as an English professor at San Francisco State College. In response, the Black Student Union, closely allied to the Black Panthers in that moment, called for a student strike that began later that fall. Among their demands, which were laid out in the ten-point format that the Black Panthers had initiated, were the reinstatement of Murray and the establishment of a Black Studies curriculum. Though Murray was never rehired, the strike concluded with an agreement to establish a School of Ethnic Studies that included Black Studies, La Raza Studies, and Asian American Studies (D13).

Yolanda Lopez and Donna Amador were at a Free Huey rally on the steps of the Federal Building in San Francisco on May 1, 1969, when they overheard the police radio reporting that an officer had been shot in the Mission District and that seven young men were wanted for the crime (two of whom were standing next to Lopez and Amador at the time!). Lopez, Amador, and others became the Committee to Defend Los Siete as the case became known as Los Siete de la Raza (D16). The Black Panthers offered support to the Committee to Defend Los Siete, including giving them several pages in the Black Panther newspaper, which after appearing for a few issues, broke out on its own as the Los Siete newspaper *Basta Ya!*

The Black Panthers had an extraordinary effect on local and national politics. They were committed to building coalitions with other groups of any race facing poverty and police repression. They galvanized the student movement, the anti-Vietnam War movement, and gave a prominent voice of self-respect and dignity to tens of thousands of black Americans who were reeling after the assassination of Martin Luther King Jr. (and several years earlier, Malcolm X) (Bloom and Martin: 2016).

D12: SAN FRANCISCO DIGGERS (1966–69)

Panhandle Park, Oak and Ashbury Streets

The San Francisco Diggers, who took their name from the revolutionary Diggers in England of the 1640s, first appeared in late 1966 as a series of broadsides on walls around town. Cloaked in mystery provided by a refusal to use their names, a fluctuating group of radicals galvanized the burgeoning counterculture in the months that led to the media-hyped Summer of Love. Peter Berg, Judy Goldhaft, Peter Coyote, Emmett Grogan, Billy

Murcott, Kent Minault, Lenore Kandel, Chuck Gould, Jane Lapiner, David Simpson, and many others came together to pioneer a politics of serious play based on the concept of "free." Free food, free music in the parks, free stores, all challenged the swirling youth culture to go beyond the predictable and ossified forms of politics, theater, art, and daily life.

Several of the original Diggers had been part of the San Francisco Mime Troupe before breaking away, finding the form and organization too constraining. They sought to engage in life theater, a form of enacting the world you wanted to live in, rather than performing for audiences or waiting for social change to be granted by authorities. San Francisco quickly became their stage, or the canvas of their radical artistic expression.

The Diggers hit upon the idea of providing free food to the influx of thousands of youth, and did this by preparing a huge pot of soup and dozens of loaves of bread to be distributed every day in the Panhandle Park at 4 p.m. This idea arose from the simple realization that there was a huge amount of food going to waste in San Francisco. In this period, people starting banding together in food conspiracies to acquire food directly from farmers and cut out the profiting middlemen. A number of Diggers started asking farmers at the Alemany Farmer's Market for their unsellable produce at the end of the day. That was the foundation for the free food project. The supplies were supplemented by various Robin Hood-like endeavors at local supermarkets, but the enormous job of cooking up many gallons of hearty soup every day was carried out in the kitchens of several Digger households, primarily by the women in the group. "Digger bread" got its name because it was baked in one-pound coffee cans and the top would spread out in a broad crusty cap, which became a recognizable emblem of their free bread.

Every afternoon at the Panhandle Park the soup and bread would arrive, and dozens of hungry young people would line up to get their serving. A couple of Diggers would stand along Oak Street where dense traffic flowed by, holding up a 6' square yellow frame made of 2×4's. In order to get your meal you had to step through this *Free Frame of Reference*, while it also framed the distribution of free food as a *tableaux vivant* of sorts, and served to highlight the challenge to daily norms they sought to mount. A small 2" version of the wooden frame was handed out to soup recipients as a lapel pin so any time they wanted to they could hold it up to the eye and change their frame of reference.

Free stores were soon opened where clothes, furniture, appliances, and even money were available to anyone who wanted it, free of charge. One older woman who was stealthily pocketing various items was confronted by a Digger, "You can't steal here." She indignantly replied, "I'm not stealing! Who you callin' a thief?" The Digger smiled and said again, "You can't steal here—because everything is free!" The woman left, only to return the next day with a flat of cupcakes to give away at the store. It didn't take long for people to adapt to the new logic (Minault: 2017).

In October 1966, the Diggers staged a *Death of Money* procession, leading to the Panhandle Park and a bonfire where money was burned as a bacchanalian dance swirled around the fire. This was the beginning of a number of events that caught the imagination of the time, and were soon being trumpeted from coast to coast. Diggers kept up a steady stream of broadsides to circumvent the efforts of the mass media to shape their narrative. After the event called *Invisible Circus* took over Glide Memorial Church in spring 1967 in an overnight festival of drugs, sex, and experimentation, the media-hyped Summer of Love kicked in. The Diggers had spent so much time serving food, organizing concerts, helping launch the Free Medical Clinic, maintaining their free stores, etc. that in the face of the mainstreaming of their efforts they were ready to hold another parade announcing *Death of the Hippie*, which they did in October 1967.

As hard drugs flooded the Haight Ashbury scene, many Diggers began to decamp to rural retreats in Northern California. Different individuals would go on to new efforts, many of them ecologically minded, in the years to come. Peter Berg and Judy Goldhaft founded Planet Drum Foundation in 1974, helping to popularize the idea of "bioregionalism," and convened the Frisco Bay Mussel Group gatherings at The Farm in 1978, an important series of public discussions helping frame radical ecological thinking at that time.

D13: San Francisco State College Strike (1968–69)

1600 Holloway at 19th Avenue

"On strike! Shut it down!" From November 1968 to March 1969, those words rang out daily on the campus of San Francisco State College near Lake Merced in the southwestern corner of San Francisco. Like clockwork,

Nesbit Crutchfield facing the San Francisco Police during the San Francisco State College strike, Nov. 13, 1968. (People's International News Service)

between noon and 3 p.m., striking students would gather at the Speaker's Platform on campus for a rally, then march on the Administration Building, intent upon confrontation with President Smith and later his successor, S. I. Hayakawa. Hayakawa famously pulled the plug on the PA system at a student rally; he rode his notoriety from the SF State strike into the U.S. Senate in 1976. The strike at San Francisco State College lasted five months, longer than any other academic student strike in American higher education history.

When English professor and Black Panther Party Minister of Education George Murray was fired on November 1, 1968, for incendiary comments he made in Cuba, the situation quickly escalated. The Black Student Union (BSU) demanded his reinstatement and called for a student strike in support of that demand, but they also developed a full set of demands, which were soon joined by the Third World Liberation Front student group and their allied demands. Amid their clamor for retention of existing professors and hiring many new ones, expanding financial aid, and admitting all black students, the key demand that altered San Francisco State and reverberated out to affect universities across the United States was for a new curriculum. The BSU demanded that "all Black Studies courses being taught through various departments be immediately part of the Black Studies Department and that all the instructors in this department receive full-time pay. . . . That there be a Department of Black Studies which will grant a Bachelor's Degree in Black Studies; that the Black Studies Department chairman, faculty and staff have the sole power to hire faculty and control and determine the destiny of its department" (Whitson: 1995).

They also demanded "that no disciplinary action be administered in any way to any students, workers, teachers, or administrators during and after the strike as a consequence of their participation in the strike." Understanding that their main behind-the-scenes enemy during the months-long dispute on campus was the system's trustees, they further demanded "that the California State College Trustees not be allowed to dissolve any Black programs on or off the San Francisco State College campus."

The Third World Liberation Front (consisting of student groups for Latinos and Asian Americans) demanded a School of Ethnic Studies be set up with the students in each particular ethnic organization to be given the authority and control of hiring and retention of any faculty member, director, or administrator, as well as the curriculum in a specific area study, and that 50 new faculty positions be allocated to the new school.

During the strike, pitched battles occurred almost daily. For months, several hundred San Francisco police, armed to the teeth, locked down the campus. With cops everywhere, no student organizations could hold a rally. There was no free speech. And there was no longer an Associated Student fund. The BSU was declared an illegal campus organization, and was kicked off campus. Many other student organizations were declared illegal, banned, and pushed off campus. This was not a symbolic show—an occupying police force was on campus for most of a school year!

The strike expanded to the faculty, first with an information picket line in early December 1968, and then with a formal strike beginning on January 6, 1969. After two months and repeated ignored court orders to end the strike, the students and faculty signed agreements with the university and ended the strike on March 20, 1969. A new School of Ethnic Studies was established, with a Black Studies department, a La Raza

Studies department, and an Asian American Studies department. Hundreds of students of color were recruited and admitted to the college in the following semesters.

Students who were radicalized by their experiences during the San Francisco State strike entered the City's tumultuous political battles of the late 1960s and early 1970s and had a major impact. From the Western Addition Project Action Committee (WAPAC) to the people behind the Patty Hearst ransom food distribution in 1974 (D19), to the I-Hotel fight (D3), Los Siete (D16), and the Black Panthers (D11)—plus neighborhood politics in Chinatown and the Mission District—every facet of local politics was affected by the strike in subsequent years.

D14: FROM UNSELLING ALCATRAZ TO THE INDIAN OCCUPATION (1969–71)

Alcatraz Island

In 1969, Texas oil industrialist Lamar Hunt proposed to buy Alcatraz Island and build a memorial museum to the Apollo space program as well as a Victorian San Francisco theme park there. The City's government approved the sale, and it would've gone through had Jerry Mander, an advertising guy, and Alvin Duskin, a clothing manufacturer, not intervened. Mander and Duskin were friends who would run into each other while separately lunching at Enrico's in North Beach. Mander was eating with magazine editor Warren Hinckle when they decided to approach Duskin with their plot. In video interviews conducted in 2009, Mander and Duskin describe how they derailed Hunt's plans by purchasing a full-page ad in the *San Francisco Chronicle* decrying the sale of Alcatraz for less than the price of Manhattan in the 1600s! Clip-off coupons at the bottom of the ad flooded into City Hall, and the ensuing uproar forced the Supervisors to rescind the contract. Later, Duskin was contacted by a member of the Inland Boatmen's Union who explained the real plan all along had been for Hunt to get the legal rights to the island and then claim that after further study the original absurd plans were unfeasible. Then Hunt would repurpose the lease to his oil business needs by converting Alcatraz into a deepwater oil tanker dock, with new oil pipelines to transport crude from giant tankers northward across the bay to the refineries in Richmond. When this idea was published in the papers, Hunt dropped his lawsuit against the City and disappeared from San Francisco forever (Carlsson: 2009).

Not long after the demise of Hunt's proposal, American Indians carried out a bold plan that had been tried in 1964 but quickly abandoned at that time. On November 9, 1969, about 250 Indians gathered at Fisherman's Wharf to boat over to Alcatraz, formerly a federal penitentiary, and claim it for the Indian people. The arranged boats never appeared, however, and the plan was scuttled. Later that night, though, a group of 14 Indians successfully landed on Alcatraz Island. It was the second attempt to take Alcatraz for the Indian people, but after a day of frantic searching by government officials and the media, they gave themselves up and left the island, planning to negotiate their now-established squatters' rights. There ensued a government runaround, and by November 20, the Indians were ready to occupy again. About 100 landed on Alcatraz, and this try was to last until June 11, 1971, when the last occupiers were escorted from the island by federal police.

Over 5,000 Indians from dozens of tribes, many displaced and living in the Bay Area, made their way to Alcatraz over the 19 months of the occupation. Efforts to present the Indians' case claiming the island led to widespread sympathetic media coverage. Cleverly, the occupiers declared themselves a "Bureau of Caucasian Affairs" and published a proclamation signed by Indians of All Tribes:

To the Great White Father and All His People:
   We, the native Americans, re-claim the land known as Alcatraz Island in the name of all American Indians by right of discovery. We wish to be fair and honorable in our dealings with the Caucasian inhabitants of this land, and hereby offer the following treaty: We will purchase said Alcatraz Island for 24 dollars in glass beads and red cloth, a precedent set by the white man's purchase of a similar island about 300 years ago. We know that $24 in trade goods for these sixteen acres is more than was paid when Manhattan Island was sold, but we know that land values have risen over the years. Our offer of $1.24 per acre is greater than the 47 cents per acre the white men are now paying the California Indians for their land. We will give to the inhabitants of this land a portion of that land for their own, to be held in trust by the American Indian Government for as long as the sun shall rise and the rivers go down to the sea—to be administered by the Bureau of Caucasian Affairs (BCA). We will further

guide the inhabitants in the proper way of living. We will offer them our religion, our education, our life-ways, in order to help them achieve our level of civilization and thus raise them and all their white brothers up from their savage and unhappy state. We offer this treaty in good faith and wish to be fair and honorable in our dealings with all white men.

We feel that this so-called Alcatraz Island is more than suitable as an Indian Reservation, as determined by the white man's own standards. By this we mean that this place resembles most Indian reservations, in that:

1. It is isolated from modern facilities, and without adequate means of transportation.
2. It has no fresh running water.
3. The sanitation facilities are inadequate.
4. There are no oil or mineral rights.
5. There is no industry and so unemployment is very great.
6. There are no health-care facilities.
7. The soil is rocky and non-productive and the land does not support game.
8. There are no educational facilities.
9. The population has always been held as prisoners and kept dependent upon others.

Further, it would be fitting and symbolic that ships from all over the world, entering the Golden Gate, would first see Indian land, and thus be reminded of the true history of this nation. This tiny island would be a symbol of the great lands once ruled by free and noble Indians.

May 31, 1970 (Eagle: 1992)

Overall the Alcatraz occupation became a turning point in federal/ indigenous relations. In the wake of the occupation, the government passed the Indian Self-Determination and Education Assistance Act in 1975, revised the Johnson O'Malley Act to better educate Indians, passed the Indian Financing Act of 1974, passed the Indian Health Care Improvement Act in 1976, and created an assistant interior secretary post for Indian Affairs. Mount Adams was returned to the Yakima Nation in Washington State, and 48,000 acres of the Sacred Blue Lake lands were returned to Taos Pueblo in New Mexico. This was the first return of land to the Indian Nations, beginning a slow process of historical reparation. During the second Christmas of the Alcatraz Occupation, President Nixon signed papers rescinding Termination stating, "This marks the end of Termination and the start of Self-determination" (Robinson: 2011).

D15: The Mission Coalition Organization (MCO) (1968–72)

23rd and Folsom Streets

The Mission District started its urbanization process back in the 1860s, and by the turn of the twentieth century it was a busy residential and industrial neighborhood, filled with a mix of Irish, Italians, Germans, and Scandinavians, both immigrants and second generation. Catholic and Lutheran churches filled the area, which encompassed the entire southern half of San Francisco. According to a map of the Mission District published by the Mission Promotion Association, founded in 1909, the neighborhood included not only today's Mission District, but also Noe Valley, Eureka Valley/Castro, Potrero Hill, and Bernal Heights, boundaries that only began to shrink after WWII and with the influx of new populations, the building of Highway 101, and other changes (Howell: 2015).

By the mid-1960s a major surge of Central American immigrants had begun to settle in the neighborhood, changing the politics and culture of the area and creating the foundation for an assertive *latinidad* that soon found its political voice (Summers Sandoval: 2013). First, the Mission Council on Redevelopment (MCOR)—a coalition that included older white business and property owners along with the Maoist Progressive Labor Party (PL), Catholic social organizations, and others—successfully organized in 1967 to block the Redevelopment Agency from bulldozing the neighborhood. After that success and the dissolution of MCOR, a new coalition formed to respond to the promise of federal Model Cities money coming to the city, which Mayor Alioto promised to dedicate to the Mission District if he could identify a properly representative organization to work with. Organizers associated with the Centro Social Obrero and Laborers Union Local 261, Arriba Juntos, and various Latino-identified political groups came together to launch the Mission Coalition Organization (MCO). Mike Miller, a staunch supporter of Saul Alinsky-style community organizing (with its hostility to the ideological Left), was hired as staff organizer, and Ben Martinez was elected president at age 24. Support from the Catholic Archdiocese, the United Presbyterian Church, Laborers Local 261, and a half dozen other groups provided essential resources and people with paid time to work on building the effort (Miller: 2009).

In October 1968, the first Convention of the MCO was held, and though it was almost derailed by the intervention of the Mission Rebels youth organization (themselves beneficiaries of Equal Opportunity federal funding), ultimately the attendees closed ranks and chose to go forward as what soon became the biggest urban coalition in San Francisco history. Focused on getting jobs for unemployed residents of the neighborhood and fighting the slumlords who were presiding over a deteriorating housing stock, the MCO built its reputation as an organization that could get things done. Over 10,000 active participants and upwards of 100 distinct organizations made for a couple of years of dynamic organizing and a string of successes in gaining jobs at local Mission businesses (such as Twinkies, Levi's, Hamm's Brewery, Best Food Mayonnaise, and many others). Rent strikes and tenant organizing led to improved conditions and greater dignity for the residents of many neighborhood buildings. By the third year, the MCO's vibrant internal democracy began to fray as the Model Cities monies they had fought so hard to control began to flow and dozens of individuals and groups began to bitterly contest how the money should be divided. During the tumultuous third annual convention of the MCO where Ben Martinez engineered the bylaw change to facilitate his ability to continue as president, many community activists and leftists walked out of the convention in disgust. By 1973, the MCO had become a shell of its former self. But many organizations that continue to this day in the Mission District—from the Mission Housing Development Corporation to the Mission Hiring Hall, Centro Legal de la Raza to the Instituto Familiar de la Raza, Arriba Juntos, and Horizons Unlimited—all played important roles or were born out of that era, and all were sustained by the Latino Mission that emerged in the wake of the MCO's remarkable (if brief) history.

D16: Los Siete de la Raza (1969–71)

429 Alvarado Street

An undercover San Francisco police officer was shot and killed on May 1, 1969, with a bullet from his partner's gun. The officers were in the midst of confronting a group of young Latino men outside a residential home at 429–433 Alvarado Street who they suspected of involvement in an alleged burglary. After the fight, the young men fled into hiding, but a region-wide manhunt caught six and jailed them to await one of the most politicized trials of the era. After a bitterly contested jury trial in June 1970, all six of Los Siete were acquitted of all charges. They were Tony Martinez, Mario Martinez, Nelson Rodriguez, José Rios, Danilo "Bebe" Melendez, and Gary "Pinky" Lescallett; Gio Lopez, the seventh suspect, escaped to Cuba and never returned (Heins: 1972).

Soon after their arrest, activists organized a defense committee, out of whose community organizing was launched a health clinic (El Centro de Salud), a restaurant, a free breakfast program at St. Peter's and St. John's churches, a newspaper (*Basta Ya!*, which was given its start by being hosted in the Black Panther newspaper), and La Raza Legal Defense (the Centro Legal de la Raza started later, in 1973, and is thriving nearly a half century later). Fusing the campaign with a variety of neighborhood political issues, the Committee to Defend Los Siete energized a grassroots opposition to the increasingly staid Mission Coalition Organization (MCO) and its incorporation into the pro-growth agenda of then mayor Joe Alioto. The self-proclaimed revolutionaries around the Los Siete campaign were not able to supplant the broad-based organizing that the MCO had been carrying out in its first dynamic years. In fact, the Los Siete committee was not even able to attract the participation of all the original defendants, several of whom were soon rearrested and suffered savage beatings at the hands of the revenge-minded San Francisco police.

Though the political aspirations of Los Siete were not achieved on their own terms, the successful campaign to defend the young men left a lasting legacy in the Mission District. The mobilization strongly contributed to improvements in legal defense, medical services, and a lasting tradition of politically engaged art, both murals and screen printing. San Francisco General Hospital has undergone many changes over the years, not the least of which was the development of a multilingual staff and the ability to provide medical services in many languages, none of which was true prior to the creation of El Centro de Salud by the Los Siete activists (D17).

D17: CHALLENGING MEDICAL AUTHORITY (1970–2018)

22nd Street/Potrero Avenue

One of the most profound consequences of the second wave feminism of the late 1960s and early 1970s was the emergence of women's self-help health-care groups, and eventually independent women's health clinics. As women came together to explore their unique experiences as females in a deeply patriarchal society, one of the earliest shared skills was to learn about ovulation and other aspects of reproductive health care (Gerson: 2011). Until the 1973 *Roe v. Wade* Supreme Court decision made abortion legal, information on family planning and contraception was difficult to get. Just learning about women's physiology was problematic given the overwhelming male focus of modern medicine, and the predominance of male doctors. But women banded together and began learning and teaching each other, helped enormously by the publication of *Our Bodies Ourselves* by the Boston Women's Health Book Collective in 1969, which rapidly became the bible of the movement. Fueled by growing knowledge and self-confidence, and the steady flow of women into medicine, the biased sexism of modern medicine was challenged at its roots.

Once the inviolable reliability of medical professionals was seriously challenged, a range of alternative approaches to health and bodies became possible. The widespread acceptance of acupuncture, chiropractic, homeopathy, and herbal medicine, among many others, was made possible by grassroots women establishing expertise through their own efforts at self-education. By the 1980s, a more critical, open-minded range of options was becoming available, even in traditional allopathic medical institutions. The delivery of all types of medicine was further broadened by the growing inclusion of multilingual services for Spanish, Chinese, and Tagalog speakers in the City, driven in part by the grassroots El Centro de Salud established by Los Siete activists in the early 1970s. The Haight-Ashbury Free Clinic, the Lyon-Martin Women's Clinic, the Martin Barros Clinic for undocumented immigrants, are all institutions that emerged to meet the needs that mainstream medical providers were failing to meet in addressing sexual, gender, and culturally diverse services.

A series of dramatic confrontations took place nationally and in the Bay Area during the 1980s over abortion rights. The Bay Area Coalition for Our Reproductive Rights trained dozens of women to defend clinics providing abortion and women's health services and frequently went head to head with militant anti-abortion activists from Operation Rescue. Bay Area clinics were targeted for over a decade until finally being checked by the consistent presence of clinic defenders. Other anti-abortion campaigners in the 1980s were financed by $5 million from the Conference of Catholic Bishops—the same ones we know now as having spent decades covering up rampant pedophilia among their ranks (Bocage: 1991).

In the 1980s, the AIDS/HIV epidemic smashed into San Francisco's gay community first. Early reports characterized it as a "gay cancer"; and the government was extremely slow to respond to the dramatic appearance of a deadly and highly contagious auto-immune disorder, and wasn't even able to properly understand it for several years. Given the homophobia of the Reagan administration at the time, stigmatization and moral condemnation came before medical attention. San Francisco's LGBTQ community responded quickly, however, setting up blood donation campaigns, hospice care services, and more. The AIDS Quilt project was launched in San Francisco, with quilt panels sewn for every person who died in the epidemic—it was taken to Washington, D.C., in the early 1990s and covered a breathtakingly large part of the mall there.

As the deaths mounted at a horrifying pace, activists took direct action. ACT-UP and Queer Nation were two organizations that were unabashed at pushing the government and public health officials to do their jobs, utilizing tactics from crashing parties and conventions to confronting individual politicians and doctors who were blocking progress. San Francisco 'zines such as *Diseased Pariah News* combined information about possible new drugs and therapies with a scathing humor that blackly laughed in the face of death. The pharmaceutical industry even came under pressure from a surging campaign demanding new solutions to be delivered at a much quicker pace in the face of the ongoing mortality. Eventually, a multiple drug cocktail was developed that has allowed many HIV+ persons to live long and relatively healthy lives in spite of their infections. But it didn't come fast enough for the tens of thousands who died in the first years of the epidemic.

The grassroots gay movement that had elected progressive Harvey Milk to Supervisor in 1977 and defeated the 1978 Briggs Initiative statewide (that would have banned gays and lesbians from teaching in schools) was harshly decapitated by the AIDS epidemic. After a decade of profound horror and fear, the survivors were exhausted. After another decade, gay politics turned toward marriage equality in lieu of a broader social agenda that also addressed racism, poverty, and war. Much of the cross-movement solidarity that characterized the 1970s gay liberationists was replaced by a strong drive toward assimilation; many in the gay community prospered in the neoliberal real estate, tech, and medical sectors of the 2000s, leaving behind the more left-wing politics of the community's origins. Feminism, too, failed to reconnect to the broader social agenda implied by the solidarity and cross-movement alliances that gave rise to its early successes.

Nevertheless, medicine would never again be left exclusively to the men in white lab coats. Deference to the power of expertise was eroded during the decades of women's activism, and then gay and lesbian activism (building on the earlier feminist successes). With the surge of women and gays in medicine, some of the long-term institutional biases and failures of the medical industry have been alleviated—with more yet to achieve.

D18: FIFTY YEARS OF MISSION MURALS (1972–2018)

Balmy Alley/Clarion Alley

Balmy Alley (formally Balmy Street) is a one-block alley between 24th and 25th Streets where murals began to appear in 1972. That year, two women who called themselves Mujeres Muralistas (the women muralists), painted their first joint mural. (Other murals in the neighborhood predated this, for example, Michael Rios's epic on the walls of the MCO office at 23rd and Folsom.) A few murals were added sporadically thereafter along the alley until 1984, when Ray Patlán brought some three dozen mural activists together and proposed a joint project in which each garage door or fence segment facing the alley would display a mural. They would be linked by dual theme: celebration of indigenous Central American cultures and protest of U.S. intervention in Central America. The organizational rubric for Balmy Alley was *Placa*, which in Spanish refers to license plate, which became the tag, plaque, or mark made by taggers.

The residents and owners whose property backed onto Balmy were mostly Latino, and while some were initially skeptical about giving permission for murals on their property, nearly all embraced the project once it began. In the summer of 1985, 27 murals were painted, and a large dedication celebration was held in September of that year. The project was funded (at $2,500!) by a single grant from the Zellerbach Foundation and a generous provision of paints by the local distributor of Politec Mural Paints. Balmy Alley became a highly influential art project, leading to the La Lucha Continua Art Park in New York City the following year, and received more publicity than any other community mural project in San Francisco's history. In the 2000s, new murals have been added to the mix in Balmy Alley, including a scathing and hilarious indictment of gentrification by Lucia Ippolito and Tirso Araiza, and Sirron Norris's surprisingly political cartoon "Victorion," turning a Transformers-like character into a gentrification-stomping but friendly monster.

In 1977, artists Luis and Susan Cervantes founded the nonprofit Precita Eyes Mural Project, and over four decades they have sponsored over 100 murals in the Mission District, including the majestic *Maestrapeace* on the Women's Building on 18th Street and the full facade of Cesar Chavez Elementary School on Shotwell Street. Artists such as Juana Alicia have had a huge impact on the neighborhood mural scene, from her role in *Maestrapeace* to the subversive *Las Lechugeras* that once depicted the aerial spraying with poisonous pesticides of women farmworkers (on Taqueria San Francisco at York and 24th Streets). After that mural was tagged and degraded, she painted a new one on the same wall, the remarkable *La Llorona* mural with water as its theme. There are many other muralists who have contributed to the Mission District murals that still fill the neighborhood.

In the 1990s, a completely different group of artists came together to transform Clarion Alley, just south of 17th Street from Mission to Valencia Streets. The Clarion Alley Mural Project (CAMP) refers to a specific place and project without historical or cultural overtones. Clarion Alley has no thematic focus comparable to Balmy Alley's. The originating group was part of a new generation of community public artists. None had participated in painting Balmy Alley, although they knew of the project. What is more, none had a background in mural painting. They brought an entirely new sensibility to the creation of a mural cluster. There is no theme or shared palette or stylistic consistency. Thus there is no claim to a unified perspective or even of agreement on what issues are important. In fact, Clarion Alley is notable (at least compared with earlier murals) in its lack of formal left-wing themes, though perhaps because of the steady turnover of artists and murals in the alley, many have come to address police violence, evictions, and the politics of a gentrifying city.

Other prominent artists who have painted large walls in the Mission with remarkable murals include Mona Caron (most of her murals are along the western edge of the neighborhood, e.g., 15th and Church Streets, 22nd and Church Streets, 24th St. Community Park, and the Duboce Bikeway), and Joel Bergner, who left several murals commenting on the influx of Central American refugees in various locations around the neighborhood, including in Balmy Alley. Eric Norberg and Mike Ramos led the youth from H.O.M.E.Y. in painting the stunning *Solidarity: Breaking Down Barriers* along the fence behind the parking lot on 24th and Capp Streets.

D19: SLA KIDNAPS AND RANSOMS PATTY HEARST: PEOPLE IN NEED (1974)

China Basin Building at 4th Street along Mission Creek

In the early 1970s, a great number of bombings were taking place around the United States, including in the San Francisco Bay Area. Different political groups claimed these attacks and offered various public communiqués to explain the rationale of their attacks. One group that emerged during this period was the Symbionese Liberation Army (SLA). They came to public attention after their November 1973 assassination of the superintendent of the Oakland Public Schools, Marcus Foster (the first African American Superintendent of the district). The SLA's communiqué explained that Foster was promoting a new student identification card and that he supported having police in schools, neither of which was actually true. They ended with the chilling slogan that reappeared on most of their communiqués: "Death to the fascist insect that preys on the life of the People!" Joseph Remiro and Russell Little were convicted of the murder and given life sentences, though Little's was overturned in 1981 and he was released. A few months later, in February 1974, the SLA kidnapped newspaper heiress Patty Hearst from her dorm apartment in Berkeley, in order to ransom her in exchange for their imprisoned comrades. When the authorities refused to release Remiro or Little, the SLA redirected their efforts to the Hearst Family. They demanded that $2 million of food be organized and distributed to poor families in the San Francisco Bay Area and Southern California.

On February 22, 1974, the first day of distribution took place, and so many people showed up that workers began throwing food from the back of the trucks. Then-governor Ronald Reagan declared publicly that he wished there would be an outbreak of botulism resulting from the free food. The SLA issued a follow-up communiqué demanding that community groups be put in charge of the food distribution, and during the following month over a million dollars' worth of food was given away, mostly from the China Basin building along Mission Creek at 4th Street. San Franciscan Darrell Rogers, who was at the time still on active duty in the Army and working at the commissary at the Presidio, personally got involved to ensure that a good mix of fresh and healthy food was made available to each person and that it was well packaged to guarantee that it could be carried home properly (Carlsson: 2016).

The unexpected outcome called the People In Need food distribution program was the shotgun marriage of various community groups who were appointed to run the program: Glide Memorial Church, the American Indian Movement, the Black Teachers Caucus, Nairobi College in East Palo Alto, the United Prisoners Union, and the National Welfare Rights Organization. As a result, a number of activists from the Haight Ashbury, the Fillmore, Chinatown, the Mission District, Bayview Hunters Point, and other neighborhoods found themselves cooperating on a complicated social service mission as volunteers. The program didn't last much beyond a month, but the relationships continued, and in early 1975, the first Community Congress was held to hammer out a political agenda for the City. The Congress resolved to support district elections for Supervisor (which began in 1977), and to back George Moscone in the coming mayoral election, an election Moscone won by a mere 4,000 votes.

Patty Hearst was held in various safe houses around San Francisco during her captivity (including some time in a closet at 1827 Golden Gate Ave.) until the shocking announcement two months after her kidnapping that she had joined the SLA and declared her revolutionary name as Tania. She was caught on video at the Hibernia Bank Branch at 22nd Avenue and Noriega Street with a machine gun helping to carry out a bank robbery. After most of the SLA members were killed in a brutal assault by the Los Angeles Police, who burned down the house they were in, the continuing

FBI hunt finally found Patty Hearst and another SLA woman, Wendy Yoshimura, in an apartment near Daly City about a year later. Hearst was tried and convicted of bank robbery and served 22 months in jail before having her sentence commuted by President Jimmy Carter in 1979; she was pardoned by President Bill Clinton on his last day in office in 2001.

D20: PLAZA SANDINO (1974–79)

24th Street BART Plazas

The 24th Street BART Station has since its 1972 opening become a gathering place for political protest in the Mission District. Unlike most of the sterile, brutalist BART stations throughout the system, the BART plazas on the southwest and northeast corners of 24th and Mission Streets are genuinely rooted in the life of the neighborhood (as are the mirror-image plazas at 16th and Mission). These functional spaces, enlivened with political rallies, religious declamation, unannounced free performances of rocking salsa and punk bands, free phone distribution, and vendors' booths, have given this place a unique personality. Decorated on its northeastern side by a 1972 fresco depicting the community resistance to the imposition of BART with its expected impacts of displacement and exploitation on the Latino neighborhood, the two diagonal plazas have been animated over the years by massive political gatherings and demonstrations.

Third Worldism fueled the politics of the 1970s, emerging forcefully from the many struggles of the late 1960s, including the Black Panthers (D11), Los Siete de la Raza (D16), Alcatraz (D14), the I-Hotel (D3), and especially the 1968–69 San Francisco State strike (D13). By the mid-1970s, local political attention was focusing on anti-apartheid and liberation movements in Southern Africa, the aftermath of the 1973 coup in Chile, the ongoing war in Vietnam, and the emerging revolutionary movements in Nicaragua and Iran.

The 24th Street BART plaza was given the moniker Plaza Sandino, named by Sandinista activists in the Mission District's large Nicaraguan community, who used the plaza to mobilize support for the revolution against the Somoza dictatorship. Recent San Francisco Poet Laureate

Alejandro Murguía and longtime Mission District veteran Roberto Vargas were both prominent pro-Sandinista activists who went to Nicaragua to fight during the revolution. Others in the neighborhood like Walter Ferretti, Raúl Venerio, Lygia S., Haroldo Solano, and Bérman Zúniga returned to play prominent roles in the revolution and post-revolutionary Nicaraguan government and military. A newspaper, *La Gaceta Sandinista*, was launched and by 1977 was distributing 5,000 copies per issue, providing news and communiqués from the Sandinista National Liberation Front in Nicaragua. In September 1976, three local activists seized the Nicaraguan Consulate in the Flood Building on Market Street to bring attention to the fight. By 1978, most of the dedicated revolutionaries in San Francisco had gone to Nicaragua to fight (Murguía: 2011).

During the same era, contemporaneous supporters of the Iranian Revolution held public demonstrations in the plaza, too. The civil war in El Salvador was boiling at the same time, and solidarity and demonstrations of mutual support between both revolutionary movements were common. As both Iran and Nicaragua won their revolutions in 1979, other solidarity movements took over the plaza in the early 1980s, notably activists protesting Reagan's illegal wars in Central America. With the influx of refugees from Central America in the 1980s, the Mission District reached its peak demographic density as a decidedly working-class, Latino cultural neighborhood. Since then, it's been the City's incubator and epicenter of Latino political and cultural resistance, from the Sanctuary City movement to Carnaval to the lowrider culture. Antiwar protesters gathered here to protest the first Gulf War in 1991, and again to protest the invasion of Iraq in 2003, while immigrants staging a massive 2006 May Day strike gathered here. The old Plaza Sandino is still a key public space for politics, music, and occasionally public discussion well into the twenty-first century.

D21: WHITE NIGHT RIOT (1979)

City Hall, 1 Dr. Carlton B. Goodlett Place

On May 21, 1979, thousands of people attacked City Hall in the wake of the voluntary manslaughter verdict handed down to former cop and right-wing city supervisor Dan White. On November 27, 1978, White went to

City Hall where he murdered Mayor George Moscone, reloaded his police handgun with six more bullets, and sought out Supervisor Harvey Milk, the first elected gay Supervisor, and shot him. Both politicians received two bullets to the head to guarantee their execution. A bizarre confession and trial followed, where White's lawyer presented the "Twinkie Defense" to argue that Dan White had been temporarily insane from eating too much junk food (among other reasons). The argument convinced a jury of white homeowning San Franciscans that Dan White, a former cop and former fireman, a good family man, hadn't committed first-degree murder. When the jury delivered a verdict of voluntary manslaughter, the City erupted.

The gay community, which quickly gathered in the Castro, marched down Market Street to City Hall. The angry mob swung into Polk Street, and after some impassioned, impromptu speeches on the steps of City Hall, began breaking windows and chasing police away. As the evening progressed, twelve squad cars were set on fire, which created a vivid scene of billowing smoke and wailing sirens. The rioters at the outset had been overwhelmingly gay and lesbian but were soon joined by hundreds of young African American men from the nearby Western Addition (Carlsson: 2019). Police managed to break up the mob after several hours. Later that night a group of officers seeking revenge for their humiliation at City Hall entered the Castro District and indiscriminately attacked people in bars (famously at the Elephant Walk bar at 18th and Castro), stores, and their homes, before being ordered to retreat by their commander. Following the riot, photocopied flyers appeared around the Castro and the Haight saying "D.I.S.H. Don't Snitch (Dangerous Information Seems Harmless)" and another portrayed a burning police car with the slogan "No Apologies!"

Less than two dozen were arrested that night, and no one ultimately went to jail for the riot. Stepped-up recruiting in the LGBTQ community led to a rising number of queer cops in subsequent years, but a long-term mistrust between the gay community and the police erupted again a decade later during the "Castro Sweep" police riot.

AIDS activists held a protest in the Civic Center on October 6, 1989, not unlike many other of the era, but this time, police took a very aggressive approach to the event. After riding herd on the marchers as they made their way from Civic Center to the Castro, with phalanxes of motorcycles filling Market and dozens of cops standing along the sidewalk with billy clubs to keep everyone off the street, angry protesters spontaneously staged a sit-in at Market and Castro, while others engaged in a die-in farther down Castro. Police eschewed their normal policy of standing by and waiting for the demonstration to end and instead mounted a frontal assault on the hundreds of demonstrators in the Castro. Sweeping down the street and sidewalks, they clubbed dozens and left many bloodied and injured. Later legal actions forced the City to pay several hundred thousand dollars in compensatory damages (Koskovich: 2002).

D22: Fleet Week and Blocking the Return of the USS *Missouri* (1983–87)

Pier 32

During the mid-1980s, a broad social campaign developed in favor of a nuclear freeze with the Soviet Union, and to urge the United States to ratchet back its military expansion and threats to use nuclear weapons in a first strike. The campaign took many forms, including petitions, peaceful marches (nearly 1 million participated nationwide in the 1982 nuclear freeze marches), and boisterous demonstrations in front of government offices, Bechtel Corporation and PG&E on Beale Street (both very involved

The Peace Navy confronts the USS Missouri *in San Francisco Bay. (© Janet Delaney)*

in the nuclear industry), and along the waterfront and on the bay. In the wake of the near-collapse of the U.S. Army in Vietnam in the early 1970s, and the broad antipathy to the military that resulted from the horrors they perpetrated in the war in southeast Asia, a purported Vietnam Syndrome had developed in which Americans refused to fight. In fact, a thoughtful rejection of the militarism that characterized U.S. foreign policy from WWII to the present was enjoying its highest popularity.

The Reagan administration came to power in 1981 determined to overcome the syndrome and embarked on a rapid expansion of military spending while aggressively amping up anti-communist rhetoric in the wake of the 1979 revolutions in Iran and Nicaragua. In 1983, Reagan sent the U.S. military to attack the tiny Caribbean island of Grenada ostensibly because it was being taken over by communists. Though barred by congressional action, the administration also illegally armed a military force to attack the Sandinista government in Nicaragua in what became known as the Contra War. Simultaneously, the U.S. government was pouring military and diplomatic resources into supporting government-sponsored right-wing death squads in El Salvador, Guatemala, and Honduras—all bordering Nicaragua.

The San Francisco Bay Area, long an epicenter of antiwar activism during the Vietnam War, again emerged as a locus for the antinuclear and antiwar movements of this era. Direct actions to block arms shipments to Central America in the eastern suburbs led to Brian Willson losing his legs to a munitions train that wouldn't stop after he laid across the tracks. Die-ins in the Financial District, a "Hall of Shame" tour in which hundreds of protesters moved from one corporate headquarters to the next in day-long demonstrations decrying the role of local companies in the war machine, and lockdowns and blockades of roads, buildings, and ports during this period, all contributed to growing opposition to the federal war efforts.

Mayor Dianne Feinstein reintroduced Fleet Week in 1981, a celebration of the Navy and the military with roots in the early twentieth century that had been cancelled for a decade. Activists opposed to the homeporting of the USS *Missouri* latched onto Fleet Week as a perfect venue to highlight their efforts. With thousands of people thronging the waterfront to visit warships and watch the Blue Angels, activists were able to explain to many the hidden plans to convert the old battleship into a nuclearized first-strike vessel. If successful, this would destabilize the mutually assured destruction doctrine that seemed to be holding the United States and U.S.S.R. in a steady-state Cold War (bad, but preferable to an actual nuclear war!). With the energy mobilized during those months, the House Armed Services Committee under Berkeley representative Ron Dellums defeated the USS *Missouri* homeporting plan, and by the end of the 1980s, nearly every military base in the Bay Area had been slated for decommissioning. In what was probably meant to be a rebuke to local antiwar sentiment, the demilitarization of so much desirable real estate actually led to an explosion of mostly new parklands, while in some areas a great deal of new housing and commercial space was created.

The Peace Navy, founded in 1983, at its peak had a fleet of over 100 privately owned boats ranging from kayaks and windsurfers to day sailors and blue water yachts, sailing under the motto *Join the Peace Navy and Save the World*. Members were boilermakers and carpenters, doctors and lawyers, students and pensioners, artists and filmmakers of all ages. Among the more dramatic actions pulled off by the Bay Area Peace Navy in conjunction with broader campaigns was the blockading of the USS *Missouri* when it steamed into harbor to promote a new homeporting in San Francisco. In 1983, some Peace Navy sailors also helped place fake harbor mines around the Alameda Naval Air Station to dramatize the illegal mining of the harbors in Nicaragua by the Reagan administration, and months later two of their activists were briefly taken prisoner by U.S.-funded Contras in Nicaragua. Collaborating with peace activists and organized labor, Peace Navy sailors showed up to protest nuclearization of the Navy, dumping of bay dredge into traditional fishing grounds offshore, discriminatory immigration policies against Haitians, arms shipments to Central America, and much more.

D23: WARCHEST TOURS 1984 AT THE DEMOCRATIC NATIONAL CONVENTION

50 Beale Street

The Democrats had chosen San Francisco's new Moscone Convention Center for their four-day National Convention in 1984, to nominate Walter Mondale for president. Activists determined to oppose the Democrats from the grassroots Left organized the Warchest Tours. They used roving guerrilla-theater nonviolent direct action to confront the corporations that funded and controlled the Democratic Party and were involved in nuclear weapons and military intervention. The form of the tour was taken from the Hall of Shame tours, which were mobile protest tours that stopped at the corporations behind the nuclear industry in the spring of 1982. They were organized by anarchists in the antinuclear power/weapons movement, who were probably inspired by the 1971 May Day protests against the Vietnam War that had paralyzed the Financial District when protesters besieged multiple corporations that were known to be involved in the war effort.

While most of the Left in the Bay Area were either supporting the Democrats or keeping silent, 455 people were arrested and many were beaten by the San Francisco police under Mayor (now Senator) Dianne Feinstein. Mayor Feinstein and the San Francisco police waged a campaign of repression to clean up and assert control over the City for the convention: attacking demonstrations; harassing homeless people, prostitutes, punks and people who lived in their vehicles; attempting to close gay bathhouses; requiring permits for street musicians; and issuing new taxi permits in opposition to the Taxi Drivers Alliance. A month before the convention an ad-hoc coalition of prostitutes, homeless people, cab drivers, street musicians, and activists were clubbed off the steps of City Hall after a protest and press conference against the clampdown and cleanup.

The Warchest Tours were also a living critique of the Left's forms of protest: monitors controlling and moving people like cattle, tactical leaders with bullhorns repeating monotonous chants, and even antinuclear sit-down-and-wait-for-the police-to-arrest-you civil disobedience that felt too much on the terms of the police. The Warchest Tours Collective encouraged avoiding arrest, nonviolent direct action, guerrilla theater, creative protest, and fun. They advertised NO MONITORS, refused to ask or negotiate permission from the police, and chose not to pursue corporate media coverage.

The first Warchest Tour began in the plaza of Bank of America world headquarters on the first day—Monday—of the convention. Two hundred people gathered and listened to one of the Warchest Tour collectives explain how the Democrats and Bank of America were involved with each other and the bank's investments in South Africa, Poland, etc. After the speech, protesters counted down "10-9-8-7-6-5-4-3-2-1!" and staged a die-in. After a minute, they jumped up to cross the street and gathered on the steps of Diamond Shamrock, producers of the cancerous defoliant Agent Orange (used in the Vietnam War and in tropical rainforests around the world), the subject of a lawsuit by Agent Orange-sickened Vietnam Vets and major contributors to the Democrats. As the information about Diamond Shamrock was being read, a line of 50 helmeted, club-wielding riot cops marched up Kearny Street and surrounded the demonstration. The Police captain announced that everyone was under arrest for "felony conspiracy to commit a misdemeanor." With no way out, demonstrators sat down and chanted "Democracy in action."

The second day of Warchest Tours went off without arrests or conflict, but on Thursday July 19, the last day of the convention, the final Warchest Tour turned into a bitter fight. It started at a Rock Against Racism/ Reagan concert on Mission Street featuring the Dead Kennedys among other bands, near the Moscone Center protest zone. The tour left with 400 people as the concert began. After several stops, they were kettled by mounted police on Kearny Street. More than half the tour ran away through a parking lot or made it through police lines, but others were arrested and some were brutalized by police. After the concert, the audience took to the streets and marched to the Hall of Justice. A satirical giant Trojan donkey (which ate mock tax dollars and shat out toy weapons) joined the march. At the Hall of Justice protesters yelled, "Set them free," facing an army of helmeted police. The police declared an unlawful assembly, and ordered everyone to disperse. Several hundred in the front sat down. The police and sheriffs moved in and arrested over 300 people. Meanwhile, in the Democratic National Convention, Walter Mondale, as expected, was nominated Democratic Party presidential candidate, with his running mate Geraldine Ferraro, the first woman ever nominated to the vice presidency.

D24: PERSIAN GULF WAR PROTESTS (1990–91)

Essex and Harrison Streets, entrance to Bay Bridge

In the late months of 1990, with the emancipation of Eastern Europe (but not yet the disintegration of the Soviet Union that would happen later in 1991), George H. W. Bush at the United Nations embraced a New World Order. Bush sought to reclaim the international spotlight from Soviet leader Mikael Gorbachev, who had originally launched a campaign for a New World Order several years earlier. Bush's speech was ultimately interpreted as a call for a unipolar world dominated by the United States—it would work with allies as able and useful, but the United States would take the lead and do what it wanted without subjecting itself to any international controls. (More than a quarter-century later, it is clear that the assertion of U.S. hegemony was a turning point (in the wrong direction). Instead of turning to a soft power strategy of building and reinforcing a more humanitarian and less militaristic world system, the attack on Iraq and the decades of war in the Middle East ever since have eroded U.S. power and made the world far less stable.)

In San Francisco, tens of thousands of people marched against military intervention in the Middle East every weekend in the last months of 1990, as the belligerence and warmongering grew louder nationally. By the time Bush invaded Kuwait and sent the air force on a "turkey shoot" over the exit route for the Iraqi Army, over 150,000 people were marching in the streets. CNN made its name as the go-to cable news source during the Shock and Awe 24-hour propaganda campaign. Meanwhile, San Franciscans marched, rode bikes, and blocked bridges, highways, intersections, and building lobbies. Paper Tiger TV-West broke the media blockade by shooting video of these protests and sharing them widely; they also broadcast footage from other cities around the United States and the world, showing how huge the antiwar opposition really was, putting the lie to the claims that everyone was patriotic and enthusiastic about the war.

The hostilities officially ended after just a few weeks. The United States withdrew its no-fly zone over Iraqi Kurdistan and allowed Saddam Hussein's air force to bomb northern Iraq to destroy the Kurdish opposition. The duplicitous instigation of the Persian Gulf War was percolating in the underground press and on email, but never made it to the mainstream news. U.S. ambassador April Glaspie had been asked directly by the Iraqi Foreign Minister if the United States "had a position on Iraq's claim to its 9th province (i.e., Kuwait)"? And she had told him clearly "no, the U.S. doesn't have a position." A few weeks later, Iraq's military rolled into Kuwait and then were surprised when the United States and its coalition partners launched a full-scale invasion to drive them back out again. Just eight years earlier, Donald Rumsfeld had been a special envoy to Hussein from President Ronald Reagan. His job had to been to arrange arms shipments and other support for Saddam Hussein in his war with

Iran. The Reagan administration was later humiliated by the Iran-Contra Scandal, wherein they authorized the sale of weapons to Iran, and took the black market money they were paid and used it illegally to fund arms for the so-called Contra rebels in Nicaragua.

President Bush lost his reelection bid to Bill Clinton in 1992, the pyrrhic victory over Saddam Hussein's Iraq providing only the briefest of bumps to his sinking popularity. But Clinton and his successor George W. Bush both kept harsh sanctions on Iraq, and eventually Bush II—with Donald Rumsfeld as his defense secretary—began the full-scale invasion of Iraq over the false assertion that Hussein was developing weapons of mass destruction.

D25: Reclaim May Day to Seattle WTO (1998–99)

Dolores Park

In 1998 and 1999, Bay Area activists organized Reclaim May Day in San Francisco, a boisterous unpermitted parade featuring homemade floats and over a dozen performances covering radical history, tenants rights and evictions, LGBTQI rights, women's rights, anti-racist struggles, and more. A dozen political groups including Art & Revolution, the Eviction Defense Collaborative, Shaking San Francisco, Wise Fool Puppet Theater, and others performed at different corners and plazas along the Mission and Market Streets parade route, highlighting a wide range of issues of the day. Each year the parade ended in a festival in Dolores Park.

Following the two Reclaim May Day parades in 1998 and 1999, many participants joined a Global Day of Action Against Capitalism on July 18, 1999. Several hundred protesters staged a new Hall of Shame tour of downtown corporations. During that July 1999 day, an anonymous group briefly shut down a key block of Montgomery Street in the Financial District, crisscrossing the street with Caution and Do Not Enter tape and hundreds of swaying neckties on rope proclaiming "Wall Street West is All Tied Up!"

In November 1999, hundreds of Bay Area activists went to Seattle to participate in the successful effort to shut down the World Trade Organization, key locals having spent a year touring up and down the West

Coast to build support for the effort. A spokescouncil met daily in the convergence center in Seattle, and out of this experience Indymedia was founded using new cheap video and Internet distribution in an attempt to overcome the self-censoring of the networks and mainstream media. (The phenomenon was soon co-opted by Bay Area tech behemoths in the form of YouTube, Facebook, and Twitter, all of which started later in the 2000s.)

D26: RESISTING THE TECH INVASION (1999–2001, 2014–18)

22nd and Mission Streets

The Mission Anti-Displacement Coalition (MAC) was officially founded in late 1999 led by activists from primarily Mission Housing, St. Peter's Housing Committee, and People Organized to Demand Environmental

A half-dozen tech buses are blocked by a pile of e-scooters in May 2018 at 24th and Valencia in the Mission District. (Chris Carlsson)

and Employment Rights (PODER). Simultaneously in that era, artists, dancers, and unaffiliated leftists were organizing against the onslaught of new restaurants, boutiques, and yuppies (young urban professionals) who were tangibly altering the texture of the neighborhood. Evictions were soaring alongside rents and the historic population of the neighborhood was being sent packing. MAC developed a list of demands with which to confront the San Francisco Planning Department: moratoriums on 1) new market-rate housing and live-work lofts in the Mission District, 2) office conversion and new digital office construction, and 3) illegal conversions and occupation of live-work lofts by Internet businesses. In addition, MAC called for the full funding of a community planning process to rezone the Mission District.

Protesters occupied the Dancers' Group/Footwork second-floor studio at 22nd and Mission Streets, and supporters spilled out into the intersection during a boisterous protest against displacement in 2000. Across the street in the Bayview Bank Building, a rare multistory office tower in the Mission District, a dot-com start-up called BigStep.com had engineered the eviction of several floors of Spanish-language media companies, nonprofits, and small businesses, sparking outrage. Almost two decades later, paint bombs that splattered the walls of the building during the protests are still visible from Mission Street.

Another site of concerted opposition was at the corner of Bryant and 20th Streets, where developers sought to demolish a large older structure full of nearly 60 small businesses, nonprofits, and artists. When the city government approved their project, the developers evicted a sweater factory, a furniture factory, a sex toy factory, a custom garment maker, a nonprofit publisher, four dozen photographers, graphic artists, sound designers, and filmmakers, including the award-winning Latina filmmaker Lourdes Portillo. After lying empty for several years, a soulless apartment building full of upscale condominiums was built and occupies the site today.

Ultimately, the vibrant mobilization that rocked the Mission District during the height of the dot-com boom of 1999–2000 subsided. Denied all efforts to block pell-mell development, organizers did gain support for a city-funded, community-based zoning and land use committee. The plans developed by this committee emerged a few years later but never galvanized the kind of widespread participation and activism that had led to its creation in the first place. The community's zoning plan addressed the eastern former industrial area near Dogpatch east and south of Potrero Hill, the North Mission's old industrial plants, and parts of western South of Market, all areas that have been radically impacted by the booming growth of Mission Bay's UCSF campus and surrounding apartments and offices. Dozens of mixed-income apartment and condominium complexes have been built in these neighborhoods during the subsequent 15 years, but the onslaught of displacement has only accelerated.

Tech Invasion II

After some years of relative quiescence, in January 2014 a few dozen spirited activists set up professional-looking traffic signs and banners to trap a Google Bus at the corner of 8th and Market. Thus began a campaign of theatrical direct action that eventually included protesters wearing official-looking yellow vests and mimes dressed as the colorful bouncing balls that were then Google's trademark, blocking private luxury shuttle buses in the Mission District and elsewhere in the San Francisco Bay Area. The months-long campaign was meant to highlight the drastic rise in housing prices and the tidal wave of evictions taking place along the routes of the new private bus lines serving the giant Silicon Valley corporations' campuses (Google, Facebook, Apple, Electronic Arts, Yahoo, and closer to San Francisco Genentech, among others). It also sought to shine a light on the absurdity of what had quietly become the norm: allowing private luxury buses to commandeer public bus stops to pick up and discharge handsomely rewarded tech workers (only employees with electronic ID badges could board any specific bus), while actual public buses serving the paying general public were delayed, blocked, and often stuck mid-street where elderly and disabled passengers struggled to access their doors. Later actions during the following year invaded the San Francisco headquarters of Airbnb, Uber, and Twitter—all scions of the new tech economy. The much-heralded "disruption" they brought to the economy generated enormous profits for investors and owners while sending thousands further into debt traps, precarious gig employment, and driving housing costs out of reach for all but the nouveaux riches.

San Francisco's long tradition of clever dissent once again got national headlines, along with denials and obfuscations by the targeted companies, and buck-passing from City Hall. A new campaign briefly erupted in early summer 2018, when three competing electric scooter companies — following the disruptive lead pioneered by Uber and Lyft—began putting thousands of their scooters around San Francisco (and dozens of other cities worldwide), blocking sidewalks, cluttering bike racks, and generally annoying far more people than they pleased. Several dozen activists gathered a bunch of scooters and occupied the intersection of 24th and Valencia Streets, using the scooters to block traffic lanes precisely as several luxury tech commuter buses were arriving. For a couple of hours about a dozen buses serving Google, Facebook, Apple, and others were stuck, unable to proceed due to the piles of scooters and protesters blocking their way. This time the outrage forced the City to impose a moratorium. The vendors had to withdraw their scooters and submit to regulations.

D27: IRAQ WAR PROTESTS (2003)

Federal Building, 450 Golden Gate Avenue

Well over 100,000 antiwar demonstrators jammed Market Street on January 18, 2003, two months before the war on Iraq started. On February 15, joining a worldwide turnout that was estimated at 12 million, another 150,000 people filled the entire length of Market Street from the Civic Center to the bay.

The Bush-Cheney administration had orchestrated a campaign of lies, insisting that Saddam Hussein's Iraq (their erstwhile ally in the 1980s) had so-called weapons of mass destruction, and that his regime was somehow involved in supporting Al-Qaeda and the attackers who staged 9/11. Both claims were blatantly false, argued protesters, and were proven so in the years that followed. But the mainstream media perpetuated the fraud, and a great many U.S. citizens fell in line with the belligerent plans of the rulers. In San Francisco, and in most cities across the country, tens of thousands of people mobilized in a new antiwar effort to block the war at home. The invasion capped more than a decade of punitive sanctions following the first Gulf War in 1991. Those sanctions had already destroyed

February 15, 2003, 150,000 people march against the Iraq War plans of Bush and Cheney. (Chris Carlsson)

much of the infrastructure of Iraq along with the basic standard of living—worse still, countless children were denied medicine and food by the decade-long economic strangulation.

Organizers of Direct Action to Stop the War planned mass action for months. Postcards flooded the Bay Area calling for people to gather at the foot of Market Street, downtown's main thoroughfare, at 7 a.m. the morning of the next business day after war began. A menu of locations was prepared to help people select targets to shut down. Affinity groups would fan out into the Financial District to carry out nonviolent direct actions, blockading dozens of intersections, war-profiteering corporations such as Chevron and Bechtel, and the local headquarters of NBC, CNN, and other media. Most of these targets were concentrated in about ten square blocks. On March 20, 2003, over 20,000 protesters appeared in free-flowing spontaneous actions that augmented the preorganized affinity groups, increasing their strength and effectiveness exponentially.

Roving groups of cyclists and pedestrians surged back and forth across downtown for hours. Police were overwhelmed and were unable to open major thoroughfares until early afternoon, and even then blockades continued until evening in many locations. For a time, the on- and off-ramps to the Bay Bridge were blocked too. It was full paralysis for downtown San Francisco, and given the numbers participating in the action, there was little the police could do. More than 1,000 arrests were made that day. The next day more blockades by far fewer people were staged, but very quickly it became apparent that there was no sustained population willing to keep up the momentum. Much to the disillusionment of everyone who had taken part in the many large mobilizations since late 2002 and ramping up to the beginning of war, the antiwar movement this time was unable to prevent or even slow down the war effort. When U.S. troops rolled into Baghdad within a few short days, and Bush foolishly declared Mission Accomplished, neither the warmongers nor the demoralized antiwar forces could imagine that the war was actually just beginning and it would go on for more than a decade, leading to over a million refugees and several hundred thousand deaths. By 2018, Iraq was still in a state of chaos in many places, its central government only marginally in control of provinces to the west and the Kurdish north, and the only glimmer of normalcy was to be found in the oil fields of the south, where British Petroleum, Chevron, and other multinational oil companies had resumed the rapid extraction and export of Iraq's oil.

D28: BAY AREA OCCUPY (2011)

Spear and Market Streets; Frank Ogawa Plaza in Oakland

During the nationwide Occupy movement that took hold in 1,600+ cities and towns during the last months of 2011, San Francisco had its Occupy encampment at the foot of Market Street, beginning at Spear and Market Streets in front of the Federal Reserve Bank building, and later spreading to the new boccie ball courts along Steuart Street opposite Justin Herman Plaza. San Jose, Santa Rosa, and Berkeley also had Occupy camps. Countless participants in Critical Mass bike rides were often central organizers in the Occupations that sprung up around the country (Blue: 2011).

Oakland undoubtedly enjoyed the most robust Occupy encampment in the Bay Area. It began in the plaza facing City Hall named after Frank Ogawa Jr. (a successful litigant against the Japanese internment in WWII) but renamed Oscar Grant Plaza by the occupiers after the young African American man who was murdered by BART police in 2009. Starting in early October 2011, Occupy Oakland became a thriving self-managed community with a nightly assembly attended by hundreds and sometimes thousands. Participant D. Scot Miller eloquently described the scene:

> What distinguished Occupy Oakland from all of the other Occupies was full community cooperation at the very beginning. Though Oakland Mayor Jean Quan is vilified now for cracking down on the movement, she was intentionally hands-off during those first few weeks. The City of Oakland provided safety for the occupiers, while the Teacher's Union donated portable toilets; the Nurse's Union contributed time and supplies; and the community at large furnished food, grills, and tarps. Twenty-four hours a day, a union member or volunteer was working the grill, handing out food, or helping out in some way.
>
> As one of the guys holding down the media center, which was powered by a bicycle generator, I covered all of the other

Occupy movements and shared information with them. Having been involved during those early days, I can say that Occupy Oakland was the most realized and comfortable Occupy site. Compared to Oakland, all the other sites—including Occupy Wall Street in New York—looked, well, busted. Just a quick glance at the Occupy San Francisco site, for example, revealed people who had to sleep under tarps on the sidewalk, who were hounded by both the police and the people already living on the streets, and who were eating cold bologna sandwiches out of paper bags. In Oakland, we had lentil soup, daycare, a library, and wide-screen movies. . . .

Occupy Oakland had people of color in key positions contributing to most of the major decisions for the first two weeks. Black people, brown people, and white people handled the kitchen, the daycare, the library, and the media center. The daily general assembly was moderated by black, brown, and white people. The march around Lake Merritt, and the nonviolent sit-in on the banks along the way, were planned by a multiracial coalition.

I was *pulled* to Occupy Oakland every day. Every free moment I had, I *wanted* to be *there*. I did not want to watch TV or surf the web. I knew where I had to be. As the debates burned in the media about intent, I was so excited about what was going on in Oakland that I could barely sleep. So much charity! So much cooperation! So many informed people! And live music! And wine! And dancing! Downtown Oakland, a district that used to resemble a ghost town after 5:00 p.m., was vibrant again. (Miller: 2012)

On October 26, 2011, the day after a brutal police attack temporarily cleared the plaza, Occupy Oakland called for a general strike. On an amazingly warm and sunny November 2, 2011, it happened. The Oakland General Strike was an opening salvo from an unexpected quarter: the *pre-cariat* (a neologism made by combing precarious and proletariat). Local unions could not formally endorse the call in such a short time, and are often bound by no-strike clauses in their contracts. Nevertheless, rank-and-file members of the Service Employees International Union (SEIU 1021), the Teamsters, the International Longshore and Warehouse Union, and others enthusiastically joined in during the daylong festival that gripped the center of Oakland, culminating in the mass marches toward dusk that shut down the Port of Oakland, the nation's fifth-largest port. But organized labor was following, not leading this general strike. The people filled the city center with music, banners, marches, humor, performance, food, yoga, meditation, childcare, art-making, and more. Rappers, hip-hop spoken word artists, and folk musicians all performed in the streets. Urban farmers showed up with free vegetables grown in the city's reclaimed lots. Free valet bike parking was provided by local bicycle advocates. Dozens of economic and environmental justice activists were in the mix. The Oakland General Strike not only halted business as usual in much of Oakland, but demonstrated practical everyday alternatives that are already well entrenched in the area.

D29: Confronting Twenty-First Century Racist Police Violence (2009–2018)

Bernal Heights ring road; 19th and Shotwell Streets

Oscar Grant was shot at point-blank range while held down by a BART policeman at the Fruitvale Station in Oakland on January 1, 2009, at 2 a.m. When cellphone video went viral in the hours that followed, protesters soon filled the streets. Since Grant's murder, at least a dozen more police killings just in the Bay Area have galvanized a growing movement for police accountability and reform—if not abolition! San Francisco and Bay Area police violence have not gotten the attention that higher-profile cases have garnered, from Mike Brown in Ferguson, Missouri, to Eric Garner in Staten Island, New York, to Philando Castile in Minnesota, but are more similar than not to those cases.

San Francisco police officers racially profile and shuffle people of color into the prison pipeline, enforcing a persistent racial inequality in San Francisco. Police violence in gentrifying neighborhoods has remained a constant theme in recent police killings. Despite hiring many people of color, and gays and lesbians, the SFPD and its political arm, the Police Officer's Association, still represent the dominant hierarchical order of straight white malehood. Police officers almost always protect each other against the public, and are further protected by state, city, and judicial standards, some dating to the late 1800s, from any significant account-ability for using violence against civilians while on the job. Current law gives them a free pass as long as they *claim* a serious threat to themselves or another. Their notorious unaccountable role as the armed City force has led to protests against police brutality in the past and present. Apparently the SFPD has stopped harassing and beating white queers only for their gender identities (as they did for decades), but there's still a long way to go toward ending police brutality against people of color and the extremely poor in San Francisco.

On March 21, 2014, Alex Nieto, a 28-year-old Chicano City College student and nighttime security guard, was killed in a hail of 59 bullets in Bernal Heights Park by four officers. Nieto was well known among Mission District community youth organizations, and there was an imme-diate community pushback against the police narrative that criminalized him. A week later, an anti-eviction protest march led by *Danzantes* snaked through the neigborhood and up to Bernal to the site of his killing. The civil rights trial two years later proved that police were drawn to the hill after two young white techies called 911 only because they feared the sight of Nieto, sitting on a bench eating his dinner. Nieto's parents and peers—Mission homegirls and homeboys—began a sustained campaign for justice and against police brutality, rooted in Mission Latino working-class expe-rience and cultural expressions that would dovetail with the Black Lives Matter movement. In March 2016, the parents of Alex Nieto lost their civil rights trial by a jury verdict. However, the story of Alex Nieto told in court revealed a one-sided gun battle by police against a man who had been eating a burrito. Later that year, the Board of Supervisors granted the par-ents the right to build a permanent memorial for their son in Bernal Heights Park.

In 2013, three radical black women organizers—longtime San Franciscan Alicia Garza, along with Patrisse Cullors and Opal Tometi—launched #BlackLivesMatter (#BLM) in response to the Florida acquittal of Trayvon Martin's murderer, George Zimmerman. The meme highlighted that black lives are systematically, intentionally, and disproportionately targeted by police violence. After Mike Brown was killed on August 4, 2014, his community of Ferguson, Missouri, rose up in a sustained popular occupation of the streets, leading to the #BLM movement exploding on the national scene.

In November 2014, Black Lives Matter activists chained themselves between the West Oakland BART station platform and a stopped train on the morning of Black Friday, the day after Thanksgiving, bringing the system to a halt for several hours. Protesting police violence and corruption in Oakland (as in many other cities around California and the country) has led to repeated demonstrations with repeated seizures of freeway stretches by protesters, blocking traffic in both directions. These tactics didn't emerge spontaneously from the Black Lives Matter movement either, but had already been used by activists going back many years.

In San Francisco between 2014 and 2016, nine out of the twelve people killed by police were Latino and black. In February 2015, Amilcar Perez-López, a 21-year-old Guatemalan Mayan immigrant worker, was shot six times in the back by two undercover officers in front of his home. In December 2015, Mario Woods, a 26-year-old African American from the Bayview District, was gunned down in broad daylight by five officers. The Mission and Bayview communities banded together to demand justice. In response, the Police Commission approved a minor change to the City's Use of Force policy, promoting de-escalation tactics.

The killings of people of color by SFPD officers were taking place in the midst of revelations of the corrupt, racist, misogynist, and homophobic culture of the department, evidenced by a series of videos and text message scandals revealed in court cases. In April 2016, not even a month after the trial of Alex Nieto and just four months after the shooting of Mario Woods, SFPD killed again, this time taking the life of Luis Góngora Pat, a 45-year-old Mexican Mayan immigrant worker, who was living homeless at the time in the Mission District. By all witness accounts, the victim presented no threat to officers when they gunned him down.

The situation in San Francisco was untenable, and five lifelong Latino and black residents of the City spontaneously started what would become the longest hunger strike in San Francisco history, lasting 17 days. They became known as the Frisco 5. At a peak moment during the hunger strike, a massive march took the Frisco 5 in wheelchairs to City Hall to the raging demand of "Fire Chief Suhr!" The day after the hunger strike ended, in early May 2016, hundreds of community members stormed City Hall, resulting in the arrest of 33 protesters, earning the label "the Frisco 500."

Mayor Ed Lee reiterated in the days that followed that the City would pursue police reform with Chief Greg Suhr at the helm. Days later, on

May 19, Jessica Williams, a young black and homeless woman, four months pregnant, was shot to death by Sergeant Justin Erb while she was sitting in a stolen car. Finally, in the wake of Williams's pointless death, Chief Greg Suhr resigned.

On March 6, 2018, Jesus Adolfo Delgado, a 19-year-old undocumented Mexican youth—raised in the Mission District—was surrounded and shot by ten officers with 99 live rounds, as he hid from them in the trunk of a car. Community members demanded accountability for the endless police killings, knowing that not a single case since 1937 had led to charges filed. In April 2018, spearheaded by the movement of Justice for Luis Góngora Pat, community members held a 24-hour vigil for the 24 lives stolen by police on the steps of the Hall of Justice on 850 Bryant Street since District Attorney George Gascón entered office in 2011. The systemic complicity of the SFPD, the Office of the District Attorney, the Police Commission, and the courts in sustaining police violence against black and brown communities is an unresolved crisis in the City at this writing.

WALKING TOURS

NEW DEAL MURALS, TRASH & ITALIANS

1. Rincon Annex
2. Embarcadero Plaza
3. Sue Bierman Park
4. 33 Pacific Ave.
5. Old Produce Market
6. Sansome & Green
7. Filbert Steps
8. Coit Tower

BUILT
WORKS PROGRESS
ADMINISTRATION
1933 — 1939

IT'S HAPPENING HERE!

MARKET STREET: THE CONTESTED BOULEVARD

1. Ferry Plaza
2. Spear & Market
3. Sansome & Market
4. Lotta's Fountain
5. Powell & Market
6. 6th & Market
7. U.N. Plaza

SCANDALOUS SOMA

1. Palace Hotel
2. 3rd & Market
3. Stevenson Alley
4. Yerba Buena Gardens
5. Carousel
6. Lapu Lapu & Bonifacio
7. South Park
8. 3rd & King

KING TIDE TOUR OF MISSION BAY

1. Pier 36 tidal columns
2. Pier 36 history kiosks
3. Pier 38
4. Ballpark on McCovey Cove
5. China Basin Building
6. 4th St. Bridge to Huffaker Park
7. Pier 52 kiosk
8. 16th & 4th Streets
9. Pier 70, 20th & Illinois

MISSION SOCIAL MOVEMENTS

1. 24th & Bryant
2. Balmy Alley
3. 23rd & Folsom
4. Folsom at 22nd
5. Mission & 22nd
6. 22nd & Bartlett
7. Valencia at 23rd
8. 21st & Valencia
9. Dolores Park
10. Women's Building
11. Clarion Alley
12. 16th & Valencia

Appendix

SHAPING SAN FRANCISCO
TOUR ITINERARIES

Starting in 1995, when the original Shaping San Francisco project was still being conceived of as a computer game, I launched a labor history bike tour to raise money for the project. Over the years I added ecological history, which eventually divided into north and south, transit history, and dissent. After many years of giving these tours in multiple variations, LisaRuth Elliott and I began offering walking tours for the many people who weren't inclined to join us on bicycle. Bike tours to accompany our four thematic chapters are at the beginning of each of them. Here are five of our favorite walking tours for those who prefer to see the city on foot. Each of these is designed to take approximately 1.5–2.5 hours. Listed under each walking tour are "stops" followed by suggested entries in the book (e.g., D18, F.24) to look at while at that location. My abbreviated notes are included in parentheses, though you won't always be able to find a direct reference in this book. For those absences, I recommend perusing Foundsf.org, where there is something to learn about each of these suggested themes.

Walking Tours

Mission Social Movements

1. Balmy Alley
    D18, E24 (food conspiracies, Mujeres Muralistas)
2. 23rd and Folsom Streets
    D15, D12 (Mission Coalition Organization, redevelopment, poverty, communes)

3. Folsom at 22nd Street
   D16, D17 (El Centro de Salud, Los Siete de la Raza, contesting medical paradigms)
4. Mission and 22nd Streets
   D26, T12 (Mission Anti-Displacement Coalition, eviction, BART construction)
5. 22nd and Bartlett Streets
   D20 (La Gaceta Sandinista, underground comix)
6. Valencia and 23rd Street
   (de)Appropriation Parklet and Democracy Wall, Third Worldism
7. 21st and Valencia
   D17, D9 (women's consciousness raising and women's newspapers, punk scene Tool and Die, TWC poetry, Editorial Pocho-Ché)
8. Dolores Park
   L9 (Berkman and Goldman at 569 Dolores, Mission High School strike 1969)
9. Women's Building
   (1970s lesbian community, Briggs Initiative, separatism)
10. Clarion Alley
    D18 (Clarion Alley Mural Project)
11. 16th and Valencia
    (Quezada Center for Culture and Politics (former CP HQ), Roxie, Gartland Pit, Esta Noche)

New Deal Murals, Trash, and Italians (Rincon to Coit)

1. Rincon Annex gathering and introduction
   D5, E13, L2, L9 (Early history of Rincon Hill, eight-hour day movement, Tom Mooney and Preparedness Day bombing)
2. Justin Herman Plaza
   D1, T7, T14 (Underground Railroad, Transcontinental railroad, Critical Mass, 1896 "good roads" movement)
3. Sue Bierman Park
   T11 (The Freeway Revolt)
4. 33 Pacific
   L3, L4, L15 (shanghaiing, Chinese in SF)
5. Old Produce Market
   E21, E15 (Italians, food, waste, redevelopment)

6. Sansome and Green
    E6, E12, E13 (Telegraph Hill quarrying, Gray Bros. Alice Griffiths and Willing Circle, wood rush/eucalyptus, native plants/invasives)
7. Filbert Steps
    E12, E19 (FUF, Grace Marchant Gardens, wild parrots, Levi's Plaza, changing sense of nature)
8. Coit Tower
    L10, D4 (1934 Big Strike, politics of New Deal murals)

Scandalous SOMA

1. Palace Hotel gathering and introduction
    D6, D1 (Ralston's Ring, William Sharon, Mary Ellen Pleasant, civil rights demonstrations)
2. 3rd and Market
    T3, T8 (transit hub/history, newspapers and dynasties)
3. Stevenson Alley
    T1, T6, E1, E7 (South of the Slot, sand dunes and steam paddys, Happy Valley, foundries and mining, 1st transit line, 3rd Street cut and Mission Plank Road)
4. Yerba Buena Gardens
    E1, E2, E13 (Rincon Hill and 2nd Street cut, wetlands (Behr), Ohlone)
5. Carousel
    L11, L10 (redevelopment, labor history, resistance, senior housing)
6. Lapu Lapu and Bonifacio
    D3, E19 (Philippine-U.S. War, Philippine immigration, mural, community garden)
7. South Park
    E1, E9 (George Gordon, sugar mill, water lot speculation)
8. 3rd and Mission Creek
    E1, E9, E10, T3 (Mission Bay, Long Bridge, Southern Pacific Terminal, United Fruit, hay wharf)

King Tide Tour of Mission Bay

1. Pier 36: tidal columns
    E1, E2, E4 (gathering and introduction, king tides, sea rise)

2. Pier 36 history kiosks
   T2, L4, E11 (South Beach, seawall construction, Port & world trade, Chinese immigration/Pacific Mail docks, Sailor's Union and shanghaiing, Belt Line Railroad)
3. Pier 38
   L3, L10 (1877 anti-Chinese riots, 1934 waterfront strike)
4. Ballpark on McCovey Cove
   T3, E1, E9 (hay wharf, old piers and warehouses, 1990s fight over future of team and stadium)
5. China Basin Building
   D19, E9, E21 (banana republics, Del Monte and United Fruit Company)
6. 4th St. Bridge to Huffaker Park
   E1, E9 (Mission Creek Conservancy, houseboats and restoration)
7. Mission Bay neighborhood walk to Pier 52 kiosk
   E10, E8 (Mission Rock grain terminal, whaling port, Santa Fe railroad, bikeway and greenbelt)
8. 20th and Illinois, Pier 70
   E13, L16, D22 (Irish Hill, shipyards, Union Ironworks and Bethlehem Steel, Military and SF economy, Restoration Hardware and new plans)

Market Street: The Contested Boulevard

1. Ferry Plaza (Harry Bridges Plaza)
   D1, T7, T14 (The eight-hour day movement and the twin railroads: the underground railroad and the transcontinental railroad—both shaped the city at the foot of Market)
2. Spear and Market, next to Southern Pacific Railroad headquarters
   L7, L9, T4, T8 (The Southern Pacific Railroad dominated state politics and owned much of the city's rolling stock in the latter part of the 19th century. After Patrick Calhoun bought up all the disparate trains, cable cars, and omnibus systems and consolidated them into the United Railroads Company in 1903, a series of strikes rocked street transit every year until a 1907 strike led to the demise of the streetcar workers union.)

3. Sansome and Market, northeast corner
   *D9, D23, D24, D27, T14 (Standing alongside "The Wall," once
   the major bike messenger hangout, we are at the site of a major riot
   during the May 5, 1971, mobilization against the Vietnam War for
   May Day. In this locale we are across the street from the former HQ
   of Chevron, and the former offices of Royal Dutch Shell are just a block
   to our north. Frequent demonstrations coursed through downtown, from
   the 1971 "Shut it Down" protests to the Hall of Shame and Warchest
   Tours of the early 1980s, to the Feb. 15, 2003, 200,000-strong
   march against the impending attack on Iraq.)*

4. 3rd/Kearny/Geary and Market: Lotta's Fountain
   *T1, D6, D8 (Lotta's fountain, the opera singer Luiza Tettrazini and
   the history of media in the streets, newspapers, etc. The three big papers
   were on this corner, the* Chronicle, Examiner, *and* Call, *representing
   the three families DeYoung, Hearst, and Spreckels. Gay Freedom
   Day and Giants World Series celebrations are examples of public
   celebrations making use of the City's main boulevard.)*

5. Powell and Market, in front of the Emporium, across from the
   Cable Car turnaround
   *L8, L10, L13 (Department store and restaurant workers staged
   dramatic strikes in the late 1930s to gain union recognition. Striking
   dept. store workers and culinary activists staged costume picket lines,
   and helped consolidate pre-WWII San Francisco as a union town.
   Along here, San Franciscans celebrated and rioted for three days at
   the conclusion of WWII.)*

6. 6th and Market
   *T7, T8, T14 (Market Street Transit Artery: Roar of the Four,
   BART's lasting effect, a history of bicycling politics)*

7. UN Plaza
   *L3, L18 (1877 Workingmen's Party riots July 25–27, anti-capitalist
   and anti-Chinese, labor politics 19th century, unemployment and
   despair, then and now)*

BIBLIOGRAPHY

Turning Shorelines, Wetlands, Creeks, Sand, and Hills into a City

Behr, Hans Herman. 1891. "Botanical Reminiscences." http://www.foundsf .org/index.php?title=Botanical_Reminiscences,_1891

Belasco, Warren J. 1989. *Appetite for Change: How the Counterculture Took On the Food Industry 1966–1988*. Pantheon Books: New York.

Bittner, Mark. 2004. *The Wild Parrots of Telegraph Hill*. Harmony Books: New York.

Blankenship, Mirjana. 2011. "The Farm by the Freeway," in *Ten Years That Shook the City: San Francisco 1968–78*, edited by Chris Carlsson and LisaRuth Elliott. City Lights Books: San Francisco.

Bodzin, Steven. 1995. "Sewerage." http://www.foundsf.org/index.php?title =Sewerage

Booker, Matthew Morse. 2013. *Down by the Bay: San Francisco's History between the Tides*. University of California Press: Berkeley.

Brechin, Gray. 1999. *Imperial San Francisco: Urban Power, Earthly Ruin*. University of California Press: Berkeley.

Brook, James, Nancy J. Peters, and Chris Carlsson, editors. 1998. *Reclaiming San Francisco: History, Politics, Culture*. City Lights Books: San Francisco.

California Coast & Ocean magazine, Spring 2001, special issue on San Bruno Mountain, http://scc.ca.gov/webmaster/coast_ocean_archives/1701 .pdf

Carlsson, Chris. Author's personal experience.

Carlsson, Chris. Various quotes taken from interviews by author for 2nd edition of Olmsted, *Vanished Waters*.

Carlsson, Chris. 1996. "Filbert Steps and Grace Marchant Gardens." http://www.foundsf.org/index.php?title=Filbert_Steps_and_Grace _Marchant_Gardens

Carlsson, Chris. 2004. *The Political Edge*. City Lights Books: San Francisco.

Carlsson, Chris. 2011. Interviews for Ecology Emerges, a project of Shaping San Francisco, with Ruth Gravanis, Karen Pickett, Judy Goldhaft, Larry Orman.

Carlsson, Chris, and LisaRuth Elliott, editors. 2011. *Ten Years That Shook the City: San Francisco 1968–78*. City Lights Books: San Francisco.

Castillo, Edward D. 1994. "The Language of Race Hatred," in *The Ohlone Past and Present: Native Americans of the San Francisco Bay Region*, edited by Lowell John Bean. Ballena Press: Menlo Park, CA.

Dillon, Richard. 1985. *North Beach: The Italian Heart of San Francisco*. Presidio Press: Novato, CA.

Dolin, Eric Jay. 2007. *Leviathan: The History of Whaling in America*. W. W. Norton: New York.

Dong, Harvey. 2011. "The Jung Sai Garment Workers Strike of 1974: 'An Earth-Shattering and Heaven-Startling Event,'" in *Ten Years That Shook the City: San Francisco 1968–78*, edited by Chris Carlsson and LisaRuth Elliott. City Lights Books: San Francisco.

Drew, Jesse. 1998. "Call Any Vegetable," in *Reclaiming San Francisco: History, Politics, Culture*, edited by James Brook, Nancy J. Peters, and Chris Carlsson. City Lights Books: San Francisco.

Dreyfus, Philip J. 2008. *Our Better Nature: Environment and the Making of San Francisco*. University of Oklahoma Press: Norman, OK.

Dyl, Joanna L. 2017. *Seismic City: An Environmental History of San Francisco's 1906 Earthquake*. University of Washington Press: Seattle.

Enders, Caty, and Jonathan Franklin. 2015. "Doug Tompkins: Life and Death of the Ecological Visionary behind North Face," in the *Guardian*. https://www.theguardian.com/us-news/2015/dec/13/douglas-tompkins-co-founder-north-face-chile-conservation

Everhart, Claude. 2009. Audio of public comments as member of Friends of Candlestick on the development of Candlestick State Recreation Area. http://www.foundsf.org/index.php?title=Candlestick_Point_State_Recreation_Area

Farmer, Jared. 2013. *Trees in Paradise: A California History*. W. W. Norton: New York.

Germain, Justin Matthew. 2016. "Housewives Save the City from the 'Cement Octopus'! Women's Activism in the San Francisco Freeway Revolts, 1955–1967." BA Thesis, History, UC Berkeley.

Gilliam, Harold. 1966, 1967. *The Natural World of San Francisco*. Doubleday: New York.

Gordon, Robert. 1999. "Poisons in the Fields: The United Farm Workers, Pesticides, and Environmental Politics," *The Pacific Historical Review* 68, no. 1 (Feb. 1999): 51/59. http://www.jstor.org/stable/3641869?origin=JSTOR-pdf

Habegger, Larry. "Gary Kray: Tender of the Grace Marchant Garden." http://www.foundsf.org/index.php?title=Gary_Kray,_Tender_of_the_Grace_Marchant_Garden

Hernandez, Roberto. 2015. "The Lot." Personal memoir. http://www.foundsf.org/index.php?title=The_Lot

Holloran, Pete. 1997. "India Basin and the Southeast Bayshore." http://www.foundsf.org/index.php?title=India_Basin_and_the_Southeast_Bayshore

Hynes, H. Patricia. 1996. *A Patch of Eden: America's Inner-City Gardens*. Chelsea Green Publishing: White River Junction, VT.

Isenberg, Andrew C. 2005. *Mining California: An Ecological History* Hill and Wang: New York.

Katz, Kathy, Mike Kavanaugh, and MaryEllen Churchill. 1995. *The Farm*. Documentary film. https://archive.org/details/FarmDoc40min

Lawson, Laura. 2005. *City Bountiful: A Century of Community Gardening in America*. University of California Press: Berkeley.

Levine-Fricke-Recon. 1997. Alternatives analysis report, Pier 98, Wetlands and Open Space Project. Prepared for the Port of San Francisco

Mann, Charles C. 2005. *1491: New Revelations of the Americas before Columbus*. Alfred Knopf: New York.

McClintock, Elizabeth, Paul Reeberg, and Walter Knight. 1990. *A Flora of the San Bruno Mountains*. California Native Plant Society: Sacramento, CA.

McKay, George. 2011. *Radical Gardening: Politics, Idealism & Rebellion in the Garden*. Frances Lincoln: London.

Meyer, Amy. 2006. *New Guardians of the Golden Gate*. University of California Press: Berkeley.

Miller, Robert Ryal. 1995. *Captain Richardson: Mariner, Ranchero, and Founder of San Francisco*. La Loma Press: Berkeley, CA, p. 57.

Milliken, Randall. 1995. *A Time of Little Choice: The Disintegration of Tribal Culture in the San Francisco Bay Area 1769–1910*. Ballena Press: Menlo Park, CA.

Myrick, David F. 1972, 2001. *San Francisco's Telegraph Hill*. Telegraph Hill Dwellers/City Lights Foundation: San Francisco.

Nelson, N. C. 1909. "Shellmounds of the San Francisco Bay Region." *University of California Publications in American Archaeology and Ethnology* 7, no. 4 (Dec. 1909): 316.

Olmsted, Nancy. 1986, 2012. *Vanished Waters: A History of San Francisco's Mission Bay*. Mission Creek Conservancy: San Francisco.

Peirce, Pam. 1993. *Golden Gate Gardening*. agAccess. Davis, CA.

Peirce, Pam. 2011. "A Personal History of the People's Food System," in *Ten Years That Shook the City: San Francisco 1968–78*, edited by Chris Carlsson and LisaRuth Elliott. City Lights Books: San Francisco.

Pollan, Michael. 2006. *The Omnivore's Dilemma*. Penguin Press: New York.

Pomerantz, Joel. Forthcoming 2020. *Seep City*, map of water in San Francisco.

Purdy, Lillian. 1902, April 13. "San Francisco's Wild Garden," *San Francisco Chronicle*, at http://www.foundsf.org/index.php?title=Lake_Merced_Wild_Garden

Quinn, Frank R. 1985. *Growing Up in the Mission District*, self-published monograph.

Rubin, Jasper. 2011. *A Negotiated Landscape: The Transformation of San Francisco's Waterfront since 1950*. Columbia College Press: Chicago.

Sacharoff, Shanta Nimbark. 2016. *Other Avenues Are Possible: Legacy of the People's Food System in the San Francisco Bay Area*. PM Press: Oakland, CA.

San Francisco Independent. 2000. "Building Resources." http://www.foundsf.org/index.php?title=Building_REsources

Schoenherr, Allan A. 1992. *A Natural History of California*. University of California Press: Berkeley, CA.

Schooley, David. 2011. "San Bruno Mountain," in *Ten Years That Shook the City: San Francisco 1968–78*, edited by Chris Carlsson and LisaRuth Elliott. City Lights Books: San Francisco.

Sloan, Doris. 2006. *Geology of the San Francisco Bay Region*. University of California Press: Berkeley.

Walker, Richard. 2004. *The Conquest of Bread*. The New Press: New York.

Walker, Richard. 2007. *The Country in the City: The Greening of the San Francisco Bay Area*. University of Washington Press: Seattle, WA.

Wolfe, Burton H. 1972. "The Candlestick Swindle." *San Francisco Bay Guardian*. http://www.foundsf.org/index.php?title=Candlestick_Swindle

Yollin, Patricia. 2004, Sept. 15. "A Little Bit of Eden in Bayview." *San Francisco Chronicle*, A1.

Whatever Happened to the Eight-Hour Day?

Bacon, David. 2017. "Hotel Workers Got It Right." http://www.foundsf.org/index.php?title=Hotel_workers_got_it_right

Bean, Walter. 1952. *Boss Ruef's San Francisco: The Story of the Union Labor Party, Big Business and the Graft Prosecution.* University of California Press: Berkeley.

Benson, Herman. 1997. *Rebels, Reformers, and Racketeers: How Insurgents Transformed the Labor Movement: The Painters Union 1962–1972.* Alliance for Union Democracy: New York.

Brecher, Jeremy. 1972. *Strike!* South End Press: Boston.

Brechin, Gray. 2015. "Trial of the Rincon Annex Murals." http://www.foundsf.org/index.php?title=Trial_of_the_Rincon_Annex_Murals

Brook, James, Nancy J. Peters, and Chris Carlsson, editors. 1998. *Reclaiming San Francisco: History, Politics, Culture.* City Lights Books: San Francisco.

California Labor School. 1957. *Once They Did It to Speak-Easies, Now They Do It to Schools.* Pamphlet accessed at the Labor Archives, J. Paul Leonard Library, San Francisco State University.

California, State of. 1940. *Handbook of California Labor Statistics.* Table 37: "Workers Involved and Man-Days Idle in Strikes, by Industry Group, California, 1927–1939" and Table 36: "Workers Involved and Man-Days Idle in Strikes, California, Los Angeles City and San Francisco Bay Area, 1927–1940."

California, State of. 1955. *Handbook of California Labor Statistics 1953–1954.* Table 54: "Number of Work Stoppages, Workers Involved, and Man-Days Idle, Major California Cities, 1941–1951."

Carlsson, Chris. Author's personal experience.

Carlsson, Chris. 2004. *The Political Edge.* City Lights Books: San Francisco.

Carlsson, Chris, and LisaRuth Elliott, editors. 2011. *Ten Years That Shook the City: San Francisco 1968–78.* City Lights Books: San Francisco.

Castillo, Edward D. 1994. "The Language of Race Hatred," in *The Ohlone Past and Present: Native Americans of the San Francisco Bay Region,* edited by Lowell John Bean. Ballena Press: Menlo Park, CA.

Churchill, Mary Ellen, 1999. "Local 2 and the Alliance of the Rank and File." http://www.foundsf.org/index.php?title=Local_2_and_the _Alliance_of_Rank_and_File

Cobble, Dorothy. 1991. *Dishing It Out: Waitresses and Their Unions in the Twentieth Century.* University of Illinois Press: Urbana & Chicago.

Cross, Ira. 1935. *The History of Labor in California.* University of California Press: Berkeley.

Enders, Caty, and Jonathan Franklin. 2015. "Doug Tompkins: Life and Death of the Ecological Visionary behind North Face," in the *Guardian*, https://www.theguardian.com/us-news/2015/dec/13/douglas -tompkins-co-founder-north-face-chile-conservation

Englander, Susan. 1992. *Class Conflict and Coalition in the California Woman Suffrage Movement 1907–1912: The San Francisco Wage Earners' Suffrage League.* The Edwin Mellen Press: Lewiston, NY.

Fradkin, Philip L. 2005. *The Great Earthquake and Firestorms of 1906: How San Francisco Nearly Destroyed Itself.* University of California Press: Berkeley.

Gentry, Curt. 1967. *Frame-Up: The Incredible Case of Tom Mooney and Warren Billings.* W. W. Norton: New York.

Glass, Fred. 2016. *From Mission to Microchip: A History of the California Labor Movement.* University of California Press: Berkeley.

Hartman, Chester. 2002. *City for Sale: The Transformation of San Francisco.* University of California Press: Berkeley.

Hinckle, Warren. 1985. *The Big Strike: A Pictorial History of the 1934 SF General Strike* with a narrative by Warren Hinckle, Silver Dollar Books: Virginia City, NV.

International Longshoremen's and Warehousemen's Union, Information Dept. 1963. *The ILWU Story.* San Francisco.

Kazin, Michael. 1987. *Barons of Labor: The San Francisco Building Trades and Union Power in the Progressive Era.* University of Illinois Press: Urbana & Chicago.

Knight, Robert E. L. 1960. *Industrial Relations in the San Francisco Bay Area, 1900–1918.* University of California Press: Berkeley.

Larrowe, Charles P. 1972. *Harry Bridges: The Rise and Fall of Radical Labor in the United States.* Lawrence Hill: New York.

Lee, Anthony W. 1999. *Painting on the Left: Diego Rivera, Radical Politics, and San Francisco's Public Murals.* University of California Press: Berkeley.

Lens, Sidney. 1974. *The Labor Wars.* Anchor/Doubleday: New York.

Levinson, Marc. 2006. *The Box: How the Shipping Container Made the World Smaller and the World Economy Bigger.* Princeton University Press: Princeton, NJ.

MacFarlane, Angus. 2017. "Pioneer Park: San Francisco's Forgotten First Ballpark." http://www.foundsf.org/index.php?title=Pioneer_Park:_San_Francisco%27s_Forgotten_First_Ball_Park

Madley, Benjamin. 2016. *An American Genocide: The United States and the California Indian Catastrophe.* Yale University Press: New Haven, CT.

Mills, Herb. 1976. "The San Francisco Waterfront: The Social Consequences of Industrial Modernization, Part One: 'The Good Old Days' . . . and Part Two: 'The Modern Longshore Operations.'" Reprinted from *Urban Life.* Sage Publications: Beverly Hills, CA.

Mills, Herb. 1996. Interview by author.

Mollenkopf, John H. 1983. *The Contested City.* Princeton University Press: Princeton, NJ.

Nelson, Bruce. 1990. *Workers on the Waterfront: Seamen, Longshoremen, and Unionism in the 1930s.* University of Illinois Press: Urbana & Chicago.

O'Connell, Jay. 1999. *Co-operative Dreams: A History of the Kaweah Colony.* Raven River Press: Van Nuys, CA.

Ovetz, Robert. 2018. *When Workers Shot Back: Class Conflict from 1877 to 1921.* Brill: Boston.

Pacific Maritime Association. 1995. *Annual Report.* San Francisco.

Pfaelzer, Jean. 2007. *Driven Out: The Forgotten War against Chinese Americans.* Random House: New York.

Pickelhaupt, Bill. 1996. *Shanghaied in San Francisco.* Flyblister Press: San Francisco.

Quin, Mike. 1948. *On the Drumhead.* Daily People's World: San Francisco.

Quin, Mike. 1949. *The Big Strike.* Olema Publishing: Olema, CA.

Resolution Film Center. 1974. "Redevelopment: A Marxist Analysis," film, 95 mins.

Rubin, Jasper. 2011. *A Negotiated Landscape: The Transformation of San Francisco's Waterfront since 1950.* Columbia College Press: Chicago.

Sandos, James A. 1997. "Between Crucifix and Lance: Indian-White Relations in California, 1769–1848," in *Contested Eden: California before the Gold Rush,* edited by Ramón A. Gutiérrez and Richard J. Orsi. University of California Press: Berkeley.

Saxton, Alexander. 1971. *The Indispensable Enemy: Labor and the Anti-Chinese Movement in California*. University of California Press: Berkeley.

Schwartz, Harvey, editor. 1995, July 20. *The Dispatcher*. "The March Inland," quoting Joe Lynch in Part IX of the ILWU Oral History Project.

Schwartz, Harvey, editor. 1995, Nov. 20. *The Dispatcher*. "Rank and File Unionism in Action," quoting Brother Hackett in Part XII of the ILWU Oral History Project.

Schwartz, Harvey. 2000. *The March Inland: Origins of the ILWU Warehouse Division 1934–38*. ILWU: San Francisco.

Schwartz, Stephen. 1986. *Brotherhood of the Sea: A History of the Sailor's Union of the Pacific 1885–1985*. Sailor's Union of the Pacific: San Francisco.

Selvin, David. 1967. *Sky Full of Storm*. University of California Press: Berkeley.

Selvin. David. 1996. *A Terrible Anger: The 1934 Waterfront and General Strikes in San Francisco*. Wayne State University Press: Detroit, MI.

Sewell, Jessica Ellen. 2011. *Women and the Everyday City: Public Space in San Francisco, 1890–1915*. University of Minnesota Press: Minneapolis.

Shoup, Laurence H. 2010. *Rulers & Rebels: A People's History of Early California, 1769–1901*. iUniverse: Bloomington, IN.

Smith, Stacey L. 2013. *Freedom's Frontier: California and the Struggle Over Unfree Labor, Emancipation, and Reconstruction*. University of North Carolina Press: Chapel Hill.

Theriault, Reg. 1995. *How to Tell When You're Tired: A Brief Examination of Work*. W. W. Norton: New York.

Tygiel, Jules. 1983. "Where Unionism Holds Undisputed Sway: A Reappraisal of San Francisco's Union Labor Party." *California History* 62, no. 3 (Fall 1983): 196–215.

Udesky, Laurie. 1994. "Levi's Too?!?" *The Nation*, May 1994.

Weir, Stan. 1967, April/June. "USA—The Labor Revolt." *International Socialist Journal* 4, no. 20 (April and June): 21.

Weir, Stan. 1996. "Unions with Leaders Who Stay on the Job," in "*We Are All Leaders*": *The Alternative Unionism of the Early 1930s*, edited by Staughton Lynd. University of Illinois Press: Urbana & Chicago.

Yellen, Samuel. 1936, 1974. *American Labor Struggles*. Monad Press: New York.

Zerzan, John. 1977. *Creation and Its Enemies: The Revolt against Work*. "Unionization in America." Mutualist Book: Rochester, NY.

Other Sources

"71% of SF Homeless Once Had Homes in San Francisco." 2016, Feb. 11, https://www.democraticunderground.com/104012742

California Indian Treaties, http://www.kstrom.net/isk/maps/ca/cal treaties.html

Guide to Subversive Organizations and Publications (and Appendices). Revised and published Dec. 1, 1961, House Un-American Activities Committee: Washington, DC.

San Francisco Chronicle. Oct. 23, 1948: 1.

San Francisco Examiner. July 21, 1901: 18.

San Francisco Labor Herald. Aug. 23, 1946, vol. 10, no. 13: 1.

TRAILS, SAILS, RAILS, AND WHEELS

Bean, Walter. 1952. *Boss Ruef's San Francisco: The Story of the Union Labor Party, Big Business and the Graft Prosecution.* University of California Press: Berkeley.

Bonnett, Wayne. 1997. *San Francisco by Land & Sea: A Transportation Album.* Windgate Press: Sausalito, CA.

Brook, James, Nancy J. Peters, and Chris Carlsson, editors. 1998. *Reclaiming San Francisco: History, Politics, Culture.* City Lights Books: San Francisco.

Carlsson, Chris. 2002. *Critical Mass: Bicycling's Defiant Celebration.* AK Press: Oakland, CA.

Carlsson, Chris. 2004. *The Political Edge.* City Lights Books: San Francisco.

Carlsson, Chris, and LisaRuth Elliott, editors. 2011. *Ten Years That Shook the City: San Francisco 1968–78.* City Lights Books: San Francisco.

Carlsson, Chris and LisaRuth Elliott, and Adriana Camarena. 2012. *Shift Happens! Critical Mass at 20.* Full Enjoyment Books: San Francisco

Caron, Mona. 1999. "The Duboce Bikeway Mural: Gateway to the Wiggle." Author's Interview. http://www.foundsf.org/index.php?title=The _Duboce_Bikeway_Mural:_Gateway_to_the_Wiggle

Chapot, Hank. "The Great Bicycling Protest of 1896." http://www.foundsf .org/index.php?title=The_Great_Bicycling_Protest_of_1896

Corbett, Michael R. 2010. *Port City: The History and Transformation of the Port of San Francisco 1848–2010.* San Francisco Architectural Heritage: San Francisco.

Dana, Richard Henry. 1840. *Two Years before the Mast*. Harpers: New York.

Elinson, Elaine, and Stan Yogi. 2013. *Wherever There's a Fight: How Runaway Slaves, Suffragists, Immigrants, Strikers, and Poets Shaped Civil Liberties in California*. Heyday Books: Berkeley, CA.

Germain, Justin Matthew. 2016. "Housewives Save the City from the 'Cement Octopus'! Women's Activism in the San Francisco Freeway Revolts, 1955–1967." BA Thesis, History, UC Berkeley.

Harlan, George H. 1967. *San Francisco Bay Ferryboats*. Howell-North Books: Berkeley, CA.

Healy, Michael C. 2016. *BART: The Dramatic History of the Bay Area Rapid Transit System*. Heyday Books: Berkeley, CA.

Henderson, Jason. 2013. *Street Fight: The Politics of Mobility in San Francisco*. University of Massachusetts Press: Boston.

Howard, Ida L. 1905, Feb. 26. "When San Francisco Was Teaching America to Ride a Bicycle," in *San Francisco Chronicle*.

Issel, William. 1999. "'Land Values, Human Values, and the Preservation of the City's Treasured Appearance': Environmentalism, Politics, and the San Francisco Freeway Revolt." *The Pacific Historical Review* 68, no. 4 (Nov. 1999): 611–646.

Jackson, Joe. 2008. *The Thief at the End of the World: Rubber, Power, and the Seeds of Empire*. Penguin Books: New York.

LaBounty, Stephen "Woody." 2009. *Carville-by-the-Sea: San Francisco's Streetcar Suburb*. Outside Lands Media: San Francisco.

Leale, John. 1939. *Recollections of a Tule Sailor*. G. Fields: San Francisco.

Matoff, Tom. 1999. *The Muni Paradox: A Brief Social History of the Municipal Railway*. SPUR Newsletter: San Francisco. http://www.foundsf.org/index.php?title=MUNI_History_I:_The_Gilded_Age--Entrepreneurial_Development,_Competition_and_Consolidation

Mumford, Lewis. 1963, Dec. 7. *The New Yorker* "The Sky Line: Not Yet Too Late."

Norton, Peter D. 2008. *Fighting Traffic: The Dawn of the Motor Age in the American City*. MIT Press: Cambridge, MA.

Olmsted, Nancy. 1986, 2012. *Vanished Waters: A History of San Francisco's Mission Bay*. Mission Creek Conservancy: San Francisco.

Reinhardt, Richard. 1973. *Treasure Island: San Francisco's Exposition Years*. Scrimshaw Press: San Francisco.

Rowsome, Frank. 1956. *Trolley Car Treasury*. McGraw-Hill: New York.

Smallwood, Charles. 1978. *The White Front Cars of San Francisco*. Interurbans: Glendale, CA.

Swan, Rachel. 2019, May 8. "Uber, Lyft Account for Two-Thirds of Traffic Increase in SF over Six Years, Study Shows." *San Francisco Chronicle*. https://www.sfchronicle.com/bayarea/article/Uber-Lyft-account -for-of-traffic-increase-in-13830608.php

White, Richard. 2011. *Railroaded: The Transcontinentals and the Making of Modern America*. W. W. Norton: New York.

DISSENTERS AND DEMONSTRATIONS, RADICALS AND REPRESSION

ACLU, 1961. "Operation Correction," public domain film published by HUAC with new soundtrack by ACLU. Part one: http://www.archive .org/details/Operatio1961 and part two: http://www.archive.org /details/Operatio1961_2

Agee, Christopher. 2014. *The Streets of San Francisco: Policing and the Creation of a Cosmopolitan Liberal Politics, 1950–1972*. University of Chicago Press: Chicago.

Barnes, Peter. 1972. "The Presidio Mutiny of 1968," from *Pawns: The Plight of the Citizen-Soldier*. Alfred Knopf: New York.

Berkman, Alexander. 2005. *The Blast: Complete Collection of the Incendiary San Francisco Bi-Monthly Anarchist Newspaper Edited by Alexander Berkman from 1916–1917 That Gave Voice to the Worldwide Anarchist Movement*. AK Press: Chico, CA, and Edinburgh, Scotland.

Bloom, Joshua, and Waldo E. Martin Jr. 2016. *Black against Empire: The History and Politics of the Black Panther Party*. University of California Press: Berkeley.

Blue, Elly. 2011. "The Occupation Will Be Pedal Powered," in *Shift Happens! Critical Mass at 20*, edited by Chris Carlsson, LisaRuth Elliott, and Adriana Camarena. Full Enjoyment Books: San Francisco.

Bocage, Angela. 1991. "Reproductive Rights Rant," in *Processed World*, no. 28, http://www.foundsf.org/index.php?title=REPRODUCTIVE _RIGHTS_RANT

Brechin, Gray. 2015. "Trial of the Rincon Annex Murals." http://www .foundsf.org/index.php?title=Trial_of_the_Rincon_Annex_Murals

Brent, Bill. 1998. *Blacksheets* magazine. Reprinted as "Society for Individual Rights" on foundsf.org. http://www.foundsf.org/index.php?title =Society_for_Individual_Rights_(SIR)

Brook, James, Nancy J. Peters, and Chris Carlsson, editors. 1998. *Reclaiming San Francisco: History, Politics, Culture.* City Lights Books: San Francisco.

Callahan, Mat. 2017. *The Explosion of Deferred Dreams: Musical Renaissance and Social Revolution in San Francisco, 1965–1975.* PM Press: Oakland, CA.

Carlsson, Chris. 1996. Interview with Tom Fleming at his home on Fillmore Street.

Carlsson, Chris. 2004. *The Political Edge.* City Lights Books: San Francisco.

Carlsson, Chris. 2009. Interviews with Alvin Duskin at his San Francisco home and Jerry Mander at his Presidio office.

Carlsson, Chris. 2016. Interview with Darrell Rogers in the Mission District.

Carlsson, Chris. 2019. Author's personal experience.

Carlsson, Chris, and LisaRuth Elliott, editors. 2011. *Ten Years That Shook the City: San Francisco 1968–78.* City Lights Books: San Francisco.

Choy, Curtis (aka Chonk Moonhunter). 1983. *The Fall of the I-Hotel.* Documentary film.

Cordova, Cary. 2017. *The Heart of the Mission: Latino Art and Politics in San Francisco.* University of Pennsylvania Press: Philadelphia.

Cornell, Andrew. 2016. *Unruly Equality: U.S. Anarchism in the 20th Century.* University of California Press: Berkeley.

Coyote, Peter. 1998. *Sleeping Where I Fall.* Counterpoint: Washington, DC.

Eagle, Adam Fortunate. 1992. *ALCATRAZ! ALCATRAZ!* Heyday Books: Berkeley, CA.

Ferlinghetti, Lawrence, and Nancy J. Peters. 1980. *Literary San Francisco.* City Lights Books: San Francisco.

Gerson, Deborah. 2011. "Making Sexism Visible: Private Troubles Made Public," in *Ten Years That Shook the City: San Francisco 1968–78*, edited by Chris Carlsson with LisaRuth Elliott. City Lights Foundation: San Francisco.

Graham, Marcus. 1933. *Man! A Journal of the Anarchist Ideal and Movement.* San Francisco 1933–34. Retrieved from San Francisco Public Library, History Center, 6th Floor.

Habal, Estella. 2007. *San Francisco's International Hotel: Mobilizing the Filipino American Community in the Anti-Eviction Movement.* Temple University Press: Philadelphia.

Harbrecht, Amanda. 2017. "New Year's Eve, Jan. 1, 1965: A Night for Gay Rights." http://www.foundsf.org/index.php?title=New_Year%27s _Eve_Jan._1_1965:_A_Night_for_Gay_Rights

Heins, Marjorie. 1972. *Strictly Ghetto Property: The Story of Los Siete de la Raza.* Ramparts Press: Berkeley, CA.

Hernandez, Roberto. 2015. "The Lot." Personal memoir. http://www .foundsf.org/index.php?title=The_Lot

Hippler, Arthur. 1974. *Hunter's Point: A Black Ghetto.* Basic Books: New York.

Howell, Ocean. 2015. *Making the Mission: Planning and Ethnicity in San Francisco.* University of Chicago Press: Chicago.

Hudson, Lynn M. 2003. *The Making of "Mammy Pleasant": A Black Entrepreneur in Nineteenth-Century San Francisco.* University of Illinois Press: Chicago.

Ignacio, Abe, Enrique de la Cruz, Jorge Emmanuel, and Helen Toribio. 2004. *The Forbidden Book: The Philippine-American War in Political Cartoons.* T'Boli Publishing and Distribution: San Francisco.

Jenkins, Becky, and Terrence Hallinan. 1994. Transcripts of eyewitness memories in public presentations at New College of California.

Koskovich, Gerard. 2002. "Remembering a Police Riot: The Castro Sweep of October 6, 1989." http://www.foundsf.org/index.php?title =Remembering_A_Police_Riot:_The_Castro_Sweep_of_October _6,_1989

Lang, Lucy Robins. 1948. *Tomorrow Is Beautiful.* MacMillan: New York.

Lee, Anthony W. 1999. *Painting on the Left: Diego Rivera, Radical Politics, and San Francisco's Public Murals.* University of California Press: Berkeley.

Madley, Benjamin. 2016. *An American Genocide: The United States and the California Indian Catastrophe.* Yale University Press: New Haven, CT.

Meeker, Martin. 2012. "The Queerly Disadvantaged and the Making of San Francisco's War on Poverty, 1964–1967." *Pacific Historical Review* 81, no. 1 (Feb. 2012): 21–59.

Mexal, Stephen J. 2013. *Reading for Liberalism: The Overland Monthly and the Writing of the Modern American West.* University of Nebraska Press: Lincoln.

Miller, D. Scot. 2012. "The Hungry Got Food, the Homeless Got Shelter." *California Northern* no. 5. http://calnorthern.net/the-hungry-got-food

Miller, Mike. 2009. *A Community Organizer's Tale: People and Power in San Francisco.* Heyday Books: Berkeley, CA.

Minault, Kent. 2017. *Diggerly-Do's.* Live performance, June 7, 2017. http://shapingsf.org/public-talks/archive_video.html#digger

Murguia, Alejandro. 2011. "Poetry and Solidarity in the Mission District," in *Ten Years That Shook the City: San Francisco 1968–78,* edited by Chris Carlsson and LisaRuth Elliott. City Lights Books: San Francisco.

O'Connell, Jay. 1999. *Co-Operative Dreams: A History of the Kaweah Colony.* Raven River Press: Van Nuys, CA.

Ramnath, Maia. 2011. *Haj to Utopia: How the Ghadar Movement Charted Global Radicalism and Attempted to Overthrow the British Empire.* University of California Press: Berkeley.

Rexroth, Kenneth. 1991. *An Autobiographical Novel.* Edited by Linda Hamalian. New Directions Books: New York.

Rhodes, Jane. 2007. *Framing the Black Panthers: The Spectacular Rise of a Black Power Icon.* The New Press: New York.

Robinson, Mary Jean. 2011. "Reflections from Occupied Ohlone Territory," in *Ten Years That Shook the City: San Francisco 1968–78.* City Lights Books: San Francisco.

Shaw, Randy. 1998. "Tenant Power in San Francisco," in *Reclaiming San Francisco: History Politics Culture,* edited by James Brook, Chris Carlsson, and Nancy J. Peters. City Lights Books: San Francisco.

Shaw, Randy. 2015. *The Tenderloin: Sex, Crime, and Resistance in the Heart of San Francisco.* Urban Reality Press: San Francisco.

Smith, Harvey. 2011. "New Deal Artists and Programs during the Depression." http://www.foundsf.org/index.php?title=New_Deal _Artists_and_Programs_During_the_Depression

Stryker, Susan, and Victor Silverman, directors. 2005. *Screaming Queens: The Riot at Compton's Cafeteria.* Frameline documentary.

Summers Sandoval Jr., Tomás F. 2013. *Latinos at the Golden Gate: Creating Community & Identity in San Francisco.* University of North Carolina Press: Chapel Hill.

Swope, Sally. 1984. "The Montgomery Washington Tower: An Historical Site and Its Artifacts." Swope Art Exhibition Services: San Francisco.

Takaki, Ronald. 1989. *Strangers from a Different Shore: A History of Asian Americans.* Penguin Books: New York.

Tussey Dan. No date. "Fireproof in SF." Guidelines, Newsletter for San Francisco City Guides and Sponsors. sfcityguides.org.

Twain, Mark. 1992. *Mark Twain's Weapons of Satire: Anti-Imperialist Writings on the Philippine-American War.* Edited by Jim Zwick. Syracuse University Press: New York.

Walker, Richard. 2018. *Pictures of a Gone City: Tech and the Dark Side of Prosperity in the San Francisco Bay Area.* PM Press: Oakland, CA.

Whitson, Helene. 1995. "Strike! Concerning the 1968–69 Strike at San Francisco State College." http://www.foundsf.org/index.php?title =STRIKE! . . . _Concerning_the_1968-69_Strike_at_San _Francisco_State_College

Zakheim, Masha. 1983, 2009. *Coit Tower San Francisco: Its History and Art.* Volcano Press: Volcano, CA.

Zimmer, Kenyon. 2015. *Immigrants against the State: Yiddish and Italian Anarchism in America.* University of Illinois Press: Chicago.

Zuboff, Shoshanna. 2019. *The Age of Surveillance Capitalism: The Fight for a Human Future at the New Frontier of Power.* PublicAffairs/Hatchette Book Group: New York.

INDEX